Business Intelligence Strategy and Big Data Analytics

Business Intelligence Strategy and Big Data Analytics

A General Management Perspective

Steve Williams

AMSTERDAM • BOSTON • HEIDELBERG • LONDON
NEW YORK • OXFORD • PARIS • SAN DIEGO
SAN FRANCISCO • SINGAPORE • SYDNEY • TOKYO

Morgan Kaufmann is an imprint of Elsevier

ELSEVIER

British Library Cataloguing-in-Publication Data
A catalogue record for this book is available from the British Library.

Library of Congress Cataloging-in-Publication Data
A catalog record for this book is available from the Library of Congress.

ISBN: 978-0-12-809198-2

For Information on all Morgan Kaufmann publications
visit our website at https://www.elsevier.com/

Working together
to grow libraries in
developing countries

www.elsevier.com • www.bookaid.org

Publisher: Todd Green
Acquisition Editor: Todd Green
Editorial Project Manager: Lindsay Lawrence
Production Project Manager: Priya Kumaraguruparan
Designer: Mark Rogers

Typeset by MPS Limited, Chennai, India

CONTENTS

ABOUT THE AUTHOR

Steve Williams is the founder and President of DecisionPath Consulting. He specializes in helping clients formulate business-driven, technically-savvy strategies for leveraging business intelligence (BI), analytics, and big data to improve profits. As a strategy consultant, he blends general management experience and education with nearly 30 years' experience in the information technology (IT) industry—the last 15 of which have been focused on BI and analytics. Steve's strong business, IT, and BI backgrounds enable him to bring a holistic, business-focused perspective that differs from the traditional technology-centric approaches to BI and analytics strategy. While technology-led innovation is a valid approach, the challenges in the world of BI, analytics, and big data are predominantly on the business and organizational side. Approaches to meeting those challenges require a general management perspective.

Over the past 15 years as a BI strategy consultant, Steve has had the privilege of working with successful companies in retail, distribution, manufacturing, transportation and logistics, consumer packaged goods, financial services, government, and utilities. His clients have included:

- ArcBest
- Heinens Fine Foods
- Louisville Gas and Electric
- Navy Federal Credit Union
- Northwestern Mutual Life
- Partners Federal Credit Union
- Pinnacle Foods Group
- Principal Financial Group
- Toronto Hydro Electric System
- United Natural Foods
- U.S. Social Security Administration
- U.S. Treasury
- Watsco

While the industries and companies are different, what has become clear through this consulting experience is that there are many common challenges when it comes to leveraging BI, analytics, and big data to enhance profitability and organizational effectiveness. Steve understands these challenges, and he provides proven methods for meeting them.

Starting in 2006 with the publication of *The Profit Impact of Business Intelligence*, coauthored with Nancy Williams, the business-driven BI and analytics strategy methods that Steve and Nancy pioneered have been the subject of many print magazine articles. A representative list of Steve's articles includes:

- "Big Data Strategy Approaches: Business-Driven or Discovery-Based?" Business Intelligence Journal, 4th Quarter 2014
- "Analytics: A Tool Executives and Managers Need to Embrace" MWorld (The Journal of the American Management Association, Winter 2012–13
- "Five Barriers to BI Success – And How to Overcome Them" Strategic Finance, July 2011
- "Power Combination: Business Intelligence and the Balanced Scorecard" Strategic Finance May 2008)
- "BI Impact: The Assimilation of Business Intelligence into Core Business Processes" Business Intelligence Journal, 4th Quarter 2007 (w/ Mohamed Elbashir)
- "Delivering Strategic Business Value" Strategic Finance, August 2004

In addition to widely sharing his thinking about BI, analytics, and big data, Steve has also served as a judge since 2001 for the annual TDWI Best Practices in Business Intelligence and Data Warehousing Competition. In this capacity, he has seen hundreds of BI case studies and worked with fellow judges who are leading instructors and consultants in the field.

Prior to founding DecisionPath, Steve worked for 20 years in several specialized consulting companies where he developed expertise in program management, systems integration, software engineering, and management accounting. He holds an MBA in General Management from the Darden School at the University of Virginia and a B.S. in Business Management from the University of Maryland.

Most executives are familiar with big data, business intelligence (BI), analytics, business performance management, business process management, and fact-based decision-making, but they are uncertain about how to best deploy them to create business value. For every organization that is doing wonderful things (think Amazon), more are struggling to effectively implement these innovations (though most are not that new).

Steve Williams' book reminds me of a meeting that I had with the CIO of a major university who wanted to discuss the development of a data warehouse and various BI applications. In the meeting I learned that the school's provost was interested in having a campus-wide scorecard system and the ability for business managers to "slice and dice" (ie, OLAP) financial and student data.

The CIO wasn't sure where to start with this request. After learning that there wasn't a good data infrastructure in place, and knowing how different the target applications were, I discussed the importance of thinking both short and long term. While both of the desired applications were feasible, they differed dramatically in terms of the scope of the data requirements, the required financial resources, the technology infrastructure, the amount of senior management support, and the demands and implications of organizational change. There needed to be frameworks and a roadmap for moving forward, along with plans for creating the required data infrastructure and developing and rolling out specific, prioritized applications that would generate quick and long-term wins. In other words, she needed to think about BI strategically.

This kind of situation is common among firms that are not far along the BI maturity curve or have approached BI in a piecemeal fashion and have not thought about BI strategically. The hype, technology, and business need are there, but it is hard to know how to proceed in a way that is logical and creates business value. Though the technological challenges seem daunting, ensuring that the work is business driven is even more challenging.

Steve Williams, along with his wife Nancy, have successfully run their own BI consulting firm for over 15 years, focusing on helping companies develop and implement BI (and now big data) strategies. In the process, he has developed frameworks and approaches and gained practical insights and experiences in numerous firms and industries.

I formally met Steve several years ago and since then he has shared his knowledge in my BI classes at the University of Georgia and in the articles he has written for the *Business Intelligence Journal* (I serve as Senior Editor) and elsewhere. I've been consistently impressed with the business sense, practicality, and clarity of his thinking and approaches, and I've integrated his materials into my BI courses. This book codifies much of what Steve has experienced and learned over the years and passes this knowledge on to the reader, whether the person is an executive or a BI/IT professional who wants to take a strategic approach to BI.

In this book you will find both content and features that will help you plan and execute BI strategically. Terms are carefully defined. The various kinds of BI applications are described and illustrated. Use cases in a variety of industries are provided so you better understand the potential use, value, and challenges of BI. Frameworks and methodologies help you to understand and execute what must be done. The links between BI and the improvement of decision making, business processes, and performance management are clearly shown. The potential barriers to success and approaches for overcoming them are presented. Key points are summarized, along with skill development opportunities to practice what you have learned. Questions are interspersed throughout the book to help you think about the materials.

Worthy of special mention is the treatment of big data and analytics. The hype around both topics is especially high, and it is easy to think that they are so new and different that they need to be treated in special ways. This book provides a clear understanding of the ways that big data and analytics both differ from the past (some of the new big data storage platforms like Hadoop) but also the many ways that they are just a logical extension of what has come before. When viewed in this context, the strategic planning for BI and analytics in the world of big data is very similar to planning for BI in general.

The frameworks, approaches, and methodologies will help you think strategically about big data.

After I read Steve Williams book, it made me think of my meeting with the university CIO. Much of the advice I gave was consistent with the recommendations and practices described in his book, though not as well thought out, organized, and presented. If you need to think about BI (and all the related topics) strategically in your company, I'm confident that you will find this book to be very helpful.

Hugh J. Watson
Professor and C. Herman and Mary Virginia Terry Chair
of Business Administration, Terry College of Business,
University of Georgia
Senior Editor, *Business Intelligence Journal*

ACKNOWLEDGMENTS

This book reflects what I think I have learned about BI, analytics, and big data over the past 15 years. It is based in no small measure on empirical evidence gained through in-depth interviews and surveys within the client companies we have served. It is also based on what I have learned from talking with smart people in the industry—some of whom are occasional competitors, and all of whom are respected peers. I would include people such as Evan Levy, Chris Adamson, Claudia Imhoff, Dave Wells, Bill Inmon, Jill Dyche, and Mike Gonzales, among many others. And I would be remiss if I failed to mention the exchanges of ideas and perspectives I've had over the years with Hugh Watson at the Terry School, University of Georgia and with Barb Wixom, now at the MIT Center for Information Systems Research.

As a consultant, I've had the privilege of working with some exceptional colleagues at DecisionPath. Our BI, analytics, and big data strategy work has always addressed technology. This includes technical readiness, technology strategy, technical risk mitigation, tool selection, and data architecture. In this area, I've learned much from Mohan Srireddy and Tom Victory—two senior colleagues who are great at explaining technical issues and the costs and benefits of the options. Over the years, they have also shared what they have learned from the technical implementation work they do for our clients, which has informed some of my perceptions about the technical implementation challenges associated with enterprise data warehousing, BI, and analytics initiatives.

I have also been fortunate to learn a lot about BI and analytics from my collaborator, business colleague, and life partner—Nancy Williams. Nancy got into the BI and data warehousing field a few years ahead of me, and I have been racing to catch up ever since. She too is a judge for the TDWI Best Practices in Business Intelligence and Data Warehousing Competition, and she is a regular instructor at TDWI Conferences, Seminars, and On-Sites. Nancy talks to many people at these venues—people from many companies in many industries—and she keeps us both up to date on the latest trends.

We've served some of the same clients, and some different clients. This allows us to see what challenges seem to be common, to share our insights from our different experiences, and to challenge and hone the thinking we bring to our clients.

Ultimately, I've learned the most about BI in the real world from the men and women in the companies we've served. Their struggles to get the information, analyses, and decision support they need to drive their companies' results persist despite widespread availability of BI products and "solutions" that have been on the market for nearly two decades. It is from their struggles that Nancy and I first saw the need for a business-driven approach to BI and analytics, and it is from their feedback that the approaches in this book have been both validated and refined.

THE CHALLENGE OF FORMULATING BUSINESS INTELLIGENCE STRATEGY

Pick up any business newspaper or periodical these days and you're likely to find an article about big data or an advertisement about cognitive business—or both. These concepts are positioned as if they represent big advancements, and it is true that there are new types of data for businesses to leverage using new kinds of analytical tools. But if we drill down below the surface, the business benefits of big data and cognitive business are the same benefits that have been delivered by business intelligence (BI) for at least 15 years.

From a business perspective, BI has always been about leveraging business information, business analyses, and decision support to improve profitability. The business benefits of BI may be couched in different business terms, such as "customer intimacy" or "supply chain agility" or the like, but there has to be a connection between achieving those things and incremental profitability. Otherwise, it is economically impossible to achieve a return on investment (ROI). So the strategic challenge for BI has always been to figure out how to leverage BI in the context of the core business processes that drive business results. We can now add the challenge of figuring out how to leverage stored digital content such as photos, texts, location data, music files, and other newer forms of data— which is the core of what is new about big data and cognitive business. That having been said, the business-driven BI strategy formulation methods described in this book apply equally well to traditional data and to big data, and they have been proven in practice since 2001. With this in mind, we'll use the term BI to include leveraging the new types of digital content known collectively as big data. Where appropriate, we'll also discuss big data and cognitive business as specific concepts.

As we explore the strategic challenges for BI, the perspective we'll take is a business-driven perspective. Many smart people have written about the technical side of BI—about how to move data from wherever it starts into an environment where it is available for BI, and subsequently delivering business information, business analyses, and decision support to the business people responsible for achieving business results. Our focus is on the business side of BI, because that is where the ROI is actually created. We can think of the technical side as creating an information asset, and the business side as leveraging the asset. From a general management perspective, pursuing BI-enabled business improvement opportunities is largely about designing the asset, creating it, and using the asset within and across the company to generate incremental profits. Accordingly, a business-driven BI strategy must address those topics.

To formulate a BI strategy, it helps to have a common understanding of what BI is. When we talk with business leaders, managers, and analysts about their BI opportunities, the picture that emerges is of BI as a multi-faceted business improvement tool kit. The specific tools include reports, scorecards, dashboards, multidimensional analyses, ad hoc analyses, advanced analytics, predictive analytics, and alerts. Accordingly, BI can be used in many different ways to achieve many different business purposes.

Since Nancy Williams and I wrote *The Profit Impact of Business Intelligence* in 2006, we have had many additional opportunities to work with leading companies in a wide range of industries. In the course of helping them formulate and execute BI strategies and program plans, we have seen firsthand that otherwise successful companies struggle in two key areas when it comes to BI:

- *BI Strategy:* understanding how they can leverage BI in core business functions such as marketing, sales, customer service, operations, distribution, supplier management, cost improvement, and financial management; and
- *BI Program Execution:* effectively prioritizing, aligning, and executing the diverse workstreams that are critical for achieving an ROI, including BI applications development, integrating BI applications into targeted business processes, and managing changes in how information and analyses are used to inform high-impact business decisions.

Essentially, we have seen that BI can deliver competitive advantages and substantial economic benefits, *but only if companies overcome these commonly-encountered challenges.* There is no shortage of excellent guidance about BI technical methods, or about BI value propositions in the abstract. What is in relatively shorter supply is experience-based information about the business side of BI—including the strategy for leveraging BI for profit improvement and the enterprise approach to executing the BI strategy. Further, there is a need for managers to fully understand that BI initiatives are really business initiatives that require business units to change how they use information and analysis to drive and improve business results—particularly profits.

Business Intelligence Strategy and Big Data Analytics is written for business leaders, managers, and analysts—people who are involved with advancing the use of BI at their companies or who need to better understand what BI is and how it can be used to improve profitability. It is also written for BI directors and enterprise data architects—the IT people who have to understand the business purposes that drive technical requirements and designs. The book is written from a general management perspective and it draws on observations at 12 companies whose annual revenues range between $500 million and $20 billion. Over the past 15 years, my company has formulated vendor-neutral business-focused BI strategies and program execution plans in collaboration with manufacturers, distributors, retailers, logistics companies, insurers, investment companies, credit unions, and utilities, among others. Through an intensive process that typically lasts 10–12 weeks, we work with business leaders, managers, and analysts across all major functions to identify specific ways that BI can be leveraged to impact business results. We also use surveys and interviews to identify any organizational, business unit, and/or technical execution barriers or risks. It is through these experiences that we have validated our business-driven BI strategy formulation methods and identified common enterprise BI program execution challenges. The ultimate goal of this book is to share methods and observations that will help companies achieve BI success and thereby increase revenues, reduce costs, or both.

OVERVIEW OF THE BOOK

Business Intelligence Strategy and Big Data Analytics is written to both advance the reader's understanding of BI and to introduce proven practical methods and frameworks for:

- Determining the strategic importance of BI in an industry and company;
- Identifying specific ways that BI can be leveraged to improve specific business processes and to automate and enhance business performance management techniques;

- Documenting and prioritizing an enterprise and/or business unit portfolio of BI opportunities;
- Articulating and documenting business-driven BI requirements;
- Identifying business and technical readiness gaps, risks, and barriers to success;
- Identifying typical execution challenges;
- Understanding the key BI program execution workstreams; and
- Understanding options and tactics for organizing and executing enterprise BI initiatives.

In addition, we provide optional "skill development opportunities" which readers can avail themselves of if they wish. These are end-of-chapter exercises that afford opportunities to practice the methods or apply the frameworks that are introduced in the various chapters.

ORGANIZATION OF THE BOOK

One of the challenges companies face when it comes to BI is developing a common understanding of what BI is and how it works as a business process and business performance improvement tool. There is a lot of hype in the marketplace for BI tools and services, driven by large advertising budgets. This causes confusion. We'll cut through the confusion in the first two chapters. *Chapter 1 — The Personal Face of Business Intelligence* uses an actual case study to illustrate what BI looks like to the business people in a company whose identity has been disguised. *Chapter 2 — Business Intelligence in the Era of Big Data and Cognitive Business* seeks to sort through the hype, provide business-oriented definitions of key concepts, and provide industry and functional views of what BI success looks like.

The next three chapters cover various aspects of BI Strategy. *Chapter 3 — The Strategic Importance of Business Intelligence* drills deeper into the multifaceted tool that is BI, and then it introduces a framework for determining the strategic importance of BI for an industry and company. *Chapter 4 — BI Opportunity Analysis* introduces proven practical methods for identifying and documenting the specific ways that BI can be used at a given company—which we call BI Opportunities, or BIOs for short. Typically, a company will identify somewhere between 8 and 15 BIOs—which collectively comprise a BI

Portfolio. *Chapter 5 — Prioritizing BI Opportunities (BIOs)* discusses factors to consider when prioritizing BIOs and introduces some methods for doing so. Applying the concepts, methods, and frameworks from these three chapters results in a specific and effective business case for investing in BI. At this stage, a company knows how it wants to leverage BI to increase revenues, reduce costs, or both.

Assuming a company can meet the technical challenges of a BI program, a topic we'll table for now, it next faces the task of leveraging BI within the core business processes that drive business results. Once one or more specific BI applications have been built, the onus for leveraging BI to create business value falls on the business unit or units for which the BI application was built. In *Chapter 6 — Leveraging BI for Performance Management, Process Improvement, and Decision Support* we use business examples to demonstrate how to leverage BI for improving the business processes that drive business results. We also show how BI can enhance business performance management capabilities. Essentially, companies need to leverage BI in ways that "move the needle" and this chapter provides frameworks for doing so.

We mentioned at the outset that many companies struggle with executing an enterprise or business unit BI program. In *Chapter 7 — Meeting the Challenges of Enterprise BI*, we share observations from our experience over the past 15 years, along with some frameworks for identifying risks, organizing for success, and synchronizing the work to be done. Many of the challenges of enterprise BI are predictable and they can be overcome by effective general management methods.

Finally, *Chapter 8 — General Management Perspectives on Technical Topics* is intended to provide business people with an overview of some of the concepts that are bound to arise when it comes to executing the technical side of an enterprise BI initiative. Business leaders and managers are often asked to endorse six-figure and seven-figure technology budgets for BI, and thus it is important to understand some of the choices and implications when it comes to BI-related architecture and technologies.

CLOSING THE LOOP

We started out by observing that companies struggle with BI Strategy and BI Program Execution. Our hope is that *Business Intelligence*

Strategy and Big Data Analytics will prepare business leaders and managers to advance the use of BI at their companies. Too often, BI is seen as an IT initiative, and it often languishes due to higher-priority or more urgent IT challenges. I argue that the business people who have to hit their numbers need to take charge of BI. From the practical perspective of applied managerial economics, revenue growth and productivity improvement can only be achieved through more effective business processes, including better performance management processes. Many of the senior business people we've worked with over the past 15 years report shocking gaps in their access to information and analysis. In an era where better information and analyses have become factors of production and competitive differentiators, BI is the right tool at the right time.

CHAPTER 1

The Personal Face of Business Intelligence

One way to develop a useful perspective about what business intelligence (BI) is and its importance in the business world is to look at what business people talk about when the subject is BI. Developing a BI Strategy using the methods we'll describe in this book is a people-intensive process—as it should be. We can leverage proven techniques, but the quality of the results depends to a significant degree on "getting into the heads" of key executives and managers. How do they see their world, what are they looking to accomplish, and how do they want BI to help them? We can build a business case that is "bullet-proof" from a logical, corporate perspective, but it also has to resonate with business people on a more intuitive level that squares with what they believe they would be able to achieve if they had better BI. So to put a human face on BI, this chapter will step through the business challenges and BI gaps identified by top executives in a manufacturing company we'll call Big Brand Foods (BBF). We'll then summarize the BI Vision and BI Portfolio that emerged from the strategy formulation process and offer some generalizations about BI opportunities (BIOs) for other manufacturing companies. While we've chosen a manufacturing company for this BI case study, the logic and process of identifying industry challenges, company strategies, functional challenges, and BIOs applies to any company in any industry. Further, the views of executives in the different business functions may be of value to executives in the same function but different industries.

1.1 BI CASE STUDY SETTING

1.1.1 Industry Setting

Food manufacturing is a large, complex industry that generates over $800 billion in annual sales. Typical food manufacturers produce hundreds or thousands of end products (called stock-keeping units, or SKUs) that are sold through a complex network of brokers, food distributors, and food service distributors to tens of thousands of retail outlets and restaurants. At the retail level, once the sole province of grocery stores and restaurants, food products are sold in many different places—by mass merchandizers, drug stores, convenience stores, and warehouse clubs, among others. Industry data suggest that less than half of food product sales are through traditional grocery stores. Other key industry trends are increased concentration of retail sales (Walmart alone accounts for over 50% of food sales), the rise of healthier products, and the diversity and increased quality of private label products that are now available. As a result of these and other trends, food manufacturers must cope with increased complexity and intense margin pressures, both of which impact profitability and customer service. Faced with these challenges, more and more food manufacturers are recognizing the strategic importance of BI.

1.1.2 Company Situation

BBF is a very successful manufacturer of widely known branded food products. Acquisition of known brands from competitors who were fine-tuning their brand portfolios allowed BBF to achieve $4 billion in revenue, and to be first or second in market share in most of the product categories in which it competed. With that growth came challenges. BBF was essentially a roll-up of acquired brands, plants, people, and systems, and it lacked the mature, well-synchronized business processes sometimes found in larger companies in the industry. BBF was addressing that challenge through an infusion of upper management talent from global competitors, such as Kraft, Unilever, Coca Cola, and Nestle. These seasoned professionals quickly figured out that BBF had substantial gaps in its ability to cope with industry complexity and manage its profitability in the face of industry dynamics. Further, they were aware that BBF was behind the times when it came to leveraging sophisticated BI and business analytics to improve profitability.

1.2 BBF BI OPPORTUNITIES

Recognizing that BI advances were critical to future business success—and to his own career—BBF's Chief Information Officer (CIO) launched an enterprise BI strategy project. His objective was to identify specific opportunities to leverage information and sophisticated analytics within BBF's major business functions and processes, such as for demand forecasting, production planning, inventory optimization, customer service improvement, revenue management, category management, trade promotion planning and lift analysis, supply chain collaboration, and cost optimization, among others. A variety of business challenges and BIOs were identified via interviews with executives, managers, and analysts across all major functions within BBF.

1.2.1 The CEO's View of Business Challenges and BIOs

After earning an MBA from a top-tier business school, John McCoy rose quickly through the ranks in sales and marketing for consumer packaged goods companies. When BBF was put together by a large private equity firm (LPE), it was with a view toward further acquisitions and eventually going public. The original CEO moved too slowly along this strategic path, and thus LPE brought in McCoy, who was known to a LPE director who had been CEO of a multibillion dollar food manufacturer.

Within less than a year, McCoy had grown frustrated. While acquisition plans were coming along nicely, BBF lacked the ability to actively manage revenues and costs. McCoy realized that execution is critical in the packaged food industry, and to get better at it he and his leadership team needed better visibility into all aspects of BBF's operations. As an industry veteran, McCoy understood that the packaged food business is complex—getting hundreds of products to thousands of retail shelves and making a profit despite fluctuating purchasing patterns and growing retailer purchasing power due to increased concentration.

As he considered what it would take to conquer complexity and move BBF to a point where all levels of the company had the visibility needed to be successful, his thoughts turned to BI and the results of a 2009 survey within the packaged food manufacturing industry. The results were troubling:

- over 50% said they wanted better information for cost and financial analysis;
- over 60% reported gaps in fundamental information and analytics needed for customer service analysis, and a third of those reported major gaps;
- over 80% reported gaps in fundamental information and analytics needed for performance management, and a quarter of those reported major gaps;
- over 80% reported gaps in fundamental information needed for sales and operations planning; and
- over 70% said that a key obstacle to BI success was lack of organizational awareness of how to use business information and analytics to improve business results.

McCoy considered these results and wondered whether the results would be the same within BBF—or even worse. At the same time, he knew that BBF's performance depended on execution, and he knew the old adage that "what gets measured gets managed." He considered where to add a BI-related objective to the BBF's overall strategic objectives, and decided that it fit under the objective "Leverage Information." With that in mind he added the subobjective "Create Business Intelligence Scorecards."

●●●──

Questions to Consider:

1. What does McCoy need to do to ensure that BBF is successful in leveraging BI and analytics to achieve its business objectives?
2. What should be the relationship between BI, analytics, and a strategy map?
3. Is it likely that people within BBF have a common definition of BI?
4. What should the dashboards display, and at what level of detail?
5. Who should be involved in dashboard design?
6. Which business functions should receive their dashboard first? Second? Why?
7. What does "visibility" mean in this context?

──

1.2.2 The Chief Operating Officer's View of Business Challenges and BIOs

After graduating in the mid-1970s with a B.S. in Industrial Engineering from a leading engineering school in the US manufacturing belt, Fred Sutcliff went to work in operations for a leading beverage manufacturer. He spent over 20 years in various manufacturing and supply chain jobs, culminating in the role of Vice President—Supply Chain. In that capacity, he was responsible for movement of products that resulted in $6 billion in revenues annually. Intrigued by what he perceived to be entrepreneurial possibilities, Fred joined BBF as Chief Operating Officer (COO).

Once onboard, Sutcliff's top priority was to put together a complete picture of the current state of operations. As an industrial engineer by training and an operations professional for over 20 years, Fred understood the importance of BI and analytics. So he hoped to quickly put his hands-on business information and analyses that would answer some of his most pressing questions:

- How are the 11 manufacturing plants performing in terms of cost, quality, safety, and customer service? What are the root causes of any unfavorable variances?
- How are plant assets performing in terms of equipment downtime and capacity utilization? What are the root causes of any unfavorable variances?
- Within the plants, which production lines are performing best? What are the root causes of any performance differences?
- Who are our strategic suppliers and how are they performing? Do we have supplier scorecards?
- How do our inbound logistics costs and service levels compare with others in our industry? With our targets? What are the root causes of any unfavorable variances?
- How are our distribution centers performing in terms of operating costs and customer service? What are the root causes of any unfavorable customer service variances?
- How is our customer service department performing against customer service metrics? What metrics are we using?
- How effective are we at demand forecasting, and at sales and operations planning process?
- What are our costs-of-goods and gross margins and trends for the last several years? Are we getting better?

What Fred found was a mixed-bag of fragmented information, mostly in the form of a monthly PowerPoint decks that contained 50 + pages of report-style information lifted from spreadsheets and traditional reports. Despite having two decades' experience, he found it difficult to see the big picture based on the PowerPoints. In frustration, he asked the VP of Finance assigned to Operations whether there were plans underway to provide the operations function with the information and analyses needed to manage the key performance variables that would determine the success—or failure—of company efforts to achieve operational excellence and meet profit objectives. Fred knew that BBF was under heavy pressure from the Board of Directors to deliver on profit targets demanded by the LPE. Without timely, accurate business information and analyses at his fingertips, Fred wondered how he could achieve what was expected of him. As a self-described "data guy," he was pleased to learn from the VP of Finance of the strategic objective to "Create Business Intelligence Scorecards." Further, he was pleased to learn that the enterprise BI strategy project was underway and that his 11 direct reports were slated to be interviewed about their views of business challenges and BI opportunities.

●●●

Questions to Consider:

1. What does Sutcliff need to do to ensure that he and his direct reports obtain the business information and analyses they require to manage the performance variables for which they are accountable?
2. By what method might they determine what information and analyses they require?
3. How should he and his direct reports determine the right set of key performance indicators?
4. For Operations, is it more important to have a dashboard or to have other forms of BI, such as advanced analytics, predictive analytics, alerts, reports, or multidimensional analyses?
5. Who should drive scorecard design?
6. Which operations function—procurement, plant operations, transportation, distribution, customer service, cost optimization, or sales and operations planning—should receive their dashboard first? Second? Why?

1.2.3 The Chief Marketing Officer's View of Business Challenges and BIOs

Rachel Smith was another hard-charging, fast-mover on the BBF management team. After graduating from a top-tier MBA program, Smith advanced through a traditional succession of marketing jobs for three different manufacturers of branded consumer products. Her many years of marketing experience were mostly in the packaged food products industry, and she was well-prepared for her new role as Chief Marketing Officer (CMO) when she joined BBF.

Much of the pressure for profits that the Board was placing on the management team fell squarely on Smith's shoulders. She was responsible for all aspects of brand portfolio management, including brand strategy, general management of brands, product innovation, consumer advertising and promotions, and brand profitability. Having come up through the marketing ranks in the 1980s and 1990s, Rachel was used to traditional sources of marketing information, such as focus group and other market research, market share data, and brand profit and loss (P&L) statements generated through laborious spreadsheet-based processes. She was not a "data" person in the same sense that the operations people were, and thus her perception was that BI and analytics were essentially better reporting. When the subject of committing her business resources to the strategic objective "Create Business Intelligence Scorecards" was raised in a meeting of BBF's Executive Team, Rachel made it clear that BI was certainly not among the top five objectives for Barry Green, her VP of Marketing.

As it turned out, however, Barry Green was very aware of the potential for BI and analytics to help meet the business challenge of optimizing the profitability of BBF's brand portfolio. His group felt the pain week in and week out of trying to make good marketing decisions without having a complete picture of current performance or the ability to effectively model the P&L impact of various courses of action. Green identified the key gaps as:

- the people in the marketing, sales, and finance departments lacked a common set of business facts, figures, and terminology for discussing actual revenues and profits in relation to the targets in annual operating plans and quarterly updates;
- due to business information gaps and inconsistencies, marketing lacked a complete picture of product shipments in its various distribution channels, making it nearly impossible to determine and respond to unfavorable volume performance in, for example, the grocery, mass merchandizer, drug store, convenience store, food service, and/or warehouse club channels;
- due to departmental boundaries and business information gaps and inconsistencies, marketing lacked a timely, automated way to determine the return-on-investment on the 40,000+ promotional campaigns BBF executed every year, which made it difficult to optimize brand P&L;
- due to business information gaps and inconsistencies, marketing lacked an automated, efficient way to manage the brand portfolio by region, customer, and SKU;
- due to departmental boundaries, information gaps, and differences in methods, marketing was not able to see inventory levels and make brand marketing plans that effectively balanced volume, share, and inventory targets to produce the optimal brand portfolio P&L; and

- the people who provide financial planning and analysis services to the marketing department have been limited by lack of investment in modern financial management systems, which means that a $4 billion company with nearly 1000 SKUs is being managed with manually intensive, error-prone, and spreadsheet-based budgeting and variance analysis processes.

In a business where small market share losses can translate to materially adverse P&L impacts, marketing execution is key, and Barry Green was sure that BBF needed to more dynamically manage its marketing activities. He was happy to provide his views of the business challenges and BI opportunities for the marketing department. At the same time, BBF was a pretty lean operation, and Green had plenty to do. The irony occurred to him that he and his marketing colleagues were so busy doing things the hard, slow way that they might not have the time needed to work with the BI team to design and deliver modern, dynamic BI and analytics. Having those capabilities would overcome fundamental gaps in marketing efficiency and effectiveness—allowing marketing managers and analysts to focus much more time on optimizing the profitability of the brand portfolio.

●●● ───

Questions to Consider:

1. What can be done to help the CMO evolve her understanding of the profit impact of BI and analytics?
2. What can the CEO do to ensure that the CMO is on board with the strategic objective "Create Business Intelligence Dashboards"?
3. What might a Brand Management Dashboard include?
4. With nearly 1000 SKUs distributed through eight major channels to customers who might operate more than 1000 stores across the United States, how could a Brand Management Dashboard be designed to "conquer complexity"?
5. For Marketing, is it more important to have a dashboard or to have other forms of BI, such as advanced analytics, predictive analytics, alerts, reports, or multidimensional analyses?
6. How hard should Barry Green push Rachel Smith to obtain BI and analytics, and what arguments might he use?

1.2.4 The Chief Sales Officer's View of Business Challenges and BIOs

Like others on the BBF Executive Team, Bob Alvarez had progressed through successively more responsible positions with larger packaged food product manufacturers. For over 25 years in sales, he had moved up the ranks by being aggressive in driving revenues to meet targets. Bob was known for his skill in developing effective professional relationships at the highest levels with key customers. By the time he joined BBF, he had also proven to be a very effective coach and mentor to his sales teams.

At BBF, the scope of the Chief Sales Officer's (CSO's) job was defined to include top-to-top sales, directing regional sales managers, managing the business relationship with their primary food broker, managing trade promotion spending in concert with brand strategies, and managing a business development organization, whose function was to translate brand strategies and plans into executable sales plans and tracking results. BBF's food broker handles sales within the grocery, warehouse club, drug store, convenience store, and military channels. BBF handles sales to Walmart and to deep discount chains, such as Dollar General and Family Dollar. BBF and its broker collaborate on brand planning, volume forecasting, trade spending, and joint sales calls. The broker handles day-to-day in-store execution of pricing actions, promotions, and merchandizing.

As Bob Alvarez settled into his position, he quickly realized that BBF could not provide the quality of business information and analyses he was accustomed to seeing at his former employer—at least not in the near term. What he received was an almost overwhelming pile of spreadsheets that looked at various performance measures in excruciating detail. Upon digging deeper, he found that there were 14 standard monthly views of sales performance, all of which contained page after page of detailed spreadsheets. Given that BBF sold nearly 1000 SKUs to hundreds of customers, at thousands of customer locations, though eight major channels, and at differing price points and promotion terms, Bob wondered how he and his team could effectively achieve revenue, share, distribution point, and other key objectives. With that concern in mind, he was happy to have his key people work with the Enterprise BI Strategy Team to discuss their business challenges and BI gaps. His people identified the following gaps:

- due to business information gaps and inconsistencies, BBF's sales teams and business development teams lacked timely, automated access to key performance measures to help them understand sales performance in relation to brand volume plans, and help them determine what actions to take to address any unfavorable performance trends;
- the current processes for trying to obtain needed business information involved extensive hunting for data and reformatting for various analytical purposes, and while this was viewed as suboptimal, getting the optimal information from the information technology (IT) department was so hard they has stopped asking and had adapted to suboptimal conditions;
- due to business information gaps, the sales teams and business development teams lacked historical performance information that would have enabled them to analyze and model the relationships between product demand and various marketing mixes, that is, price, trade promotions, consumer promotions, and merchandizing;
- due to business information gaps and overreliance on the spreadsheets described above, the sales teams and business development teams were not able to leverage dashboards to "manage by exception" and quickly focus in on the performance variances that were the most important and had the greatest financial impact—it was too hard to separate the wheat from the chaff;
- due to business information gaps, and because the sales, business development, and finance departments lacked a common set of business facts, figures, and terminology, it was very difficult to manage product profitability, that is, timely and accurate product-level profit measurement was very difficult to deliver for the nearly 1000 SKUs, and thus it was hard to determine the impact of varying the marketing mix on product profitability;
- while many in the industry were talking about supply chain collaboration between retailers and manufacturers, BBF business development teams lacked consistent access to its customers' Point-of-Sale data and inventory levels, which made it difficult to get a true picture of demand for each of the nearly 1000 SKUs;
- due to departmental boundaries and business information gaps and inconsistencies, the business development teams lacked a timely, automated way to determine the return-on-investment on the 40,000 + promotional campaigns BBF executed every year, which made it difficult to optimize the marketing mix and brand P&L;

- due to business information gaps, the business development teams lacked a timely and efficient way to measure, manage, and improve in-store execution of trade promotions by BBF's broker and the fields sales teams, and to measure incremental volume and lift; and
- due to business information gaps, it was very laborious to measure and track trends for key performance indicators (KPIs), such as cost per incremental case, cost per shipped case, cost per consumed case, merchandizing efficiency, ROI, share-of-market, distribution points.

As Alvarez looked at the list of gaps, he was impressed that his sales teams and business development teams were able to perform as well as they were. At the same time, he wondered how much revenue and profit was being left on the table due to all of the fundamental gaps in BI and analytics—and it occurred to him that without better BI and analytics it would be nearly impossible to figure that out.

●●●———————————————————————————

Questions to Consider:

1. Assuming that BBF will invest in creating a Sales and Business Development Dashboard, how might the dashboard be designed to help the CSO and his direct report manage by exception?
2. What might be the key ways to look at performance variances?
3. With nearly 1000 SKUs distributed through eight major channels to customers who might operate more than 1000 stores across the United States, how could a Sales and Business Development Dashboard be designed to "conquer complexity"?
4. To what degree might the Brand Management Dashboard and the Sales and Business Development Dashboard overlap in the business information and analyses to be presented?
5. For Sales and Business Development, is it more important to have a dashboard or to have other forms of BI, such as advanced analytics, predictive analytics, alerts, reports, or multidimensional analyses?

1.2.5 The Chief Financial Officer's View of Business Challenges and BIOs

Like many Chief Financial Officers (CFOs), Steve Hayes earned his CPA and started his career with a major public accounting firm. Within 5 years, he had moved up to become CFO of a consumer packaged goods company focused on over-the-counter health and wellness products. Upon joining BBF in the early 2000s, Steve took on the responsibility for financial operations, treasury, tax, and IT. One of his first major initiatives was reducing IT and operating costs, which provided him with a deep understanding of how the company worked day in and day out and allowed him to contribute to meaningful improvements in profitability.

The scope of Steve's responsibilities made him both a producer and a consumer of BI and analytics. On the producer side, he was counting on the CIO—one of his direct reports—to lead the charge in formulating the Enterprise BI Strategy. As CFO, Hayes had a lot on his plate, including a directive from the Board to shift the mix within the $900 million advertising and promotion budget toward a more balanced allocation between trade promotion spending and consumer advertising and promotion. At the same time, he was concerned because his CIO was more of an operations professional and less so an IT strategist/technologist or BI visionary. The CIO's strong background in operations had been extremely useful during Steve's early effort to reduce supply chain and operations costs. That background had also been useful because BBF managed IT as a cost to be minimized rather than as a profit enabler.

As a consumer of BI and analytics, Hayes knew there were big gaps at BBF, and he was concerned about the CIO's ability to successfully close the gaps and meet his needs and those of his peers on the Executive Team. On the other hand, with BBF's yet-to-be-announced acquisition of a well-known maker of packaged food products about to be announced, and with all the postmerger integration work to be done, Hayes felt he had bigger fish to fry than pushing ahead with BI and analytics. Even so, he had his direct reports meet with the enterprise BI strategy team and lay out the business challenges and BI opportunities. His people identified the following gaps:

- due to business information gaps and processing inefficiencies, the plant controllers reported that it was difficult for plant managers to manage the various drivers of plant profitability—including such variables as production costs, batch yields, and equipment effectiveness—in relation to forecasted and actual order volumes and mixes;
- due to information gaps, plant managers and plant controllers lack standardized historical information about performance, making it hard to conduct trend analysis for sales volume, product production volume by SKU, and actual raw materials usage;

- due to information gaps, plant managers and plant controllers lack standard automated variances analyses in relation to operating budgets, quarterly budget updates, and standard costs;
- due to information gaps and processing inefficiencies, senior financial planning and analysis professionals were handcuffed in their ability to dynamically measure, manage, and improve the financial performance of BBF's supply chain and production operations—the monthly cost-of-goods sold report consisted of 50+ pages of spreadsheets that was hard to produce, delivered more information than could be usefully consumed, and provided no ability to manage by exception; and
- due to information gaps and processing inefficiencies, senior financial planning and analysis professionals were handcuffed in their ability to dynamically support marketing, sales, and business development teams with SKU-level and customer-level P&L statement and variance analyses in relation to annual operating plans, brand plans, and quarterly updates.

As Steve Hayes reviewed these gaps he knew there were others, but the list did a good job of reflecting the fact that BBF lacked ready, efficient access to vital cost and financial information about the guts of the business. Manufacturing, supply chain, and sales and marketing expenses were a huge portion of the company P&L and BBF needed to improve and optimize those expenses in order to meet Board profit expectations.

●●●——————————————————————————

Questions to Consider:

1. How can Hayes balance the need for better BI and analytics across BBF with the demands of postmerger integration and the fact that the CIO is not a BI visionary or IT strategist?
2. In the role of producer of BI and analytics for BBF (through the CIO), how might Hayes think about priorities between his own needs as a consumer and the needs of his peers on the Executive Team? What factors should be considered when setting priorities?
3. Is there a systematic way to evaluate which business requirements for BI and analytics are common among the various BBF business units?
4. How might BBF's overall IT budget be set, and what portion of that budget should be invested in BI and analytics?

1.2.6 The CIO's View of Business Challenges and BIOs

Ralph Milan was a key player in BBF's strategic objective—Create BI Scorecards. His background in supply chain systems, enterprise operations planning, project management, and information systems had allowed him to make important early contributions to improvements in BBF's supply chain and operations performance. Further, he had a prior 4-year working relationship with his boss, Steve Hayes (the CFO), and they were philosophically aligned with the idea of managing IT as a cost. Like most of BBF, the IT department ran lean, and Milan ran his 70-person department without the benefit of an administrative assistant.

BBF's primary foray into BI and analytics was embodied by a 10-year old marketing data warehouse (MDW), which had been developed and delivered by a prominent public accounting firm. The information in MDW was pulled from BBF's enterprise resource planning (ERP) system and from its trade promotions management system, a nightly process that took over 8 hours due to flaws in the original design and approach to refreshing the MDW. The information in MDW was a key input to a large number of reports generated by BBF business units using outdated BI tools—reports that provided raw data to business users across BBF for the various manually intensive, department-specific monthly reports prepared in standard spreadsheet templates. Milan was aware that BBF was falling behind in its use of modern BI and analytics, and thus he launched the 3-month Enterprise BI Strategy project. The project produced a number of key deliverables, including an assessment that identified the following technical gaps and challenges:

- reports take a long time to run;
- a typical data usage scenario is that business users pull data from the data warehouse into the BI tool, cut and paste data from a BI report into a spreadsheet, combine data from multiple reports and spreadsheets into a single spreadsheet for formatting and calculations, and then cut and paste information from spreadsheets into PowerPoint presentations;
- business users want dashboards and reports where they can use pick-lists to specify and filter what information is to be presented;
- business users want prestaged information about key performance metrics and they want that information to be standardized across BBF;

- business users want to leverage alerts and management by exception;
- business users want to leverage automated variance analyses; and
- business users want to have standardized, automated P&L statements and associated drill-downs.

As Milan looked the list, it seemed to him that many of the business users' wishes could be met by upgrading to a modern BI tool that enabled user self-service. He knew there were power users in the key department, and he believed that if they were armed with a better BI tool that they could create BI dashboards for their purposes. While not an official member of the Executive Team, Milan also knew that a major acquisition was about to be announced, and he had been through a postmerger integration before. He wondered if the business community would engage as needed to develop BI dashboards. With these considerations in mind, Milan approved an acquisition of a modern BI tool and then decided to sit back and gage business interest in BI Scorecards before pushing ahead.

Questions to Consider:

1. Is it likely that deployment of a new BI tool will enable BBF to overcome the business challenges and capitalize on the BI opportunities described in the CEO, COO, CMO, CSO, and CFO sections of this chapter?
2. Based on the information presented, what do you believe is likely to happen at BBF with respect to the strategic objective—Create Business Intelligence Dashboards?
3. How important does BI appear to be in the food manufacturing industry?
4. If BI is important, how might the CIO proceed to create BI dashboards?

1.3 THE BBF BI VISION AND BI OPPORTUNITY PORTFOLIO & BUSINESS CASE

Based on the business challenges and BI opportunities identified through interviews and a web-enabled survey of BBF executives, managers, and analysts, the enterprise BI strategy team produced a BI Vision and a BI Opportunity Portfolio & Business Case. The BI Vision described a desired future state for BI and analytics at BBF. The BI Opportunity Portfolio & Business Case described key business-driven opportunities to leverage BI and analytics and the value proposition for doing so. Highlights from these BI Strategy documents are provided below.

1.3.1 The BBF BI Vision

The BBF BI vision is intended to describe a general direction for how BI will be leveraged to improve business performance. Specific BIOs and projects will be described in Section 7.3.2.

1. Automate and improve information-intensive aspects of recurring business planning, performance management, variance analysis, root cause analysis, and corrective action planning. Current processes are inefficient, error-prone, inflexible, and suboptimal for managing the complexities of our business.
2. Automate and accelerate timely generation of enterprise and business-unit dashboards and KPIs to focus our attention on key customers and channels that drive our desired results, measure our performance against established KPI targets, and leverage management by exception strategies. Our current manually intensive performance reporting processes are slow and expensive.
3. Automate trade promotion effectiveness analysis in order to cope with the volume of trade promotions being executed and enable a surgical approach to shifting trade support to consumer advertising and marketing. There is a "huge opportunity" to leverage BI for promotion level analysis and scenario planning in relation to specific situations, brands, and customers so that our substantial investment in trade support achieves optimal results.
4. Deliver standardized and comprehensive historical business information/facts as inputs for the various enterprise plans and budgets and for short-interval control. Having ready access to transactional details and relevant summaries of gross revenues, shipments, consumption, market share, trade spending, net sales, production volumes and yields, inventory levels and ages, costs of products manufactured/sold, operating expenses, and other operational and financial information would enable efficient and effective planning and control.
5. Enable timely and cost-effective monitoring of our business and financial performance through standardized yet dynamic views of

profitability and performance by customer, segment, category, brand, product, SKU, plant, and channel. Managing profitability at granular levels, for example, by customer, would enable us to be more proactive in managing the business situations, relationships, and processes that have a substantial impact on sales, costs, service, and profits.

6. Deliver business information and business analytics in ways that match the usage preferences and styles of the various constituencies in the business community. Our business professionals report a range of usage preferences, including standard reports, ad hoc access to large data sets, slice-and-dice and drill down/across (OLAP), scorecards and dashboards, and predictive analytics. In general, most users want simple, easy-to-use screens that allow them to specify variables of interest and "as-of" dates on reports and analyses that run quickly.

7. Renovate the current data warehousing and reporting processes to mitigate or eliminate performance problems with the current environment. Many reports take far too long to run, and in some case the reports are not available in a timely fashion, which drives the need for workarounds and hampers business performance in cases where more timely information makes a difference.

When the BBF BI Vision is fully realized:

• If they so choose, BBF executives will be able to easily monitor enterprise and functional performance via scorecards, dashboards, and exceptions-based alerts presented on their desktops and/or laptops. They will also have the option to drill down on any KPI of interest, to see such information as customer, brand, segment, product, and plant performance and P&Ls, and to monitor leading indicators, such as brand equity, distribution, and pricing. For executives who are not as hands-on with computers, all this information will be staged so that it can easily be delivered by static reports.

• Directors and managers will have role-based access to the same information as BBF executives, with the ability to rapidly assess business performance, drill down into root causes, and identify potential courses of action. Providing these front-line professionals with easy access to timely, specific, and reliable information will enable us to increase our ability to execute operational changes in response to specific situations with consumers, markets, customers, products, plants, inventory, channels, and so forth.

- Customer-facing and market-facing professionals will have complete views of customers, categories, brands, trade spending, and products so that they can more effectively manage key relationships and programs and achieve brand marketing and sales plans, including volume objectives, price points, and distribution objectives.
- Power users and analysts in all areas of the company will have access to prestaged business information (cubes) so they can write their own ad hoc queries and so they can perform true OLAP analyses. These users will be able to easily access time series data for user-specified periods of interest, to access data for planning, budgeting, and forecasting purposes, to access data for deep-dive variance analyses, for modeling scenarios, and many other data-intensive analyses.

To achieve this broad vision, we have defined specific BIOs that can be prioritized and sequentially delivered. These are discussed below.

1.3.2 The BBF BIO Portfolio
The BIOs that BBF professionals identified are discussed and defined below.

1. *Enterprise Performance Scorecards and Dashboards.*
   This BIO would implement custom-designed scorecards, dashboards, and exception reporting to compare planned versus actual performance in financial and operational terms for key dimensions of business performance, including performance with customers and by brands, plants, carriers, distribution centers, and so forth.
2. *Revenue Management Analytics.*
   This BIO would integrate and deliver timely, granular information about revenues, shipments, volume, prices, consumption, share, margin, inventory, and net sales—which is essential for enterprise demand planning, brand planning, customer service analysis, category analysis, price and promotion optimization, budgeting, financial analysis, and variance analysis. This BIO will help drive revenue growth and help to effectively manage revenue attainment on a customer-by-customer basis across all channels of distribution.
3. *Trade Promotion Analytics.*
   This BIO would integrate trade spending, IRI, and ERP data as needed to automate promotion level analysis and deliver promotion performance metrics. Having ready access to such information will benefit BBF during market and brand planning processes and during the process of targeting trade support toward programs and customers

whose performance has been proven. There is a huge opportunity to more effectively allocate the $900 million in trade support investments by leveraging BI to automate the postpromotion analysis process and view promotions by customer and type. This will allow us to accurately judge trade promotion effectiveness, profit, lift, and ROI by customer, brand, product, channel, and other relevant dimensions.

4. *Inventory Management Analytics.*

This BIO would integrate and deliver timely and granular inventory information for supply planning, customer service, and inventory optimization purposes. It would also enable adoption of customer service and inventory optimization techniques that would allow BBF to differentiate its service to the top customers who drive the preponderance of its revenue and profits, assuming that suitable process changes are also adopted. Further, it would also provide inventory availability information for comparison to projected demand to better avoid or manage stockouts.

5. *Cost and Financial Analytics.*

This BIO would enable deeper understanding of the operational drivers of BBF's costs so they can be actively managed and optimized. Further, it would stage cost and financial information for planning, budgeting, cost estimating, establishing standard costs, cost analysis, variance analysis, financial modeling, and other financial management purposes—all tools that are needed to more tightly and cost-effectively control productivity, profit and free cash flow.

6. *Supply Chain and Operations Analytics.*

This BIO would integrate fundamental operating information from our ERP, logistics, human resources, timekeeping, process control, and factory execution systems to provide a comprehensive, end-to-end picture of BBF's supply chain and operations performance and productivity. The information and analytics delivered would be used to improve supply planning, vendor negotiations, capacity planning, warehousing and transportation performance, productivity, plant and copacker performance, and customer service.

7. *Enterprise Planning and Budgeting.*

This BIO would provide standard historical information for planning and budgeting, automate sales and operations planning processes and exception reporting, and automate conversion of operating plans expressed in case volumes to financial plans expressed in dollars.

The prioritized BIOs, illustrated by Fig. 1.1, were used to drive a multiyear BI Program Plan.

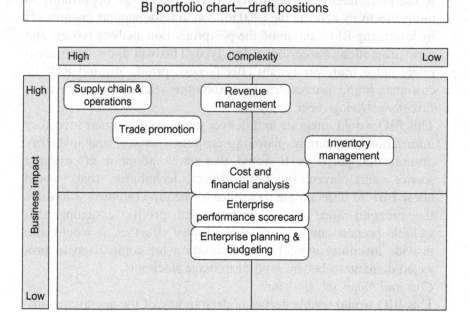

Figure 1.1 A BI Portfolio Diagram guides BIO prioritization.

In the next subsection, we will highlight how the BIOs identified at BBF may also be applicable for other manufacturers outside of the food manufacturing industry.

1.4 GENERALIZING FROM THE BBF CASE—BI APPLICATIONS FOR MANUFACTURERS

The BBF case provides useful examples of how BI can be leveraged by manufacturers to increase revenues, reduce costs, or both. BI can be the heart of an enterprise performance management system, and the business information and analyses BI delivers can be used to drive operational improvements in key value chain processes—improvements that result in positive financial results. A high-level "menu" of BI applications for manufacturers is shown in Fig. 1.2.

We used the term "menu" to indicate that there are a lot of possible BIOs for any manufacturing company, and the choice of what is important is influenced by the actual industry and how the company competes. For a packaged food company like BBF, trade promotional spending is a large percentage of revenues and thus obtaining

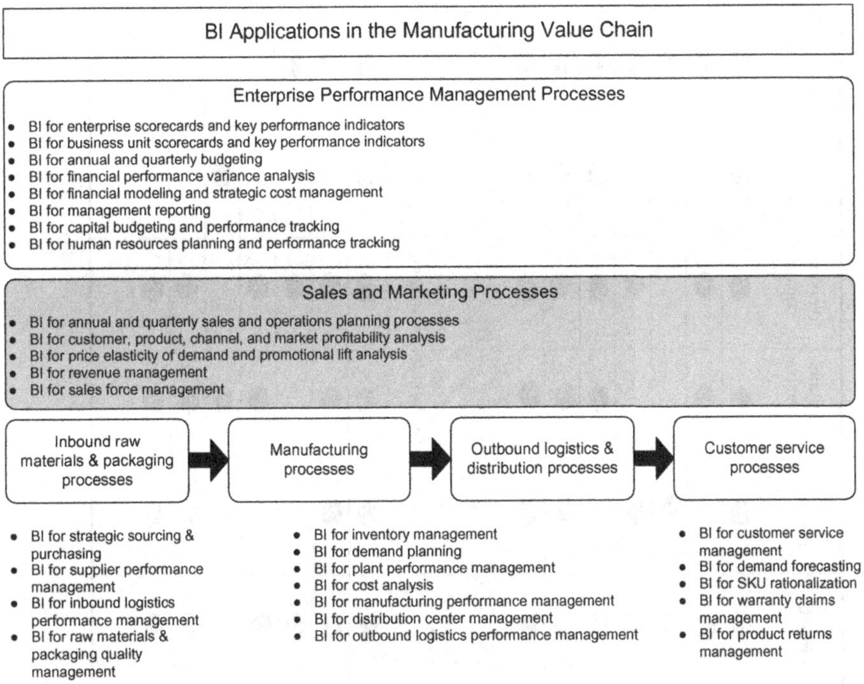

Figure 1.2 Manufacturers have many opportunities to leverage BI.

suitable lift from the 40,000 + campaigns they run every year is important to manage, and BI is critical for that purpose. For consumer electronics companies, the product lifecycle is extremely short, so it is
critical to get new products out into the retail channels quickly. That
makes BI for the function that is called "sales operations" essential for
managing inventory levels, distribution, and product returns. Since
consumer electronics companies typically outsource product
manufacturing, BI about manufacturing performance might be less
important due to lack of direct control of that function. In contrast,
companies who manufacture military equipment are required to report
very specific and comprehensive manufacturing performance information, so BI about cost, schedule, and technical performance is essential.
These are but a few examples of how the industry in which a manufacturer competes and its business model influence BIOs and priorities. In
general though, BI can influence financial and operational performance as shown in Fig. 1.3 below—using the BBF BIOs for illustration purposes.

BBF BI opportunities impact financial performance

	Net sales	Cost of goods	Gross margin	Profits	Inventory	Accounts receivable	Working capital	Fixed assets	Return on assets
Performance scorecard/dashboard	●	●	●	●	●	●	●	●	●
Revenue management analytics	●		●	●		●	●		●
Trade promotion analytics	●			●	●				●
Inventory management analytics	●	●	●	●	●		●		●
Cost & financial analytics	●	●	●	●		●	●	●	●
Supply chain & operations analytics		●	●	●	●	●	●	●	●
Enterprise planning & budgeting		●	●	●	●	●	●	●	●

BBF BI opportunities impact operational performance

	Strategic & operational alignment	Growth	Productivity & cost effectiveness	Customer retention & profitability	Demand forecasting	Supply chain effectiveness	Planning & scheduling	Product portfolio management	Sales & marketing effectiveness
Performance scorecard/dashboard	●	●	●	●	●	●	●	●	●
Revenue management analytics	●	●		●	●	●	●	●	●
Trade promotion analytics	●	●		●			●		●
Inventory management analytics	●		●			●	●		
Cost & financial analytics	●		●					●	
Supply chain & operations analytics	●		●	●	●	●	●		
Enterprise planning & budgeting	●	●			●	●	●		

Figure 1.3 BI done well favorably impacts financial and operational performance.

Ultimately, BI and analytics are about increasing revenues, optimizing costs, and thereby improving profits. A simple way for manufacturers to start homing in on where their most important BIOs might lie is to look at the cost drivers for the expenditures that are the largest proportion of operating income, and to look at the performance of the business processes that have the greatest impact on customer satisfaction. The menu provided by Fig. 1.2 is a useful way to start. In the following section, we'll revisit BBF and use the case to illustrate some of the strategic barriers to BI success.

1.5 LESSONS LEARNED FOR BI STRATEGY—BBF BI PROGRESS

At the time of the case, BBF was on the verge of a $1 billion plus acquisition, which went through just as the enterprise BI Strategy project was wrapping up. As might be expected, postmerger integration activities consumed much of the bandwidth of BBF's key business leaders and managers for over a year. Additionally, pressure for profits coming from private equity backers certainly didn't abate, and thus the Executive Team kept a clear focus on blocking and tackling—particularly in sales, marketing, and manufacturing cost improvement. As a lean company, BBF's top executives and their direct reports were spread very thin. As a Senior Vice President (SVP) in financial management put it, "I'm assigned to three business improvement projects, and on each I'm supposed to be half time. I do my regular work on Sundays, and I'm not doing any of these well." As a result of these factors, for a couple of years BBF made almost no meaningful progress on realizing the BI Vision and capitalizing on the BIOs identified by the enterprise BI strategy team.

As the executive team emerged from the rigors of postmerger integration, there started to be rumbles at the SVP and VP level about needing better information and analyses in order to meet profit expectations. Recognizing the need for action and his own lack of experience in the BI arena, a Director of BI Strategy was hired. In this newly created role, Carol Penner was charged with the strategic objective "Create Business Intelligence Scorecards"—the same objective that CEO John McCoy had established a few years back. Penner did her best to move things forward, and soon encountered some barriers to BI success.

1.5.1 Lesson 1—Lack of Understanding of BI Makes the Value Hard to Determine

One of Carol Penner's first steps was to have introductory meetings with executives at the Executive Vice President, Senior Vice President, and Vice President level, some of whom had been interviewed during the BI strategy project. What she found was that some of these senior people lacked a clear understanding of what BI is and what it can do. Several suggested that some education about BI would be useful, and Penner took steps to make that happen. In the end, however, the management bandwidth was still an issue at BBF and the executives wouldn't or couldn't engage to become educated about BI. This lack of understanding is a strategic barrier to BI success because it translates to inaction—in the form of insufficient funding and/or insufficient commitment of business people to BI projects. Top executives won't act if they don't understand how value would be created with BI, and this is clearly a barrier to BI success.

1.5.2 Lesson 2—The Mission and Importance of BI Is Not Clear

While CEO John McCoy was on the mark in understanding that BBF needed to conquer complexity and simplify how the company operates, and while he understood the idea that BI could help, his background had not prepared him to understand the complexity and general management challenges of an enterprise BI initiative. He was frustrated with the inability of some of his direct reports to provide answers to his questions about various aspects of enterprise performance. At the same time, BBF's strategic objectives encompassed six major performance areas and numerous subobjectives, and his attention was naturally drawn to revenue and profit performance. The impact on the BI initiative is that it received almost none of his management attention for over 2 years. He did not establish a clear mission for the BI initiative, he did not ensure that his best people understood that BI was important given the complexity of the industry, and he did not incorporate making progress on the BI front into the individual performance plans and bonus structures of the executives whose support of the BI initiative was critical to its success.

1.5.3 Lesson 3—No Sense of Urgency Among Upper Management

Given the bandwidth issues at BBF, it was no surprise that the urgent drove out the important, and that BI fell pretty low on executives' lists of priorities—clearly a barrier to BI success. The enterprise BI strategy team had produced a BI Vision and a BIO Opportunity Portfolio that had: (1) established a clear link between BI and BBF's business strategies and critical business processes and (2) described a better future state whereby BBF's executives, managers, and analysts would have the information and analyses they needed at their fingertips. On the other hand, the lack of understanding of BI (Lesson 1) and the absence of clear mission and stated importance for BI (Lesson 2) contributed to a lack of urgency among BBF's top people. From an external perspective, while BBF faced the same margin pressures and operational challenges as its competitors, it still held the leading or second-place share-of-market in almost all of the packaged food categories in which it competed. In the absence of an externally induced "burning platform," the BI initiative was thought to be lower on the list of priorities than other profit improvement opportunities BBF was pursuing—most of which were aimed at growing sales volume and improving manufacturing efficiency. The irony was that BI could have been instrumental to achieving both those objectives.

1.6 QUESTIONS TO CONSIDER FOR YOUR COMPANY OR FUNCTION

1. How complex is your industry and/or your business model within the industry?
2. Is BI strategically important to your company or function?
3. From a competitive perspective, is it safe for your company to be a laggard?
4. From a competitive perspective, do you need to be leaders, or is parity OK?
5. Which of the BI applications described in Sections 1.3 and 1.4 make sense for your company or function?
6. Has your company pursued BI, and if so has it faced any of the barriers discussed in Section 1.5? What might be done to overcome the barriers?

CHAPTER 2

Business Intelligence in the Era of Big Data and Cognitive Business

Business executives, managers, and analysts have wrestled for over two decades with the problem of understanding how to leverage data to improve business results. For much of that time, the umbrella term "business intelligence"—or "BI" for short—has been used to describe a family of business analysis techniques ranging from standard reports to highly sophisticated advanced statistics. More recently, terms like "big data" and "cognitive business" have been introduced into the business and technical lexicon. Upon close examination, the newer terminology is about the same thing that BI has always been about: analyzing the vast amounts of data that companies generate and/or purchase in the course of business as a means of improving profitability and competitiveness. Accordingly, we will use the terms BI and business intelligence throughout the book, and we will discuss the newer concepts as appropriate.

Whether we call it BI, data mining, big data, cognitive business or whatever, the business challenges for realizing business value are the same:

1. helping business executives, managers, and analysts in companies sort through the confusing array of terminology to understand what is real, what is hype, and how to leverage data throughout the enterprise to improve business results;
2. ensuring alignment between business strategies, the core business processes that execute the strategies, and the use of BI to improve those core business processes—processes such as marketing, sales, customer service, and operations that ultimately determine the economic results for the business; and
3. managing the complex organizational factors that determine how effectively BI applications are developed and how effectively they are adopted within business processes to increase revenues, reduce costs, or both.

Because of struggles in these regards, BI is underutilized within companies where it could have a substantial impact—at a time when information and analysis have become critical factors in business success. A key aspect of the problem has to do with lack of clarity about what BI is, what BI they should have, and how BI is related to analytics, big data, data warehousing, and other related topics. With this in mind, it is important to clarify some of the terminology we will use throughout the book. We'll also explore what BI success means to different people in different industries and job functions.

2.1 GETTING CLEAR ABOUT TERMINOLOGY—BUSINESS DEFINITIONS OF BUSINESS INTELLIGENCE AND RELATED TERMS

Having worked with business executives, managers, and analysts in well-known companies in a wide range of industries, I can say with certainty that they are often unclear about both the terminology and the value propositions associated with BI. It's no surprise given the confusing array of BI-related terminology to which they are exposed, as exemplified by Fig. 2.1[1].

With this in mind, we'll use the following business-oriented definitions throughout the book[2]:

- *Business intelligence (BI)*: An umbrella term that encompasses provision of relevant reports, scorecards, dashboards, e-mail alerts, prestructured user-specified queries, ad hoc query capabilities, multidimensional analyses, statistical analyses, forecasts, models, and/or simulations to business users for use in increasing revenues, reducing costs, or both.
- *Analytics*: A subset of BI and an umbrella term that encompasses provision of relevant statistical analyses, forecasts, models, and/or simulations to business users for use in increasing revenues, reducing costs, or both.
- *Big data*: Large amounts of rapidly generated pictures, video clips, location (geospatial) data, sensor data, text messages, document images, web logs, and machine data traditionally captured and used

---

[1]From Williams S. 5 Barriers to BI Success and how to overcome them. Strategic Finance, July 2011.
[2]Adapted from Williams S. Big data strategy approaches: business-driven or discovery-based? Bus Intellig J 19(4).

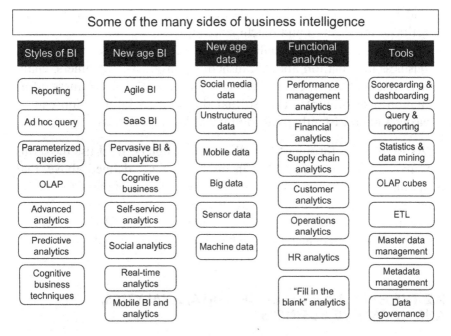

Figure 2.1 BI terminology can be confusing for those who don't work with it day-in and day-out.

by social media and Internet-based businesses and more recently being leveraged by early adopter mainstream businesses.

- *Big data analytics*: Analysis of stored big data content of various kinds to supplement BI and traditional analytics for use in increasing revenues, reducing costs, or both. Also useful for nonbusiness uses, such as public safety and national defense.
- *Structured data*: The typical business data used by companies for decades—represented as numerical values, calculated measures and metrics, and business facts such as financial results, customer characteristics, factory output, or product characteristics—and which has been typically stored in relational databases.
- *Unstructured data*: Digital content such as pictures, video clips, text messages, document images, and web logs. "Unstructured data" is substantially equivalent to "big data"—but differs in that sensor data, location data, and machine data are typically structured data and are included as examples of the variety of data that collectively constitute big data.
- *Cognitive business*: The use of structured and unstructured data and highly sophisticated analytical techniques to identify, evaluate,

and recommend business courses of actions. Related terms include artificial intelligence and machine learning.

- *Data warehouse*: A specialized database used to store important business information about transactions, products, customers, channels, financial results, performance metrics, and other business information over multiple years so that the business information can be easily and consistently used to improve business results.

As we proceed through the forthcoming chapters, we'll use the terms "business intelligence" and "BI" in the broad sense defined above, that is, as an umbrella term. We will also use it to encompass the newer concepts—big data, big data analytics, and cognitive business. Where appropriate to the context, we will distinguish between BI in general and a specific type of BI—such as analytics or multidimensional analysis.

2.2 THE HYPE AROUND BI, BIG DATA, ANALYTICS, AND COGNITIVE BUSINESS

Every day, executives and managers at leading companies are bombarded with claims about BI, big data, analytics, and cognitive business. Many business people are a skeptical lot when it comes to potential business improvements enabled by information technology. They need to have a concrete idea of how BI, analytics, cognitive business, and/or big data would actually help them in their specific business before approving multimillion dollar budgets. As one client put it, "we need to sort through what is hype and what is real for our specific business context." Prompted by this need, I suggest the following considerations.

It might be hype if... the smartest, most experienced business people at your company cannot explain very specifically how having *better information and analyses* would enable the company to capture incremental revenues and/or reduce expenses. In our professional opinion, the "true North" by which to navigate the hype is whether or not there is a clear, concrete connection between a proposed use of BI and an important company business process that makes a difference to customers and company economics. In this case, "better information" typically means transactional history, product/service holdings, plus customer demographic information about each and every individual customer, automatically available on a daily basis, and organized for reuse across the company on a daily/weekly/monthly basis whenever such information is needed to run the company and improve profits. Unless that connection can be made in a very specific and detailed way, it might be hype.

It might be hype if... there is a big gap between the visionary and poetic language being used to describe benefits of a BI, big data, or cognitive business product offering and the actual products and services being sold. We worked with a $2 + billion company in 2011/12 that was trying to figure out what to do in the BI and analytics space so they asked leading BI vendors what they should do. One prominent vendor known for flashy ads aimed at business executives submitted a proposal that:

- was mostly about selling licenses for commodity BI tools that have been on the market for over a decade and
- hoped to sell some 2000 full-featured BI tool licenses to a company that was not likely to need that many licenses for years to come, if ever.

The business benefits being touted were couched in high-level business terms like agile business and customer intimacy, but what was being sold was a package of canned reports with little connection to the business benefits being claimed. If you perceive this kind of gap, it might be hype.

It might be hype if... you're being sold a race car and your company is just learning to ride a bike. When it comes to BI, big data, analytics, and cognitive business, even the most successful companies in many industries are just starting to move up the maturity curve. One of our clients was being pushed by a leading vendor to purchase roughly $500,000 in advanced enterprise analytics hardware and software, when what the client really needed to get started was two desktop licenses for a standard statistical analysis package—for a total of roughly $24,000. If you feel you are being sold a package that represents what your company *might* need after several years of getting its feet wet, it might be hype.

It might be hype if... the topic is big data, big data analytics, or cognitive business. The "next big thing" in BI comes along every couple of years and then fizzles. Pushed by big consulting firms, big vendors, and prominent analyst firms, these latest concepts are all the rage at a given point in time. Now of course the proponents point to case studies that back up their claims, but many cases are really just about creative uses of BI and analytics using traditional data that we've had for decades. Our experience with traditional Fortune 1000 and mid-cap companies is that:

1. many successful big companies haven't even leveraged regular data yet, let alone big data or cognitive computing;
2. the most valuable data for BI and analytics are generally the common, mundane transactional data, customer data, and financial data that companies have had for years—data that is the key to understanding the economic performance of the company and what drives it;
3. big data in the form of unstructured digital content such as pictures, video clips, text messages, and document images is of unproven value in many traditional (non-Internet based) companies; and
4. many traditional companies do not generate unstructured digital content in the normal course of their business, though marketers are starting to leverage web and social media data.

If the value of big data is not clear to the smartest, most experienced people in your company, it might be hype.

It might be hype if... you hear the term "out of the box" in relation to any BI, analytics, big data, or cognitive business software product or service. Software vendors design standard products that they hope to license to millions of users. While there is some tailoring of the products to industries and/or job functions, these products are simply pre-packaged capabilities that have the *potential* to help companies leverage business information and analytics to create business value. That "out of the box" potential means nothing without intelligent use of the potential to create incremental revenues and/or reduce or optimize expenses. Vendors are sophisticated at convincing business executives and managers that their "solution" reduces risk, speeds up time to value, and creates competitive advantage—out of the box and without any customization. In other words, their product is a silver bullet for solving all manner of complicated business challenges. If this sounds too good to be true, it might be hype.

It might be hype if... a technology vendor conveys the idea that all one needs to do is buy their product and the company will obtain benefits like improved profits. BI, analytics, big data, and cognitive business need to be business-driven initiatives, not technology-driven. If a company can develop a clear vision and concrete strategy for leveraging business information and business analyses, the technology piece can be figured out and is generally low-risk if one uses tools that have been around for a long time. There is no substitute for aligning BI, analytics, big data, and/or cognitive business applications with core business process, managing process and cultural change, and driving adoption of the applications by business users. If a vendor claims that the technology delivers the BI benefits, it might be hype.

As we noted at the outset, there is a lot of hype around BI, analytics, big data, and cognitive business. This makes it hard for business professionals to understand their true opportunities, understand the risks, and formulate pragmatic strategies and program plans. We hope this book will paint a picture of what is possible with BI and what may make sense for your industry, company, and job function. Armed with this information, you'll be in a stronger position to sort through the hype. And if your company has been paying BI consultants and/or BI vendors, you'll be in a better position to judge whether your company is better off for having done so.

2.3 A BUSINESS VIEW OF BIG DATA[3]

From a business perspective, what's really new and important about big data? The most widely communicated concept of big data holds that it differs from traditional data in its volume, variety, and velocity. Let's examine those in turn.

Data volume. There is no argument that the Internet and the social media revolution have spawned vast amounts of new kinds of data. And new technical approaches to storing and managing these vast volumes of new data have evolved to make the cost of keeping that data much less expensive. So we can store big data cheaply, but the "garbage in, garbage out" maxim still applies. *From a business perspective, what is important is determining the utility of that data for creating business value.*

Data velocity. A good example of the change in velocity of data is provided by the electric utility industry and its adoption of smart meters. A utility with 700,000 customers might have obtained 700,000

[3]Ibid.

meter readings a month in the past. With smart meters, that same utility might obtain 700,000 meter readings a minute. More broadly, the explosion of social media activity and Internet commerce means that there are hundreds of millions of pieces of data created every second. *From a business perspective, what is important is determining whether and how high data velocities are relevant and useful for creating business value.*

Data variety. What is supposedly new with big data is the capture and storage of unstructured data or semistructured data—all of it digital but much of it not really "data" in the traditional sense of the word. The pictures, video clips, text messages, document images, and web logs stored today could arguably be called "content" or "digital content" rather than data. In fact, in the document management and workflow worlds, many of these types of unstructured data are considered content. Insurance companies for years have captured pictures and copies of documents and stored them within workflow-oriented claims processing systems. In the banking world, the Check 21 initiative was based on storing check images on optical disks. In the manufacturing world, statistical process control methods that generate large volumes of sensor readings have been in use for decades. *From a business perspective, what is important is determining how these various forms of "big data content" can be used to create business value.*

Based on the above, it seems fair to conclude that the volume and velocity of digital content creation is indeed new, and that there are new varieties of digital content—with text messages and web logs (less new) being good examples. As to the business importance of big data, we might reasonably point out that:

- new *varieties* of digital content will be important if they can be used to increase revenues, reduce costs, or both—and this will depend on industry-specific and company-specific factors;
- increased *volumes* of digital content will be important if the content can be used to increase revenues, reduce costs, or both—otherwise one could be spending money to store ever-increasing volumes of trash; and
- increased *velocities* of digital content will be important if the content can be used to increase revenues, reduce costs, or both and its utility for doing so is time-dependent—otherwise one could be spending money to accumulate trash more quickly.

With all of the foregoing in mind, and giving due recognition to the fact that big data *might* be valuable, the potential competitive implications of big data suggest that companies systematically evaluate big data opportunities when formulating their BI strategies—or as extensions to existing BI strategies. Such an evaluation should consider:

1. alignment with any ongoing enterprise, business unit, or functional uses of BI;
2. how big data content—pictures, video clips, location (geospatial) data, sensor data, text messages, document images, web logs, and machine data—can be used to increase revenues, reduce costs, or both; and
3. whether to invest in capturing and storing big data content "on the come"—by which I mean ahead of any clear idea of exactly how that content will be used to increase revenues, reduce costs, or both.

There is nearly 20 years of history of companies using BI, data warehouses, and traditional analytics to create business value—with many successful companies still needing to do more to fully leverage these proven tools. And there are proven methods that can be applied for analyzing how big data content can be used to create business value—about which we will say more in chapter "The Strategic Importance of Business Intelligence." From a BI perspective, big data is simply another potential source of useful information and digital content that might be useful for analytical purposes aimed at improving the business processes that drive economic results.

2.4 A BUSINESS VIEW OF COGNITIVE BUSINESS

The field of cognitive science draws on disciplines such as neuroscience, psychology, artificial intelligence, statistics, mathematics, and computer science. Cognitive business is simply the use of cognitive science techniques and methods to address complex, dynamic, and/or ambiguous business situations. Since many business situations and decision contexts have those characteristics, the thinking is that using cognitive science for business purposes can result in better business performance than would otherwise be possible.

If we look at the idea of cognitive business from a BI perspective, we can compare the two as shown in Table 2.1.

Table 2.1 Cognitive Business Techniques Add New Analytical and Decision Support Tools to the BI Toolkit

	Business Intelligence	Cognitive Business
Business outputs		
Reports	X	
Scorecards and dashboards	X	
Multidimensional analysis	X	
Ad hoc analysis	X	
Advanced analytics	X	X
Predictive analytics	X	X
Alerts	X	
Visualization	X	
Relationship to business processes		
Information and analysis about process performance	X	
Information and analysis used within processes	X	X
Information and analysis for process control	X	X
Data inputs		
Traditional structured data	X	X
Unstructured data		X
Platform		
Company premises	X	X
Cloud based	X	X

The circled portions of Table 2.1 highlight similarities and differences as follows:

1. Similarity—both BI and cognitive business encompass the use of standard mathematical and statistical methods to perform analyses in the context of various business domains. For example, advanced analytics (backward looking, such as trend analysis) and predictive analytics (forward looking, such as simulations and optimizations) have been considered a subset of BI for decades. Cognitive business is mainly about such analytical methods, although it may bring more advanced techniques to bear than have traditionally been used in business. Arguably, any analytical technique employed by cognitive business applications and applied to structured data can also be used

by data scientists and business domain experts working with analytics platforms such as SAS and SPSS.

2. Difference—traditional BI tools are used to analyze structured data, whereas cognitive business applications would have both structured and unstructured data as inputs. Given the need to analyze unstructured data, there are a variety of tools that are used to basically take unstructured data and describe it in ways so that it can be processed by computerized algorithms.

From a business perspective, what might be important is if your particular company needs to move beyond more traditional BI and analytics to analyze large amounts of unstructured data in order to improve some relevant business process in a way that increases revenues, reduces costs, or both. In an industry where there are such needs, it would also be important to consider the competitive implications of cognitive business techniques. From a strategy perspective, there is a need to evaluate cognitive business applications developed by vendors versus building a customized application. In the latter case, a company's internal domain experts would work with data scientists and leverage packaged analytical components (eg, text analysis software) to weave together cognitive business algorithms. From a BI strategy perspective, from this point forward we will consider cognitive business applications to be a type of BI—an extension of traditional analytics and a subset of BI.

2.5 BI AND ANALYTICS—IS THERE A DIFFERENCE?

For our purposes, business *analytics are data-based applications of quantitative analysis methods* in use in businesses for decades. There are hundreds of books that apply various quantitative analysis, operations research, and discrete mathematics methods to specific business domains, ranging from sophisticated customer segmentations and predictions of customer lifetime value to demand forecasting and supply chain optimization. So analytics, per se, are not new. Rather, proven quantitative analysis methods have been implemented as packaged software applications and bundled into "analytics platforms" that are used to build a wide range of analytical applications that address common business challenges. SAS and SPSS are well-known examples of companies that sell analytics platforms, and there are many others.[4]

---

[4]This paragraph is excerpted from Williams S. Analytics: a tool executives and managers need to embrace. MWorld, J Am Manage Assoc, Winter 2012–2013.

More broadly, we previously defined *BI as an umbrella term that encompasses provision of relevant reports, scorecards, dashboards, e-mail alerts, prestructured user-specified queries, ad hoc query capabilities, multidimensional analyses, statistical analyses, forecasts, models, and/or simulations to business users for use in increasing revenues, reducing costs, or both.* Typical business intelligence (BI) applications—all of which leverage business data and provide analytical perspectives—include:

- REPORTS: standard, preformatted information for *backward-looking analysis* of business trends, events, and performance results;
- MULTIDIMENSIONAL ANALYSES: applications that leverage a common database of trusted business information and that fully automate information slicing and dicing for *analysis of the underlying drivers of business events, trends, and performance results*;
- SCORECARDS and DASHBOARDS: convenient forms of *multidimensional analyses* that are common across an organization, that enable rapid evaluation of business trends, events, and performance results, and that facilitate use of a common management framework and vocabulary for measuring, monitoring, and improving business performance;
- ADVANCED ANALYTICS: automated applications that distill historical business information so that past business trends, events, and results can be summarized and *analyzed* via well-known and long-used statistical methods;
- PREDICTIVE ANALYTICS: automated applications that leverage historical business information, descriptive statistics, and/or stated business assumptions to predict or simulate future business outcomes that can be *analyzed* for their business impact; and
- ALERTS: automated process control applications that *analyze* performance variables, compare results to a standard, and report variances outside defined performance thresholds.

Ultimately, all of these forms of BI deliver business information for decision-makers to use to analyze past performance and its root causes, model and analyze various courses of actions, predict future results and analyze economic impacts, and make decisions that are informed by underlying data and sound analytical techniques. From this business perspective, advanced analytics and predictive analytics are a subset of BI, and the various kinds of BI leverage business information and analyses to inform decisions and drive business results. When it comes to formulating a BI strategy, companies should consider all forms of BI—including analytics. When it comes to defining BI requirements, it is important to be clear about what type of BI is needed, for example, a scorecard or a report or an analytical application such as a forecast or a sophisticated customer segmentation application. In the end, BI has always been about analysis, and much of the "buzz" in the BI field these days is around a narrower conception of analytics—one centered on advanced analytics, predictive analytics, and big data analytics.

2.6 BEYOND THE HYPE—WHAT BI SUCCESS LOOKS LIKE

BI is used to create business value by enabling increased revenues, reduced costs, or both—thus leading to increased profits. It is like a carpentry toolkit, where what needs to be built depends on the needs of the customer. With a carpentry toolkit, I can build a shed, a closet, a cabinet, a house, or whatever. With a standard BI toolkit, we can build custom BI applications that are designed to meet industry-specific and job-specific business challenges. Accordingly, BI success is a function of meeting those challenges. Success is demonstrated through improved business performance for the key business functions and processes of the firm, and thus it looks different to different executives and managers within different industries.

2.6.1 Industry Views of BI Success

A central objective of BI is to provide executives, managers, and knowledge workers with information and analyses they can use to create positive business results. The information and analyses that are relevant in one industry may not be relevant in a different industry. For example, operations managers in a product distribution company are keenly interested in inventory levels, inventory turnover, and customer service trends because optimizing inventory in relation to customer service goals is critical to economic results. On the other hand, operations managers for a retail bank are primarily interested in serving customers quickly and cost-effectively and in offering additional products to customers based on what they are likely to need. BI for inventory analysis is critical for a distribution company, and is relatively less important for a retail bank. Because the uses of BI that are relevant differ by industry, BI success looks different depending on the industry in which a company operates. While not every company in an industry competes in the same way or has the same role in the value chain, we can still paint industry views of BI success using broad brushstrokes.

For manufacturing companies, BI success consists of having the ability to actively manage and improve performance in the core areas that impact customer service and financial performance. A manufacturing company that has achieved a reasonable measure of BI success will have deployed the following BI applications:

1. Enterprise and business unit performance dashboards that are updated on a timely basis and that identify the unfavorable performance variances that require immediate management action— typically those variances related to revenues, product manufacturing costs and output, logistics performance, customer service, key supplier performance, and inventory. The variances displayed are typically for the top 10 or so contributors to the unfavorable variances, and the variances are calculated year-over-year, in relation to an annual operating plan or budget, in relation to updated operating plans or budgets, and by key dimensions such as customer, product, and channel.

2. Analytical dashboards that are reached from the performance dashboards and that allow managers and analysts to drill-down into the details of unfavorable variances so that corrective actions can be quickly identified, evaluated, decided upon, and acted upon. For example, if the performance dashboard identifies that two major customers are buying less and that product distribution in a targeted channel is below target, the analytical dashboard is the launching pad for identifying the root causes of the unfavorable variances. In our example, perhaps Customer A buys 10 products from us, and has decided to switch to a competitor's product for two of the products. The analytical dashboard allows an analyst to see that Customer A is no longer ordering Products X and Y. Armed with this information, corrective action strategies are devised quickly and efficiently.

3. BI applications for enabling demand analysis and demand forecasting—typically a data mart with order and order line history and a combination of standard multidimensional analysis capabilities and an advanced and predictive analytics tool, such as SAS, SPSS, or a low-cost alternative. The demand analysis capability makes recurring processes, such as budgeting, sales and operations planning, setting inventory targets, establishing manufacturing plans,

developing distribution plans, analyzing production capacity utilization, and developing brand/product plans and strategies, much more efficient. The demand forecasting capability is a key tool in company efforts to optimize costs, productivity, and asset utilization in relation to market and customer service requirements.

The above BI applications enable manufacturers to actively measure, manage, control, and improve business performance in all the core business processes that determine customer service levels and revenue growth. They are high-level examples of the kinds of BI capabilities manufacturing companies require. Companies that have met these BI requirements can be said to have achieved BI success.

For financial services companies, BI success typically consists of having the ability to offer personalized services and conduct intelligent, focused multichannel marketing campaigns that reach the right customers with the right offers and the right time. With possible exception of the investment banking and wealth management segments of the industry, financial services companies provide products and services that are generally commoditized, which means that competitive differentiation depends to a large degree on being able to offer differentiated customer service. Whether we're taking about credit and debit cards, retail banking services, consumer lending, property and casualty insurance, or retirement and investment products, financial services companies face the challenge of treating large numbers of customers in a way that conveys that they know who they are and understand their individual needs. In this environment, financial services companies that have achieved a reasonable measure of BI success will have deployed the following BI applications:

1. BI applications that enable a so-called 360° view of each individual customer. This view provides basic information such as the customer's name, address, and so forth. More importantly, it provides information about all aspects of the business relationship with the customer—such as account balances, loan balances, product/service holdings, loan payment history, credit and/or debit card transactions, deposits, withdrawals, and so forth. Also, it provides a complete record of all customer service and marketing interactions—including calls to a call center and their resolution and a record of all marketing offers made, which channel was used

to make the offer, and whether the offer was accepted. This information is updated on a real-time or near real-time basis.

2. BI applications for multidimensional analysis of business performance by geography, market, location/office/branch, product, customer segment, and channel. Financial services companies are increasingly complex—with thousands or millions of customers, dozens of product variations, and an increasing number of digital interactions. Understanding how and where growth is being achieved, which products/services are doing well with which customers, and the trends in digital channel usage is fundamental to managing and improving customer service and business results.

3. BI applications for multidimensional analysis of marketing results and predicting customer propensity to purchase specific products and services. For years, financial services companies have used life stage and income as the primary bases for customer segmentation. The emergence of digital channels and the ability to mine call center records enables BI applications for more sophisticated segmentation, more personalized offers, more efficient list generation, and more real-time tracking of marketing campaign results. Further, the use of advanced and predictive analytics enables applications of segmentation based on predicted customer lifetime value and differentiated marketing and customer service tactics.

The above BI applications enable financial services firms to cope with the inherent complexity of their business and to offer high-quality personalized customer service. They are high-level examples of the kinds of BI capabilities such companies require. Companies that have met these BI requirements can be said to have achieved BI success.

For distributors, BI success typically consists of having the ability to effectively leverage information and analysis to manage margins, inventory levels, and customer service in a complex, dynamic, and low-margin environment. While system distributors sometimes have a less complex environment, many distributors offer thousands of products to hundreds of customers who require delivery to thousands of endpoints. Product manufacturers offer a wide array of promotional deals, which distributors pass along in whole or in part to downstream distributors or retailers. The distributors themselves also offer deals—typically volume-based but also time-based and other variants. The net effect of this is that the distributor's true product cost and true realized revenue on any given product is often unknown for weeks or months. This makes it hard to optimize pricing and promotions to achieve margin targets. This complexity is coupled with an often incomplete view of true demand at retail, which makes it difficult to understand price elasticity of demand and to optimize inventory in relation to customer service level requirements. In this environment, distributors that have achieved a reasonable measure of BI success will have deployed the following BI applications:

1. Executive and distribution center performance dashboards that are updated on a timely basis and that identify the unfavorable performance variances that require immediate management action— typically those variances related to revenues, product movement volumes, margins, inbound logistics performance, distribution center productivity, inventory levels, outbound logistics performance, product damage and returns, and customer service. The variances displayed are typically for the top 10 or so contributors to the unfavorable variances, and the variances are calculated year-over-year, in relation to an annual operating plan or budget, in relation to updated operating plans or budgets, and by key dimensions such as customer, product, and channel.

2. Analytical dashboards that are reached from the performance dashboards and that allow managers and analysts to drill-down into the details of unfavorable variances so that corrective actions can be quickly identified, evaluated, decided upon, and acted upon. For example, if the performance dashboard identifies product movement volume through a new channel is 30% below the targeted volume, the analytical dashboard is used to drill-down into the root causes of the variance. In this hypothetical, the analytical dashboard allows an analyst to see that the pricing used in an established channel was carried over to the new channel, and that has hindered product uptake. Armed with this information, corrective action strategies are devised quickly and efficiently.

3. BI applications for demand analysis and forecasting and for multidimensional analysis of marketing performance. Demand forecasting at the product and/or product family level is essential to optimizing purchasing quantities and inventory levels in relation to customer service requirements. Demand analysis is critical for optimizing pricing, promotions, and margins in relation to various demand scenarios. Multidimensional analysis of promotional performance provides

critical insight into what promotion structures work best for which products, customers, channels, and geographic regions.

The above BI applications enable distributors to cope with the inherent complexity of their business and to optimize margins, volume, inventory, and customer service. They are high-level examples of the kinds of BI capabilities such companies require. Companies that have met these BI requirements can be said to have achieved BI success.

For utilities, BI success typically consists of having a robust and comprehensive set of system and plant operating performance information, detailed cost information, and customer service information—all of which allow the utility to meet targeted system reliability and customer service goals at costs that were assumed in rate justifications to regulatory bodies. Further, BI success for utilities includes extensive engineering information about assets—generation plants, substations, poles, underground wires, trucks, and so forth—for use in capital planning, project planning, maintenance planning, and predicting restoration times in responsive to outage events. Utilities operate in what amounts to a fixed-price environment where all constituencies want highly reliable supplies of electricity, natural gas, and water and very fast restoration times in the event of outages—all for low rates. In this environment, utilities that have achieved a reasonable measure of BI success will have deployed the following BI applications:

1. Executive and business unit performance dashboards that are updated on a timely basis and that identify the unfavorable performance variances that require immediate management action—typically those variances related to restoration times during outage events, system reliability, customer service, preventative maintenance progress, construction progress, energy costs, and safety performance. The variances displayed are typically for the top 10 or so contributors to the unfavorable variances, and the variances are calculated in relation to an annual operating plan or budget, in relation to updated operating plans or budgets, and by key dimensions such as customer type, power generation plant, geographic location, and distribution system asset (eg, electrical system substations and circuits, gas lines, water lines).
2. Analytical dashboards that are reached from the performance dashboards and that allow managers and analysts to drill-down into the details of unfavorable variances so that corrective actions can be

quickly identified, evaluated, decided upon, and acted upon. For example, if the performance dashboard identifies that overall system reliability is below the targets projected in justifying the rates, the analytical dashboard allows managers and analysts to drill-down to specific outage events—including location, duration, the assets involved, the priority given to repair, the crew assigned to repair, the extent of the damage, and the predicted time to repair based on established work standards. Armed with this information, corrective action strategies are devised quickly and efficiently.

3. BI applications for demand analysis, predicting demand, predicting the cost of producing power or purchasing power, asset reliability analysis, and asset condition. Achieving customer service and system reliability objectives at the fixed cost assumed during the rate justification process is a complex task. Variances between assumed demand and actual demand induces revenue variances that create pressures on costs due to the need to achieve a return for shareholders. System reliability is impacted by investments in preventative maintenance, the effectiveness of which is impacted by asset conditions and complex decisions as to which assets to maintain and which to run to failure. System reliability is also impacted by outage events and vegetation management processes. Multidimensional analysis, advanced analytics, and predictive analytics are used to understand tradeoffs and take effective asset management and customer service actions.

The above BI applications enable utilities to cope with the inherent complexity of their business and to optimize customer service and system reliability at a predetermined cost. They are high-level examples of the kinds of BI capabilities such companies require. Companies that have met these BI requirements can be said to have achieved BI success.

For retailers, BI success typically consists of having a comprehensive and specific view of product movement (demand), customer purchasing behavior, product costs, and the impact of price and promotion on product movement—all by store, department, product category, and time of year. Retailers who are advanced with BI leverage point-of-sale (POS) data and syndicated data about product movement to develop a deep understanding of the relationships between product movement, price/promotion, and margins. For retailers who self-distribute and who may manufacture some of their own products, the POS data and syndicated data (demand data) are also used to optimize cost and customer service across the value chain. Further, this same demand data is used with key suppliers to achieve the same goal and avoid stockouts while not holding excess inventory. In this environment, retailers that have achieved a reasonable measure of BI success will have deployed the following BI applications:

1. Executive and store performance dashboards that are updated on a timely basis and that identify the unfavorable performance variances that require immediate management action—typically those variances related to sales, margins, labor utilization, expenses, inventory shrinkage, category performance, and product performance (movement, contribution margin). The variances displayed are typically for the top 10 or so contributors to the unfavorable variances, and the variances are calculated in relation to year-over-year, in relation to an annual operating plan or budget, in relation to updated operating plans or budgets, and by key dimensions such as store, department, subdepartment, product category, and customer segment.
2. Analytical dashboards that are reached from the performance dashboards and that allow managers and analysts to drill-down into the details of unfavorable variances so that corrective actions can be quickly identified, evaluated, decided upon, and acted upon. For example, if the performance dashboard identifies that same-store sales are off on a year-over-year basis, the analytical dashboard allows the analyst to easily identify which store or stores comprise the bulk of the variance and then drill-down to identify departments, categories, and products that are part of the root cause of the variance. Armed with this information, corrective action strategies are devised quickly and efficiently.
3. BI applications for demand analysis, predicting demand under various price and promotion tactics, evaluating product movement trends and category contribution margins, evaluating assortments and product ranges by store, and segmenting customers so that appropriate and personalized rewards, trial offers, and retention offers can be made to optimize customer lifetime value. Many retail businesses are complex because they must stock and sell thousands or tens of thousands of distinct items in a way that results in having the right product and the right price at the time of need for thousands of customers whose needs vary. With fixed shelf space,

companies that tie up space with products that don't move run the risk suboptimal profits in what is often a tight-margin business. On the other hand, being out-of-stock generates an immediate opportunity cost and may eventually result in customer defections. BI applications for multidimensional analysis, advanced analytics, and predictive analytics are used to understand the fundamental relationship between product, price, promotion, merchandising, and margin so that optimal actions can be taken to retain customers, grow market baskets, and make a reasonable profit.

The above BI applications enable retailers to cope with the inherent complexity of their business and to optimize customer retention and company profitability. They are high-level examples of the kinds of BI capabilities such companies require. Companies that have met these BI requirements can be said to have achieved BI success.

2.7 SUMMARY—INDUSTRY VIEWS OF BI SUCCESS

The above examples illustrate that what BI success looks like depends on the industry in which a company operates. While the BI tools may be common—dashboards, multidimensional analysis, advanced analytics, predictive analytics, and so forth—*the way that the tools are used must be relevant to the industry and the manner in which the company competes in the industry*. And while we have focused on five particular industries and the types of BI applications that are relevant for those industries, companies in other industries can leverage well-established business-driven techniques for determining an overall BI vision and identifying which uses of BI are most relevant in their specific cases. These techniques set the stage for BI success and they are subject of the remainder of this book.

2.7.1 Job Function Views of BI Success

Our discussion of what BI success looks like in different industries also provided a glimpse of how BI success varies by job function. While the BI needs of people in different job functions within a company are not mutually exclusive, there are definitely BI applications or uses that are job-specific. For example, a plant manager may want a BI application for measuring, managing, and improving plant output by shift and production line. That application would be of limited value to a sales manager. On the other hand, it is not uncommon for sales people, customer service people, and operations people to have a common interest in inventory on hand if the company fulfills orders out of inventory. At a high level, we can generalize that[5]:

- For the Chief Financial Officer (CFO) and financial management professionals, BI success means such things as having a precise and granular understanding of the relationship between operational performance and financial results, having better tools for performance management, having high-quality historical facts at their fingertips for planning, forecasting, and budgeting, and having better information and analytical tools for working capital management.
- For the Chief Operating Officer (COO) and operations management professionals, BI success means such things as having precise and granular information available for cost analysis, having analytical tools for monitoring and improving customer service and product quality, and having high-quality historical facts about demand readily available for demand management and capacity planning.
- For the Chief Marketing Officer (CMO), sales leaders, and marketing professionals, BI success means such things as having complete information about individual customers to enable better customer segmentation, more precise campaign targeting, improved customer service and customer retention, more timely campaign lift analysis, improved ability to determine customer lifetime value, a better understanding of the price elasticity of demand, improved tools for category management, and tools for performance management.
- For the Chief Information Officer (CIO), BI directors, and BI team, BI success means being able to measure BI usage and BI impact, being able to do a better job of meeting the demands of business users, moving beyond being order takers for standard reports, and being able to operate with a solid business case and adequate time and money to be effective in helping improve business performance and profits.

The above examples are just a sample of what BI success looks like to the people in companies who are charged with meeting business objectives, delivering profits, and/or meeting competitive challenges. Ultimately, BI success is measured in improved business performance and profitability. Those are the subjects of the rest of this book.

---

[5]Portions of this discussion are taken from Williams S. 5 Barriers to BI success and how to overcome them. Strategic Finance, July 2011.

2.8 RECAP OF SOME KEY POINTS

1. The terms "business intelligence" and "BI" mean different things to different business people. Lack of a common understanding of what BI is and what it can do is an impediment to BI success.
2. There is a lot of hype in the marketplace about BI, big data, and analytics. This confuses business executives, managers, and analysts about the value proposition for BI—which impedes adoption and/or results in ineffective capital investments.
3. Big Data is a combination of traditional business data and new types of "data." Many of the new types of "data" are actually digital content—like text messages, digital images, music files, etc. This new digital content is referred to as "unstructured data." To obtain value from unstructured data, it has to be leveraged within a business process that increases revenue, reduces costs, or both.
4. From a BI perspective, big data is simply another source of data and digital content that *might* be useful for analytical purposes.
5. The primary raw materials for cognitive business are structured and/or unstructured data, computing power, and complex mathematical and statistical methods that are woven into algorithms.
6. The algorithms are designed in conjunction with people who are experts in the relevant business domain, for example, inventory management, insurance fraud detection, operations management, and so forth.
7. Predesigned cognitive business applications will be similar to packaged software, that is, they will be designed by vendors to deliver a standard business technique to as many companies as possible.
8. Custom-designed cognitive business applications will be based on the knowledge about a relevant business process held by people within a given company. For example, a cognitive inventory management application would incorporate knowledge and practices of inventory managers in the given company.
9. Despite the allure of terms like machine learning, artificial intelligence, and mathematical optimization, cognitive business still comes down to applying programmed business logic to data as a means of improving business results.
10. Analytics are not new, though we have better tools for applying them than we did 20 years ago.
11. Historically, analytics have been considered a subset of BI.
12. BI has always been about analysis.

13. All forms of BI—including analytics—should be used as appropriate within the core business processes that drive increased revenues, optimized costs, and overall profitability.

14. BI is a general purpose tool that must be applied in different ways for different job functions and industries. For example, a relevant and appropriate BI application for retail grocery store operations improvement will be different from a BI application for customer segmentation for a life insurance company.

15. Because BI must be applied differently in different business contexts, BI success will look different in its specifics depending on the industry, company, and function wherein BI applications are being used.

CHAPTER 3

The Strategic Importance of Business Intelligence

The global business environment is one where leveraging business information, business analyses, and decision support—that is, business intelligence (BI)—is an increasingly important factor of production. Companies that excel in their deployment and use of BI have achieved competitive advantages in a number of industries. At the same time, the strategic importance of BI varies by industry, company, and company business model—and it is also affected by competitors' actions. In general, the more complex and information-intensive an industry is, the greater the strategic importance of BI and the greater the opportunity for competitive differentiation. Accordingly, it is important for companies to determine the strategic importance of BI in their industry and for their business model, because that determination should drive the formulation of enterprise BI strategies and the definition of a mission for the BI organization. These considerations affect the pace of capital investment, the funding models for the BI program, the pace of resource acquisition and/or utilization, the pace of BI deployment, and ultimately the pace and magnitude of business value creation.

When determining the strategic importance of BI, an important first step is for companies to understand what BI is from a business perspective and to understand the mechanism by which BI can be used to increase revenues, decrease costs, or both. We'll cover those topics in Sections 3.1 and 3.2. Armed with those understandings, companies can then use the framework detailed in Section 3.3 to determine the strategic importance of BI for their industry and company, to assess their BI capabilities in relation to competitors and/ or BI norms, and to decide on a BI mission that is supportive of their business strategies.

3.1 A BUSINESS VIEW OF BI

There are many definitions of BI, many of which are "systems oriented" and/or vendor-defined. In order to determine the value of BI, it needs to be understood from a business perspective. Here are a few examples.

Forrester Research Definition: "Business Intelligence is a set of methodologies, processes, architectures, and technologies that transform raw data into meaningful and useful information used to enable more effective strategic, tactical, and operational insights and decision-making."

Howard Dresner 1989 Definition: "BI is an umbrella term to describe concepts and methods to improve business decision making by using fact-based support systems."

Another business-driven view of BI is as follows:

BI is the use of business information, business analyses, and decision-support techniques in the context of primary business processes in order to increase revenues, reduce costs, or both.

This business-driven view of BI is illustrated by Fig. 3.1.

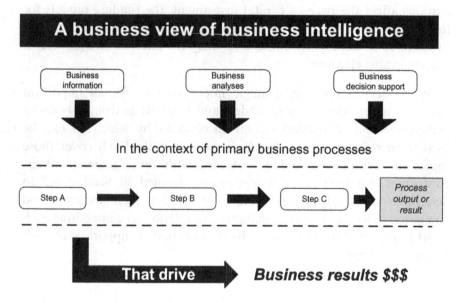

Figure 3.1 An investment in BI needs to increase profits if it is to generate a return on investment.

3.1.1 Styles of BI

BI uses a combination of historical information about past transactions or events and reference data about, for example, customers or products, to enable a wide variety of analyses and decision support techniques.

A "what you get" or output view of BI includes the typical BI applications described below.

- *Reports*: Standard, preformatted information for backward-looking analysis.
- *User-defined analyses*: Prestaged information where "pick lists" enable business users to filter (select) the information they wish to analyze, such as sales for a selected region during a selected previous timeframe.
- *Ad hoc analyses*: Power users write their own queries to extract self-selected prestaged information and then use the information to perform a user-created analysis.
- *Scorecards and dashboards*: Predefined business performance metrics about performance variables that are important to the organization, presented in a tabular or graphical format that enables business users to see at a glance how the organization is performing.
- *Multidimensional analysis (also known as On-line analytical processing)*: Flexible tool-based user-defined analysis of business performance and the underlying drivers or root causes of that performance.
- *Alerts*: Predefined analyses of key business performance variables, comparison to a performance standard or range, and communication to designated business people when performance is outside the predefined performance standard or range.
- *Advanced analytics*: Application of long-established statistical and/or operations research methods to historical business information to look backward and characterize a relevant aspect of business performance, typically by using descriptive statistics.
- *Predictive analytics*: Application of long-established statistical and/or operations research methods to historical business information to predict, model, or simulate future business and/or economic performance and potentially prescribe a favored course of action for the future.

Business analyses come in a wide range of types and uses, ranging from simple analyses such as accounts receivable aging reports to the sophisticated antifraud analytics used by major credit card companies. Table 3.1 shows the styles of BI and the typical uses of those styles by various kinds of business people.

Table 3.1 BI Delivers Different Kinds of Information and Analyses to Different Business Users According to Their Roles and Preferences

BI Is Used to Measure, Manage, Improve, and Control Enterprise Performance, Revenue Growth, and Operating Performance

	General Management Executives	Functional Executives	Functional Directors and Managers	Analysts
Standard, preformatted reports	Used to present basic high-level information about business performance, revenue growth, and/or operating performance in order to detect problems and/or opportunities. Often requires lots of manual data acquisition and manipulation by analysts to generate such reports.			
User-defined analyses	Analyses performed by others are presented to executives. In some cases, executives do their own analyses because tools are easy to learn.		Used to determine root causes of problems in business performance, revenue growth, and/or operating performance. Also used to understand opportunities where performance is much better than expected.	
Ad hoc analyses	Analyses performed by others are presented to executives and managers as part of the process of responding to problems in business performance, revenue growth, and/or operating performance.			Analysts directly access data to assess problems and opportunities with respect to business performance, revenue growth, and/or operating performance.
Scorecards and dashboards	Performance scorecards and dashboards present executives with the big picture of business performance, revenue growth, and/or operating performance, highlighting unfavorable variances for prompt attention and identifying opportunities for management consideration.		Analytical scorecards and dashboards are the launching pad for prestaged multidimensional analyses used to determine root causes of problems in business performance, revenue growth, and/or operating performance. Also used to understand opportunities where performance is much better than expected.	
Multidimensional analysis (OLAP)	Analyses performed by others are presented to executives. In some cases, executives do their own analyses because tools are easy to learn.		Advanced OLAP tools enable users to explore and analyze business performance, revenue growth, and/or operating performance problems and/or opportunities from multiple user-defined perspectives.	

(Continued)

Table 3.1 (Continued)

BI Is Used to Measure, Manage, Improve, and Control Enterprise Performance, Revenue Growth, and Operating Performance

	General Management Executives	Functional Executives	Functional Directors and Managers	Analysts
Alerts	Often used in customer-facing and operating processes for short-interval control of business performance or operating performance. For example, alerts can be set to be triggered if: (1) a customer service performance metric falls below a company-defined threshold; (2) if revenues/day/region fall below a defined threshold; and/or (3) if production output/hour/plant falls below a defined threshold.			
Advanced analytics Predictive analytics	Sophisticated analyses of performance problems or opportunities with respect to business performance, revenue growth, or operating performance are presented to executives and managers, many of whom will never perform these kinds of analyses themselves.			These sophisticated analytics are applied in data-intensive environments to develop even-deeper understandings of business performance, revenue growth, and/or operating performance problems or opportunities. Examples include demand analysis and forecasting, market basket analysis, customer lifetime value predictions, and many more.

3.1.2 An Effective BI Environment Provides Integrated Operational and Financial Views of Facts About Business Performance

Many organizations struggle to develop a cohesive view of organizational performance on a timely basis during a given month and after the monthly close. Further, experience at many companies suggests that executives, managers, and analysts are often handcuffed when it comes to continuously improving the business processes that drive operational and financial results. For example, a manufacturing plant manager operating with inadequate BI might lack basic information and analyses about the drivers of manufacturing performance. Looked at more broadly, companies with inadequate BI may be slow to react to unfavorable performance variances, and they may have to guess at what the optimal corrective actions might be. Lack of an effective BI environment also hinders companies' ability to inject BI into core business processes to increase effectiveness and/or efficiency. For example, a consumer lending company with inadequate BI might make more bad loans or might turn down too many good loans, both of which adversely impact earnings. Fig. 3.2 provides a conceptual illustration of the kinds of business facts and the various analytical perspectives that an effective BI environment can deliver.

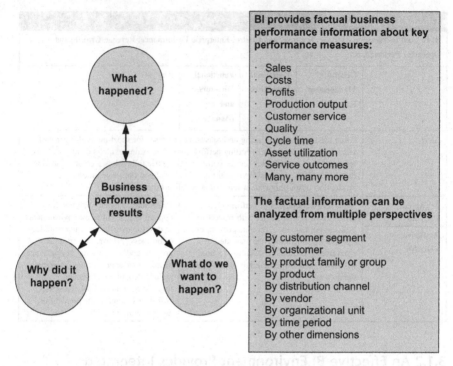

Figure 3.2 BI provides an integrated view of business performance.

3.2 HOW BI ENHANCES BUSINESS PROCESSES AND BUSINESS PERFORMANCE

BI is used to create business value by increasing revenues, reducing costs, or both. The manner in which this can happen is by appropriately leveraging BI in its various forms to inform key business decisions and actions. Those decisions and actions are taken in the context of specific business processes and then executed by those business processes. Accordingly, there needs to be a specific linkage between key business processes, the key decisions that need to be made in the context of those processes, and the kind of BI that is most appropriate for enabling fact-based, analytically supported business decisions. When those links are made, BI can help executives and managers increase revenues, reduce costs, or both. The linkage between business processes, business decisions, and BI applications is illustrated in Table 3.2.

Table 3.2 categorizes business processes into three basic groups, as shown in the left-hand column. For each group, we have provided examples of business processes in the second column. The names of

Table 3.2 BI Applications Used Within Core Processes Can Enable More Impactful Business Decisions			
Business Processes	Business Process Examples	Examples of Related Business Decisions	Examples of Related BI Applications
Management processes	Planning, resource management, budgeting, performance measurement, variance analysis, strategic cost analysis	Performance goals and objectives, hiring targets, capital budgets and projects, operating budgets, responses to unfavorable performance variances	Performance management scorecards and dashboards, multidimensional analytical scorecards, strategic cost models, project performance scorecards and dashboards, project portfolio analytics, business unit performance scorecards and dashboards
Revenue generation processes	Demand forecasting, marketing, sales, customer service, product development	Demand targets ($, units, volume), prices, promotional plans, product cost targets, service cost targets, customer service budgets, salesforce goals, margin goals	Demand trend analyses, customer lifetime value models, customer retention alerts, customer segmentation—clustering and collaborative filtering, price elasticity of demand models, promotional effectiveness scorecards and dashboards, product/service cost models, sales performance scorecards and dashboards, multidimensional sales performance analytical scorecards, cognitive business applications for pretransaction analysis
Operating processes	Demand forecasting, purchasing, inbound logistics, order management, planning, manufacturing, distribution, outbound logistics, service operations	Demand plans, distribution plans, logistics plans, manufacturing plans, operating plans, resource plans, responses to unfavorable performance variances, cost targets	Volume variance analyses, operations performance scorecards and dashboards, operating cost models, multidimensional analytical scorecards, alerts, warranty claims analyses, product/service quality analyses, call center performance scorecards and dashboards, distribution network cost models

those examples are generic, so what your company might call a given process might be different. For example, some companies might use the term "inbound logistics" and others might use the term "inbound transportation." Also, some readers may see the term "marketing" and think of it as a function. In the figure, I've used that term as shorthand for all the specific business processes that the marketing function typically performs—such as demand forecasting, customer segmentation, promotion planning, customer retention, and so forth. For any given business process, we can also identify business decisions that typically need to be made in the context of those processes, examples of which are shown in the third column. Lastly, I've provided examples of BI applications that can bring facts and analyses to the table for decision-makers to use in conjunction with their experience and intuition. We will dig much deeper into this subject in chapter "Leveraging BI for Performance Management, Process Improvement, and Decision Support." That having been said, it is important to understand the basic BI value-creation mechanism as part of the broader determination of the strategic importance of BI. We'll provide an overview below.

3.2.1 Review of Business Processes Improvement Thinking

Regardless of the business process, a key to process improvement is to identify performance gaps and envision an improved future state process. Performance gaps for any process can be measured using the common characteristics that all processes: they cost money, they take time, they achieve a service level, they achieve a quality level, they use assets, and they provide outputs to internal and/or external customers. Performance gaps can also be assessed by different process characteristics, such as scalability, flexibility, and manual intensity. These ideas are shown in Fig. 3.3.

Over the past 20 years, BI has proven to be highly useful in improving many different business processes:

- Management processes—like strategic planning, budgeting, performance measurement, controlling, and performance variance analysis.
- Revenue generation processes—like market research, customer segmentation, sales planning, revenue budgeting and management, pricing, promotions planning and execution, product development, service development, customer order processing, and so forth.
- Operating processes—like purchasing, supplier management, inbound logistics, manufacturing, operations, inventory management, distribution center management, outbound logistics, quality assurance, order fulfillment, customer service, and so forth.

In broad terms, a well-designed BI environment serves as a powerful multifaceted tool for performance measurement and process improvement. This idea is illustrated by Fig. 3.4.

BI *about a process* is used to measure process performance and identify performance variances for use in gap analysis and continuous improvement. BI *within a process* is used to improve the effectiveness and/or efficiency of one or more steps within the process.

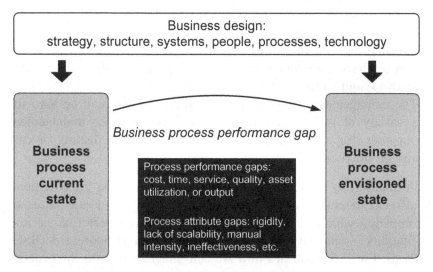

Figure 3.3 *BI is instrumental for improving the business processes that drive business results.*

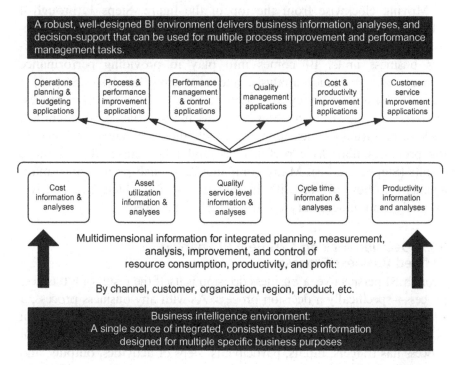

Figure 3.4 *BI delivers integrated multidimensional information that serves multiple business improvement purposes.*

Working from the bottom of the drawing up:

1. The BI environment provides various types of consistent, high-quality business information.
2. The information provided is essentially management accounting information—blended financial and operational information for cost analysis, asset utilization analysis, quality analysis, cycle time analysis, and so forth.
3. The management accounting information—or BI—can be used for a variety of process improvement and performance management purposes, for example, operations planning and budgeting or cost and productivity improvement.

In addition to serving as a powerful tool for process improvement, BI also enhances the business performance management capabilities of a company—which should translate into improved performance and profitability. Using an example based on Balanced Scorecard (BSC) methods, Fig. 3.5 illustrates how we can integrate BI into the broader performance management framework.

Moving clockwise from the top of the figure, Steps 1 through 4 reflect a typical BSC approach, which ends up with performance objectives, targets, and key performance indicators established for the various business units. BI comes into play in providing performance measurement, variance analysis, and root cause analysis (Step 5)—typically on a monthly cycle. Based on results, BI is used for process analysis and improvement (Step 6) as discussed earlier. Thus there is a cycle of performance measurement, which allows managers to focus on the processes that drive performance and take actions that enhance results (Steps 7 and 8). Many companies approach performance management without BI or with limited use of BI, which is expensive, untimely, and unnecessary given what BI can deliver.

3.2.2 Decision-Making Can Be a BI-Enabled, Defined Business Process

From a BI perspective, a business decision is itself the result of a business process—specifically a decision process. As with any business process, a decision process can be formal or informal and its efficacy (results) can be monitored and sometimes measured. And like all processes, a decision process has triggers, inputs, participants, steps or activities, outputs, and customers (internal or external). For example, manufacturers who fulfill

A performance management framework that integrates the use of BI provides more robust capabilities for strategic and operational performance measurement and performance improvement.

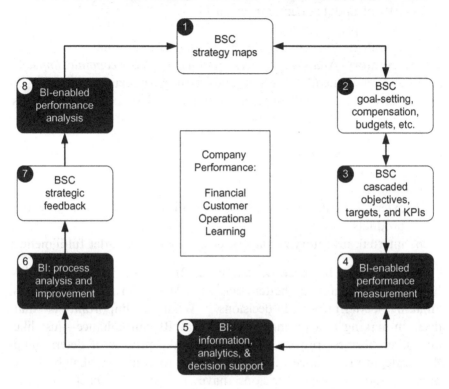

Figure 3.5 BI enables closed-loop performance measurement and improvement aligned to strategic goals and objectives.

orders out of inventory typically adjust inventory targets on a regular recurring basis. Since inventory levels have a substantial impact on profitability, a given company might wish to specify an "inventory decision process" along the lines of the very simplified example below:

1. Participants: EVP Operations, VP Inventory Management, VP Customer Service, and Inventory Analyst.
2. Inputs:
   a. from ERP system: inventory balances,
   b. from company plans: current manufacturing, inventory and product promotion plans; annual inventory goals,
   c. from BI: updated demand forecast; inventory fulfillment performance scorecard; customer service scorecard; forecasted

fulfillment and ending inventory at current manufacturing plan and updated demand forecast; forecasted fulfillment and ending inventory at current manufacturing plan and ± 1%, 5%, and 10% of updated demand forecast.

3. Process steps:
   a. Inventory Analyst assembles and analyzes all inputs.
   b. Inventory Analyst prepares options, *models economic impacts*, and recommendations and sends to all participants.
   c. Participants meet in-person and/or by video conference, discuss options, and determine new targets by consensus.

4. Outputs:
   a. updated inventory targets,
   b. decision memo for the record.

5. Customers:
   a. external: customers (business or end-consumers) who buy the products,
   b. internal: inventory managers, customer service/order fulfillment.

Much of what has been written about BI over the past two decades has seen BI as enabling "better decisions." We prefer to express this as "making better-informed decisions." What is important is that decision-making is a business process that BI can enhance—just like any other business process. So as part of the process of determining the strategic importance of BI, it is useful to consider what business process and business decisions have the most impact in your company's industry and for your company's business strategies.

3.3 THE STRATEGIC IMPORTANCE OF BI[1]

The road to BI success is like that of any other enterprise performance improvement initiatives. Whether the goal is improved enhanced customer service, reduced operating costs, or any other improvement initiative organizations undertake, success demands very skillful general management and change management. It also demands a clear vision of the desired future state and a compelling strategic argument for achieving the future state. For enterprise BI initiatives, top management must provide leadership and they must invest in BI, which they will be more inclined to do if they believe BI is strategically

---

[1]Portions of this section are excerpted from Williams S. 5 Barriers to BI Success and how to overcome them. Strategic Finance, July 2011.

important to their organizations and in the industries in which they operate. The strategic importance of BI then establishes the mission for the BI initiative—whether it is to become an industry leader in the use of BI, to establish competitive parity, to be a fast follower, or to be a late adopter.

3.3.1 Some Examples of the Strategic Importance of BI

3.3.1.1 Financial Services Industry

Even small credit unions and retail banks have thousands of customers and dozens of products/services, and their larger competitors have millions of customers. We all use financial services companies, and we expect them to provide us with highly personalized service. We expect them to know the full extent of our business relationship, and we don't want to be bombarded with marketing offers that are not relevant to us. BI enables financial services companies to provide personalized service, and those companies who cannot are at a competitive disadvantage.

3.3.1.2 Grocery Stores

A typical average-sized grocery store carries 40,000 different products and sells them to thousands of customers. With store loyalty card programs, store operators have better insight into what is being purchased by their regular shoppers. As with the financial services industry, shoppers expect some level of personalized service, generally in the form of coupons for products they actually buy and rewards for their loyalty. BI enables grocers to understand who their best customers are, what they buy, and what their economic value is as customers over the long haul. This enables better customer segmentation and the use of more targeted promotions, and this is strategically important in a competitive field where customers have many convenient options with other grocery stores and with many nontraditional channels, such as drug stores, convenience stores, club stores, and mass merchandisers.

3.3.1.3 Government Agencies

Federal, state, and local governments generally have some organizational units that process cases of some kind—such as disability claims, unemployment claims, business license applications, and legal cases to name but a few. Case processing is typically a complex multistep process and there may be thousands of claims to be processed—and thus it is important to have visibility into claim processing performance. BI enables agencies to track and manage such key performance variables as elapsed time, quality, the number of cases completed, case backlog by type of case, and processing cost. BI also enables agencies to build operating budgets based on the number of cases processed and projected.

3.3.1.4 Manufacturers

Manufacturers are typically concerned with productivity, customer service, inventory, and logistics. Those that operate multiple production lines, plants, and distribution centers and that make many products for many customers face a high level of complexity. BI enables manufacturers to cope with complexity by providing high-quality information and analyses about all key facets of operations—and by providing the means to analyze those facets by plant, customer, product, business unit, and so forth. With better BI, manufacturers can improve productivity, a key to competitiveness and customer service.

●●●———————————————————————————————————

Factors That Influence the Strategic Importance of BI
- The number of individual customers a company serves.
- The number of products and/or services a company offers.
- The number of suppliers from whom a company obtains products and/ or services.
- The number of geographies in which a company operates.
- The number of business units a company has.
- The variability of the demand for a company's products or services.
- The number of industries in which a company operates.
- The position of the company in the supply chain.
- How competitors are using BI to an advantage.

———————————————————————————————————————

Essentially, BI is more strategically important in more complex businesses and industries, and less so in more straightforward business. A simplified example would be if a company makes one product for one customer and delivers it to one location. In that case, BI might not be strategically important. At the other extreme, BI may be very strategically important for a consumer packaged goods manufacturer with hundreds of products manufactured at a dozen plants and distributed to hundreds of customers with thousands of locations.

Vignette: BI for Personalized Interactions With Customers

A very successful financial services company recognized the strategic importance of personalizing its interactions with its millions of customers. The company offered a wide range of products, which were sold through hundreds of intermediaries of various types and that had varying degrees of market reach. The demand for the company's products varied by life stage and income level. As with many of its similarly situated competitors, the tendency was to use shotgun marketing approaches, which were expensive to execute and which posed difficulties when it came to evaluating the economic impact of marketing campaigns. Further, the traditional shotgun approach meant that marketing campaigns often communicated offers to individuals for products that were not appropriate for their life stage and/or income level. This communicated the message that the company did not really know individual customers, whereas more and more financial services were leveraging BI and analytics to personalize their interactions with customers. Accordingly, BI was and is strategically important as a means to reduce the inherent complexity of their business, respond to competitive dynamics in the industry, and to treat millions of customers in a highly personalized way.

Determining the strategic important of BI and the resulting BI mission is an important part of the BI strategy formulation process. A simple framework for deciding upon a BI mission is shown in Fig. 3.6.

Business executives, managers, and analysts can consider the complexity of their industry and company and use that as a proxy for the strategic importance of BI. They can also consider competitors' uses of BI, to the extent that such information can be had. Absent specific competitor information, companies' BI capabilities can be compared to the descriptions of what BI success looks like as found in chapter "Business Intelligence in the Era of Big Data and Cognitive Business." Yet another way to gage the competitiveness of a company's BI capabilities is to use BI Maturity and/or BI Readiness assessment instruments. More broadly, a company with competitive BI capabilities will have:

- the ability to define, align, and govern a portfolio of BI opportunities over 3 to 5 years,
- the ability to perform the technical work required to deliver BI applications to business users,
- the ability to integrate BI applications into to core business processes that drive business results.

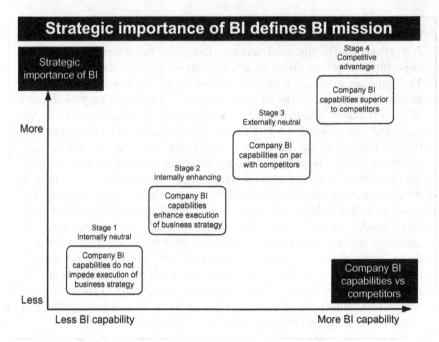

Figure 3.6 Setting a BI Mission guides key business decisions about BI strategy and execution.

Once the strategic importance of BI and the comparative BI capabilities have been determined, the BI strategy team can use the framework shown in Fig. 3.6 to define a BI Mission and use that mission to guide decisions about funding, pace of BI development and deployment, and governance of the BI initiative.

3.4 SKILL DEVELOPMENT OPPORTUNITY: THE STRATEGIC IMPORTANCE OF BI

3.4.1 Objectives

1. Determine the strategic importance of BI for your company.
2. Consider how your company's use of BI helps or hinders its business strategies.
3. Use the framework depicted by Fig. 3.6 to assess your company's current position and ideal position.
4. Outline a high-level strategic argument to top management about the strategic importance of BI.

A. Consider the factors below and decide which ones present the most complexity for managing your company, improving core processes, and/or enhancing profitability.

- number of individual customers,
- number of products and/or services,
- number of suppliers,
- number of company and customer locations,
- number of business units and/or industries,
- variability of the demand,
- other factors.

B. What difficulties does complexity present at your company? Is BI strategically important? Why or why not?

C. How do you think your company's BI capabilities stack up against those of your competitors? How might you benchmark your company's BI capabilities?

D. Outline a high-level strategic argument to top management about the strategic importance of BI to your company. In your argument, try to provide examples of how BI could enable better execution of key business strategies and processes. Also try to provide examples of how insufficient BI hinders business performance.

3.5 SUMMARY OF SOME KEY POINTS

1. BI is about leveraging information; data warehouses and data marts are simply BI enablers.
2. BI encompasses various ways of using information and analyses to improve business results.
3. BI means different things to different business people.
4. It is useful for organizations to develop a common understanding of styles of BI.
5. With sound alignment with core business processes, BI can result in increased revenue, decreased costs, or both.
6. BI enhances business decision-making by supplementing experience and intuition.
7. BI creates value by enabling more impactful decisions that improve the effectiveness of core business processes, including business performance management processes.

8. BI is a decision support, process improvement, and performance management tool.
9. The strategic importance of BI varies by industry and by company business model.
10. Business complexity elevates the strategic importance of BI.
11. Competitor uses of BI may elevate the strategic importance of BI.
12. The strategic importance of BI influences the BI mission within an enterprise.

CHAPTER 4

BI Opportunity Analysis

To succeed in leveraging business intelligence (BI) to increase revenues, reduce costs, and improve profitability, it is critical to move beyond vague generic value propositions. Most executives who have to approve BI investment budgets do not resonate with purported benefits, such as enabling better decisions, increasing customer intimacy, or enhancing supply chain agility. They want to understand—in very concrete terms—how proposed investments in BI relate to enterprise and/or functional business strategies, which business processes will be improved and by what type of BI, how their ability to drive business performance will be enhanced, and what economic return they can expect over what general timeframe. Accordingly, to obtain funding and shape an effective BI program, it is necessary to identify, define, and document BI opportunities, or BIOs for short. Once identified, these BIOs provide the investment hypotheses, value propositions, and/or business cases for investing in BI to improve profitability. The process of identifying BIOs is called BI Opportunity Analysis, and there are a number of proven techniques that can be used. These are the subject of this chapter.

4.1 BI OPPORTUNITY ANALYSIS PROVIDES THE ECONOMIC RATIONALE FOR BI

Technically speaking, to create value, investments must increase net after-tax cash flows into the business. Most companies use a formal capital budgeting process that provides a framework for deciding whether and how much to invest in business improvement opportunities. While formats, frameworks, and degree of rigor varies, capital budgeting processes are all aimed at determining the economic impact of proposed investments. Toward that end, key capital budgeting questions typically include:

1. What is the general nature of the proposed investment—for example, is it to extend the useful life of an existing business asset/capability, replace an obsolete asset/capability, satisfy the requirements

of an important customer/customer segment, increase revenues, improve productivity, enhance customer service, or what?
2. How does the proposed investment relate to our business strategy?
3. In what ways, if any, will the proposed investment improve our competitive posture?
4. Which of our business processes will be impacted by the proposed investment, and how much change will be involved?
5. How much must be invested to realize the proposed opportunity?
6. How long until the investment breaks even?
7. What is the total expected return on the investment?
8. How much time must our business and IT people invest over what timeframe?
9. How much risk does the proposed investment entail, and what is the nature of the risk or risks?
10. What are the critical success factors and how well are we prepared to meet them?

Depending on the company and business, company sponsors of any given capital budget request may spend weeks, months, or even years doing the research and analysis required to obtain objective, defensible answers to such questions. For potential investments in BI, the BI Opportunity Analysis is a proven, structured approach to identifying and documenting the specific ways that BI can be used to increase revenues, reduce costs, or both. Done well, the analysis provides answers to questions 1 through 4 above, and it provides the starting point for drilling down to obtain answers to remainder of the questions. Accordingly, BI Opportunity Analysis provides much of the business-driven economic rationale for a proposed investment in BI.

Because BI is the use of business information, business analyses, and decision-support techniques in the context of primary business processes, the overarching goal of BI Opportunity Analysis is to develop answers to the following questions:

1. What business information do we need?
2. What business analyses do we want to be able to do using the business information?
3. What business decisions do we want to support using the business information and analyses?
4. Which core/key business processes would be improved by leveraging better information and more robust analyses?

5. What would be the potential business/economic impact of improving those business processes?
6. How much change to people, process, and technology would be involved?
7. How long will it take to recover our investment and start to create value?

There are a number of useful methods for obtaining insights into and answers to these questions, and we will dig into those in the next few sections of this chapter. These include:

- Top-Down BI Opportunity Analysis
- Structured Interviews
- Analyzing Strategy Maps and Balanced Scorecards
- Using Industry and Company Research

These methods are not mutually exclusive and are often used together to identify a robust set of BIOs that are aligned to business strategies, functional strategies, and core business processes.

Vignette: BI for Enterprise Performance Management

A successful building products distributor operated through several wholly owned operating companies. Collectively, the operating companies sold thousands of products, parts, and supplies to building contractors through a network of over 400 local and regional distribution centers. To complicate matters, the operating companies were aligned with different original equipment manufacturers, each of which required that their licensed distributors sell their products exclusively within stipulated geographic territories—though the operating companies could sell some of the same parts and supplies. In order to more effectively manage enterprise financial performance, the company used BI Opportunity Analysis to identify and prioritize the ways it could leverage BI and analytics. At the core, the company needed to integrate sales, product, and customer information and develop BI applications for revenue management, supply chain optimization, enhanced purchasing leverage, and customer marketing. Enhanced BI was seen as a means to move beyond decision-making based on intuition and guesswork toward more fact-based and impactful decisions. This would require some significant changes to business processes, and in some cases meeting substantial training needs. If successful, the company believed BI would generate a substantial competitive advantage in their industry—as well as delivering increased profitability.

Importantly, the BIO methods we will describe are all business-driven approaches, which differ from the "data subject" approach because they identify specific BI applications that aim to impact specific business processes in defined ways and that will generate a targeted return. In contrast, the data subject approach focuses on, for example, customer data or product data. The tendency with the data subject approach is to: (1) amass more data than is necessary or useful for BI purposes—just in case that data might be needed; (2) rely on generic value propositions that fail to provide a basis for a company-specific return-on-investment analysis; and (3) spend more money on moving data around than is needed. Further, the data subject approach fails to provide a specific business context for integrating data—for example, customer data, product data, and channel data. It fails to answer the questions: what are we trying to analyze, for what business purpose, with what analytical method, that requires what data, and to what economic end. Absent such business context, efforts to integrate data for BI purposes tend to devolve into technical arguments that impede progress, or data are integrated in ways that don't make sense to the business users. Business-driven approaches overcome these shortcomings.

4.2 TOP-DOWN BI OPPORTUNITY ANALYSIS

A fundamental precept for formulating an enterprise BI strategy is that potential investments in BI should be responsive to industry drivers and support enablement of enterprise business strategies. Accordingly, the analytical framework and flow for Top-Down BI Opportunity Analysis is as shown in Fig. 4.1. The work to conduct this analysis can be done by a team or by an experienced business analyst, with the outcome documented as described later in this chapter. This often entails doing industry research and company research. Useful sources for this research include:

1. company annual reports,
2. public company filings with the Securities and Exchange Commission,
3. company presentations to securities analysts,
4. industry trade associations,

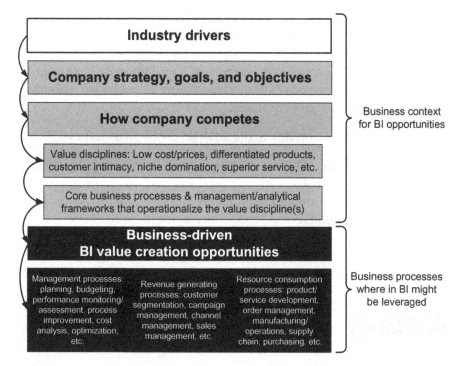

Figure 4.1 Top-Down BI Opportunity Analysis ensures strategic alignment between business strategies and BIOs.

5. articles in the business press,
6. company internal business documents—strategies, plans, organization charts, etc.

These sources provide insights for the top-down analysis flow shown in Fig. 4.1.

Starting at the top of Fig. 4.1, the arrows on the left side of the graphic indicate the top-down analytical flow. By systematically developing an understanding of the linkages between industry drivers, company strategies, how the company competes, and the core business processes that are essential to how the company competes, we have a foundation for identifying potential uses of BI to improve the effectiveness of those core processes—and thereby create business value. The boxes in the top portion of the graphic are the business context for BI strategy formulation and BIO identification, as indicated at the right-hand side of the graphic. The boxes at the bottom are where knowledge of what BI can do and knowledge of company business processes need to come together to come up with specific, concrete BIOs for specific core business processes. To illustrate this more concretely, Fig. 4.2 is a simplified example of Top-Down BI Opportunity Analysis from the perspective of a manufacturer of packaged consumer food products sold in grocery stores.

Working from the top down, the analysis could go as follows:

1. The three Industry Drivers each put pressure on margins. Private label products compete with our products and are generally priced lower. Rising raw materials prices elevate our cost of goods sold, and retail consolidations gives grocers more purchasing power, which results in price pressures.
2. Our Company Strategies aim to offset these margin pressures. Winning at supply chain execution will reduce our cost of goods

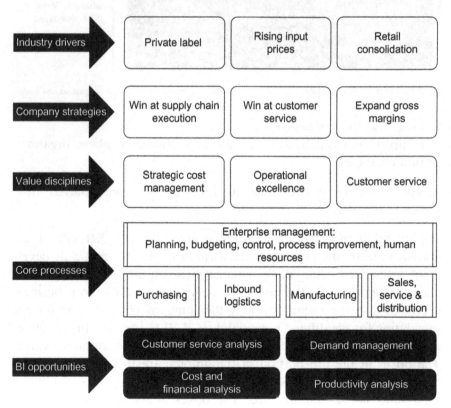

Figure 4.2 Top-Down BI Opportunity Analysis identifies opportunties to leverage BI within the core processes that drive business results.

sold. Winning at customer service will broaden our customer relationships and help offset their purchasing power. Systematically focusing on our cost structure—such as the cost of ingredients—offers additional opportunities for margin improvement.

3. Our Value Disciplines are aligned to our Company Strategies. Strategic cost management capabilities will help us expand gross margins by aligning our plants and distribution in a way that optimizes costs while also supporting winning at supply chain execution and at customer service. Operational excellence capabilities will help us expand gross margins by keenly focusing on the productivity of our manufacturing plants and distribution centers. Customer service capabilities will help us expand gross margins by allowing us to differentiate our service levels and collaborate with customers on win—win supply chain improvements.

4. Our Core Processes are the means by which we leverage our Value Disciplines and realize our Company Strategies. We look here for BIOs.

5. Based on all of the above, our key BIOs are targeted on offsetting margin pressures and capturing margin improvement opportunities. Demand Management BI will help us cope with demand variability, optimize supply chain processes, enhance customer service, reduce inventory, and achieve more optimal manufacturing and distribution plans. Productivity Analysis BI will help us optimize manufacturing performance and reduce costs. Cost and Financial Analysis BI will help us optimize supply chain and manufacturing costs. Customer Service BI will help us focus on continuously improving our performance on behalf of our customers and end consumers.

4.3 USING STRATEGY MAPS TO DISCOVER BIOs

Another way to identify BIOs is available to companies who employ strategy maps and/or enterprise scorecards. This approach is similar to Top-Down BI Opportunity Analysis in that it works from business strategies to the core processes through which the strategies are realized and then identifies opportunities where BI can be leveraged to improve those core processes. We will use Fig. 4.3, which is a hypothetical strategy map for a grocery retailer, to illustrate this method.

A strategy map is a means of aligning business strategies, goals and objectives with: (1) the company's value propositions for its

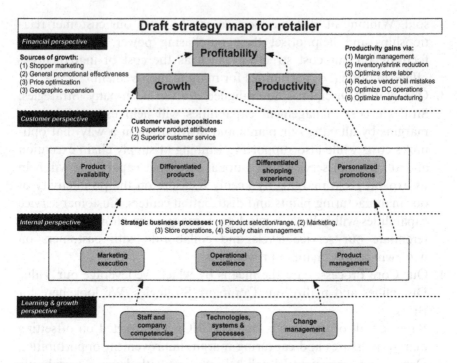

Figure 4.3 Strategy maps and/or enterprise scorecards are a solid starting point for BIO analysis.

customers; (2) the internal business processes through which customer value propositions are achieved; and (3) the internal processes by which the company develops itself and its people. The framework assumes that business performance should be managed from four key perspectives:

1. Financial Perspective;
2. Customer Perspective;
3. Internal Perspective; and
4. Learning & Growth Perspective.

Much of the value of a strategy map lies in the collaboration across the company in developing it, and in its ability to represent and communicate the company's strategy throughout the company. Working from the top down, we can see from Fig. 4.3 that:

1. Growth and Productivity contribute to Profitability, and that there are specifically identified sources of growth and productivity gains.
2. Customer Value Propositions are superior products and superior customer service, attainment of which is enabled by Product

Availability, Differentiated Products, Differentiated Shopping Experience, and Personalized Promotions. Realizing these value propositions supports Growth.

3. Strategic Business Processes and various internal disciplines (eg, Marketing Execution) support delivery on the Customer Value Propositions and contribute to Productivity.

4. That developing: (1) Staff and Company Competencies; (2) Technologies, Systems, and Processes; and (3) Change Management are necessary for enhancing the performance of strategic business processes and developing internal disciplines such as Operational Excellence.

Based on the strategy map, we can identify BIOs that correspond with the four perspectives and with the various value propositions and business capabilities. Some examples include:

- BI applications to support price optimization and promotional effectiveness;
- BI applications for measuring, monitoring, and improving productivity;
- BI applications for measuring, monitoring, and improving store operations;
- BI applications for aligning product assortment with customer demand;
- BI applications for measuring, monitoring, and improving distribution to stores;
- BI applications for analyzing and forecasting product sales trends;
- BI applications for revenue management;
- BI applications for enterprise performance management; and
- many, many more.

By aligning BIOs to the various parts of a strategy map, we help ensure that potential investments in BI are tightly coupled to the business strategies, processes, goals, and objectives that management feels are vital to company success. That alignment is useful for value creation purposes, and it has the added benefit of making it easier to communicate the business case for BI in a way that business leaders and mangers can relate to since they are already familiar with the strategy map. The degree to which business leaders can relate to the BI business case affects funding decisions and the degree of support for the BI initiative. Vague value propositions tend to die on the vine.

4.4 USING STRUCTURED INTERVIEWS TO DISCOVER BIOs

As with the other methods used for BI Opportunity Analysis, the goal is to identify opportunities to leverage BI to improve one or more business processes—and thereby increase revenues, reduce costs, or both. Accordingly, structured interviews are essentially business conversations and brainstorming sessions about business strategies, functional strategies, core business processes, and the use of business information and business analyses to enhance business performance. The general logic for the conversation follows the Top-Down BI Opportunity Analysis. That said, the interviews enable a deeper dive into the particulars of core business processes, key business/functional challenges, and gaps in information for analysis and decision-making—gaps that hinder the ability to drive business results.

4.4.1 Typical "Conversation Starters" for Structured Interviews

- What is your business unit and your role therein?
- What are the key business processes/tasks/activities performed by your unit?
- How is business unit and individual performance measured?
- What performance metrics are used, and how do they relate to company performance metrics?
- What business information and analytical tools do the people in the business unit use, for example, reports, ad hoc analysis, scorecards, dashboards, alerts, predictive analytics, etc.? What do they want?
- What gaps are there in business information and analytical tools, how important are the gaps, and what would be the business impact of overcoming those gaps?
- If you could run your unit however you wished, what information and analyses would you have available, and what would be the potential business impact?
- What barriers exist to successfully getting the business information and analytical tools (BI) you need, and how could they be overcome?

The information obtained from the interviews is used to formulate and document BIOs for review, evaluation, and validation by business leaders, mangers, and analysts.

4.5 FACTORING IN BIG DATA AND COGNITIVE BUSINESS OPPORTUNITIES

The primary difference between big data and the traditional data businesses have always had lies with the availability of unstructured data. The ability to leverage such data for business purposes is elevated by the availability of cognitive business techniques. Examples of these techniques include natural language processing, visual recognition, language translation, customer sentiment analysis, machine learning, and image indexing. As this is written in 2015, these cognitive business techniques and their application to unstructured data are in the very early experimental stages of adaptation to business situations. Accordingly, there are both risks and potential rewards for businesses that seek to leverage unstructured data.

At a strategic level, companies face a choice of strategies for leveraging unstructured data. Sales pitches for big data tend to be vague and supported by "success stories" that may or may not be relevant to a given company or industry. What is often pitched is that companies should store unstructured data cheaply and then turn "data scientists" loose to discover ways to use it to create business value. The basic premise is that it is a certainty that unstructured big data has value, and it simply needs to be discovered. This "discovery-based strategy" is different than the business-driven strategy that is at the heart of this book, as shown in Table 4.1.[1]

The perspective we advocate is business-driven, and the approaches to discovering BIOs discussed so far in this chapter can be applied just as well to unstructured data as to traditional data. Throughout this chapter, we have argued that using BI to create a rerun on investment requires solid alignment between business strategies, business processes, and BIOs. By focusing on business processes, we can also systematically evaluate whether different types of unstructured and/or big data could be used to improve a given business process. An example of this is provided by Table 4.2.

To illustrate this approach, we can focus on the top portion of the graphic, which shows how a retailer of consumer packaged goods might evaluate the potential relevance of different types of big data to its

---

[1]Adapted from Williams S. Big data strategy approaches: business-driven or discovery-based. Bus Intellig J 19(4).

Table 4.1 Factors to Consider When Choosing a Strategy for Leveraging Big Data and Cognitive Business Techniques

Comparison of Strategies for Leveraging Unstructured Big Data

Comparison Factor	Business-Driven Big Data Strategy	Discovery-Based Big Data Strategy
Basic premise	We can figure out in advance how various types of big data content can be used within our business processes to increase revenues, reduce costs, or both.	We can't know in advance how various types of big data content can be used to create business value—that needs to be discovered.
Investment hypothesis	Leveraging specific types of big data content will improve one or more core business processes, which will increase profits and enhance strategic performance.	There are case studies that illustrate how big data content creates value, so we know big data has value, and we need to discover what that value is or risk falling behind.
Strategy formulation approach	Structured up-front analysis of relevance of each type of big data content to each core process that impacts revenue growth, cost reduction, or both.	Discovery model *is* the strategy.
Role of cognitive business techniques	Relevant to both types of strategies. Advanced analytical techniques can be applied to both traditional structured business data and to unstructured data such as images, video clips, text, and audio files.	
Primary business paradigm	Business process improvement, profit optimization	Research and development
Primary skill sets	Typical business analysis and process improvement skills coupled with suitable technical skills to manage big data content.	PhD science skills coupled with suitable technical skills to manage big data content.

business processes. High-level business processes are shown in the rows within the far left column, and different types of big data (mainly unstructured or partially structured) are arrayed across the other columns. Per the legend provided at the upper left, we can use symbols to map the degrees of fit between business processes and big data types. For example, we see that Marketing processes might be a good fit for leveraging data from web-logs, text messages, and social media. In fact, some retailers are doing just that to try to discover potential shoppers' interests and intent so that they can try to influence an eventual purchase. On the other hand, analysis of images and audio files do not appear to be that relevant to various supply chain processes. Once areas of potential fit have been identified, we can then determine which analytical techniques we want to apply, potentially including cognitive business techniques. For example, we might use sentiment analysis to analyze the text messages of potential customers as part of an attempt

Table 4.2 A Business-Driven Technique for Identifying Big Data and Cognitive Business Opportunities Avoids the Risk of a Discovery-Based Strategy

INDUSTRY & POTENTIAL USAGE		TYPES OF UNSTRUCTURED DATA FOR BI/ANALYTICAL PURPOSES							
★ = good potential fit / = low potential fit	? = possible fit	web-logs	sensor/machine	images	audio files	video files	text	social	geoloc
CPG-RETAIL									
BUSINESS PROCESSES									
Marketing	Loyalty, Category Mgmt, Merchandising, Returns	★		?	?		★★	★★	?
Sales	Circulars, Co-op Ads, Promos, Pricing	★★	?	?			★★	★★	?
Supply Chain	Purchasing, DSD, DC Ops/Inventory, Distribution		?						
Store Operations	Revenue, Shrink, Inventory, Labor, Maintenance		?						
Department Mgmt	Demand Management, Ordering, Labor								
Financial Mgmt	Performance Management, Profit Management					★			
Human Resources	Skill Base, Training, Compensation	?							
CPG-MANUFACTURING									
BUSINESS PROCESSES									
Marketing	Brand Mgmt, Product Mgmt, Category Mgmt	★		?	?		★★	★★	?
Sales	Trade Mgmt, Broker Mgmt, Forecasting	★★	?	?			★★	★★	?
Supply Chain	Purchasing, Inbound/Outbound Logistics, DC Ops/Inventory		? ★						
Operations	Manufacturing, Safety, Quality, Yield, Maintenance								
Financial Mgmt	Performance Management, Profit Management					★			
Human Resources	Skill Base, Training, Compensation	?							

to influence their purchases. This assumes, of course, that we actually have access to prospective customers' text messages.

This same business-driven technique can be applied in any company and industry as part of a structured enterprise process of identifying BIOs that align to business strategies and core business processes—and that have a strong potential for delivering business value.

4.6 DOCUMENTING BIOs

BI Opportunity Analysis results in identification of BIOs. Each individual BIO should be documented in a concise fashion that presents a qualitative business case for investing in the BI required to realize the BIO. The format for documenting BIOs is flexible and should be tailored to your company's style. Here is a sample topical outline with short content examples.

1. *Bio name*: Store Operations Improvement.
2. *Scope*: The scope of this BIO encompasses store operations and the major key performance indicators (KPIs) that market, store, and department managers are collectively expected to influence, including sales, margin, labor utilization, employee development, controllable expenses, and contribution to profit.
3. *Value proposition*: This BIO will quickly and effectively stage detailed operational and financial information that helps enable Store Operations efficiently and effectively plan, budget, monitor, assess, improve, and control store operations performance across all markets, stores, departments, and their associated KPIs.
4. *Informational and analytical capabilities*: This BIO will enable a rich set of information and analytical capabilities, including: (1) multidimensional scorecards and dashboards that allow responsible managers to quickly take the pulse of their operation and (2) consistent timely access to transaction-level and item-level information, for example, increases or decreases in average basket size, top movers by department, subdepartment, and category, changes in top movers, labor cost trends, shrink trends, etc.
   Armed with these BI capabilities, the Store Operations team will have an enhanced ability to "move the levers" that have the most favorable impact on the KPIs for which they are accountable.
5. *Gaps with current state*: Current BI is insufficient for efficient monitoring of store performance on a short interval (weekly) basis,

which means that unfavorable sales and margin trends could go weeks before being detected and corrected.

6. *Alignment to business units and business processes*: This BIO is primarily intended to benefit all levels of the Director of Store Operations business unit in its execution of the following business processes: (1) annual planning and budgeting; (2) sales performance management; (3) inventory and shrink reduction; (4) store labor optimization/labor mix management; (5) staff development; (6) margin management; and (7) price optimization.

4.7 SKILL IMPROVEMENT OPPORTUNITY: DISCOVERING BIOs AND MAPPING TO BI STYLES

4.7.1 Key Objectives

1. Review the case information provided below using the Top-Down BI Opportunity Analysis framework.
2. Identify potential BIOs and the styles of BI that could be useful for improving the business process targeted by the BIO.
3. Alternatively, do a Top-Down BI Opportunity Analysis framework for your company or business function, or one that you know.

4.7.2 Case Study Information (Sourced From Public Documents)

Industry setting: Consumer packaged goods (food)

- Complex industry:
    - thousands of products (stock-keeping units, SKUs),
    - tens of thousands of retail points of purchase,
    - powerful retailers with different business practices,
    - emergence of nontraditional channels.
- Drivers and challenges:
    - product portfolio management,
    - private label products versus branded products,
    - retailer power, for example, Walmart, Kroger's, Safeway,
    - shifting consumption patterns (health, value),
    - competitive intensity and consumer options,
    - coping with rising input prices,
    - coping with item proliferation,
    - improving supply chain performance,
    - meeting customer service demands,
    - managing and optimizing inventory levels and costs,

- managing pricing and product lifecycles,
- improving forecasting, planning, and control of business processes and performance,
- creating innovative products to meet dynamic consumer demands.

Company setting:

- Large manufacturer of branded and private label (store brand) foods.
- Four reportable business segments:
  - cereals,
  - frozen bakery products—pancakes, rolls, deserts,
  - snacks—crackers, cookies, nuts, and candy,
  - sauces/spreads—peanut butter, jelly, sirups, dressings.
- Competitors:
  - all major CPG food manufacturers plus some private label manufacturers.
- Strategies:
  - increased sales—existing and new products,
  - emulation of branded products, new product development,
  - enhancing employee productivity,
  - cost control,
  - improving manufacturing and distribution efficiency,
  - aggressive pricing and promotion.
- Production and inventory:
  - multiple plants encompassing over 150 production lines,
  - use some comanufacturers,
  - mix of make-to-order and make-to-forecast,
  - hold some inventory, for example, cereal products, predictable frozen items.
- Channels/customers:
  - grocery, mass merchandisers, drug chains, clubs, supercenters, foodservice,
  - Walmart.
- Distribution:
  - company-owned warehouses,
  - third party distribution centers,
  - use independent truck lines,
  - direct ship from factory,
  - direct store distribution.

- Sales:
  - internal sales staff,
  - independent sales agency,
  - food brokers.
- Employees:
  - over 9000 worldwide, mostly in the United States,
  - numerous collective bargaining agreements.

4.8 SUMMARY OF SOME KEY POINTS

1. To create value, investments must increase net after-tax cash flows into the business.
2. Companies spend millions to provide information and analyses (BI) for running the business and improving results.
3. BI Opportunity Analysis provides the economic rationale and business case for investing in BI. The primary assumption is that strategies and financial results are realized through business processes, and BI can be leveraged to improve business processes.
4. The goal of BI Opportunity Analysis is to align business strategies, functional strategies, business processes, and potential investments in BI—which we call BI Opportunities, or BIOs for short.
5. Once we have identified and documented BIOs, we have a business-driven rationale for investing in BI and a hypothesis for how the investment will generate an economic return.
6. BI Opportunity Analysis is a business-driven, process-focused approach to identifying ways that BI can be leveraged to improve business results, that is, BIOs.
7. BI Opportunity Analysis differs from a "data subject" approach because it identifies specific BI applications that aim to impact specific business processes in defined ways that generate targeted economic results.
8. Industry research is used to gain insight into industry drivers and how companies compete. Company research is used to gain insight into a company's business strategies. Interviews with business leaders, managers, and analysts are used to validate industry and company research, to identify key processes, and to brainstorm BIOs.
9. BI Opportunity Analysis can also be done using structured group and/or individual interviews with executives, managers, and business analysts. Ideally, interviews should be with business people from all core business units and business functions and should

include company executive management, their direct reports, middle managers, and business analysts who are "close to the data." To make best use of time, it helps if the interviewer/facilitator has done industry and company research ahead of time.

10. A Strategy Map communicates how a company intends to compete and achieve economic results—and thus it reveals what business processes are important to measure, manage, and improve. We can map BIOs to the Strategy Map.

11. BI Opportunity Analysis results in identification of BIOs. Each individual BIO should be documented in a concise fashion that presents a qualitative business case for investing in the BI required to realize the BIO. The format for documenting BIOs is flexible and should be tailored to your company's style.

12. Opportunities for leveraging big data and cognitive business techniques may be discovered by focusing on how unstructured data could be used within core business processes to increase revenues, reduce costs, or both.

13. Some businesses generate unstructured data as part of their basic business models and thus they already have it—think Facebook, Google, Twitter, etc. If your company doesn't generate unstructured data as a matter of course, where would you get it and what kind would you buy for what business purpose?

CHAPTER 5

Prioritizing BI Opportunities (BIOs)

Most companies are able to identify multiple business intelligence opportunities (BIOs)—opportunities to leverage BI to increase revenues, reduce costs, or both. Realization of these BIOs requires a joint effort between business sponsors, business subject matter experts, and the technical teams who execute BI projects. Given finite resources, the identified BIOs need to be prioritized for execution over time—typically via a series of rapidly executed projects over the course of a few years. There are a number of factors that can be considered when prioritizing BIOs, and different companies employ differing degrees of formalization in doing so. For some companies, structured conversations about the BIOs are sufficient for agreeing on the priorities. For others, more rigorous multiattribute scoring techniques are favored. And of course many companies require some form of return-on-investment (ROI) analysis. This chapter discusses some of the considerations and approaches companies use to evaluate and prioritize their BIOs.

5.1 BI PORTFOLIO PLANNING AND THE BI PORTFOLIO MAP

Since developing and deploying BI applications and underlying data structures is typically a 3–5 year journey, the BIOs are typically prioritized and managed as a portfolio of investments. The primary BIO prioritization tradeoff is between the potential business impact (ROI) and the execution risk of any given BIO. The BI Portfolio Map is a way of depicting the relative positions of the various BIOs with respect to business impact and execution risk so that these characteristics can be discussed as part of the prioritizing process.

5.1.1 Business Impact Versus Execution Risk

The process of identifying BIOs is a systematic approach for gauging business impact—usually in qualitative terms and sometimes in quantitative terms, depending on the company. Balanced against the hypothesis of business impact for any given BIO is the uncertainty of success. This uncertainty can be thought of as Execution Risk, and there are three general types:

1. *Governance risk.* Simply put, can the company govern and manage a multiyear BI program with constancy of purpose, consistency of funding, and an ability to learn and adapt?
2. *Business risk.* Achieving a business impact depends on one or more business units: (1) engaging during the requirements, design, and testing phases of BI application development; (2) adapting their business processes to leverage the BI application(s) as intended; (3) managing change; and sometimes (4) changing the culture around the use of data and analysis in deciding what business actions to take under various circumstances.
3. *Technical risk.* The ability to design, build, deploy, maintain, and enhance BI applications that realize BIOs depends on: (1) having an appropriate technical infrastructure; (2) having a sound data architecture; and (3) having appropriate technical skills, tools, and methods.

In chapter "Leveraging BI for Performance Management, Process Improvement, and Decision Support" we will discuss a formal method for assessing Execution Risk, the results of which provide survey/opinion data from within the company that is used to augment the discussions about BIOs and priorities. This same method is also used for risk identification so that risks can be mitigated as part of the broader BI program management approach.

More broadly, the process of prioritizing BIOs is one of balancing relative risks and relative rewards among the identified set of BIOs. It is not an exact science, and in some cases the decision about which BIO to pursue first comes down to factors such as which business unit wants to go first and has the bandwidth to do so, or which BIO would be easiest to do quickly in order to get an early win.

5.1.2 The BIO Portfolio Map (Also Known As BI Portfolio Map or BI Portfolio)

Fig. 5.1 is a sample BI Portfolio Map for an electric utility. In simplified form, it shows BIOs in various draft positions, that is, in tentative relative positions as a means to start discussions about business impact and execution risk. Please note that in this version, the high-risk

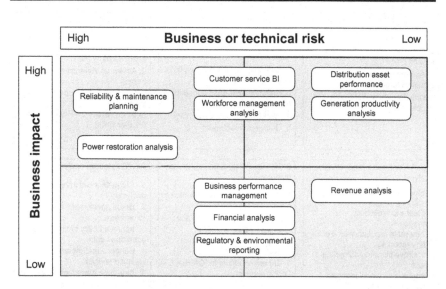

Figure 5.1 The BI Portfolio Map facilitates prioritization of BIOs.

high-reward quadrant is the upper left and the lower-risk high-reward quadrant is the upper right. This is done this way because many people assume that the upper right quadrant is the "best" quadrant to be in, so we structure the portfolio map to meet that assumption. In the example below, the Distribution Asset Performance BIO (upper right) is felt to be high impact and relatively lower risk. In contrast, the Power Restoration Analysis BIO (middle left) is felt to be moderate impact and relatively higher risk. The positions on the Portfolio Map can be determined using qualitative discussions or formal scoring methods or both, depending on the company culture for group decision processes.

When using the BI Portfolio Map to frame the prioritization discussion, it is important to have the participants review the BIO documentation—or a summary thereof—so that there is a common understanding of what it meant by the short BIO names used in the portfolio map, for example, Customer Service BI or Power Restoration Analysis. For example, "Power Restoration Analysis" could encompass performance scorecards, root cause analyses, and analytics for predicting the mean-time-to-repair of various components of the electricity distribution grid—all based off of integrated repair history data that could be

Sample of capsule descriptions of BIOs		
BIO#1 Customer service analysis 1. Automate KPI reporting 2. Demand/capacity balancing by service type 3. Automate variance analysis—actual vs target 4. Drill-down to specific units and people	**BIO#2 Workforce management analysis** 1. Demand prediction for types of work 2. Statistics/standards for types of work 3. Enhanced expense budgeting & management 4. Workforce capacity planning 5. Outage management	**BIO#3 Business performance management** 1. Automate scorecards and dashboards 2. Automate variance analysis vs targets 3. Drill from top to bottom of "data pyramid" [n.b.: this BIO will be done as part of other BIOs]
BIO#4 Generation productivity analysis 1. Fleet wide productivity analysis/monitoring 2. Fleet wide reliability management 3. Automate regulatory/enviro/safety reporting 4. Improve planning/budgeting inputs 5. Improve variance analysis (operations and $)	**BIO#5 Reliability & maintenance planning** 1. Automate RCM calculations, eg, MTBF, MTTR 2. Automate failure modes and effects analysis 3. Automate economic impact calculations 4. Enhanced inputs for CAPEX & OPEX budgets	**BIO#6 Financial analysis** 1. Stage financial information for analysis 2. Stage operational information for analysis 3. Improve ability to link $ and operations data 4. Enhance budget analysis & variance analysis 5. Automate margin analysis

Figure 5.2 Capsule descriptions of the BIOs facilitate discussions of the merits and risks of various BIOs.

analyzed by component type and manufacturer, location, duration of outage, time of year, work crew, and other relevant dimensions. An example of a BIO "cheat sheet" is provided by Fig. 5.2.

5.2 FACTORS TO CONSIDER WHEN PRIORITIZING BIOs

There are a variety of factors companies can consider when prioritizing BIOs within the BI Portfolio. While these vary by company, there are many that get taken into account more often than not.

5.2.1 Some Business Factors to Consider

1. Which BIO, if any, is most urgent for competitive reasons or for customer service reasons?
2. If a quick win is needed to establish credibility for the BI initiative and enhance executive support, which BIO best fits that need?

3. For any BIO under discussion, what would the actual BI application be, who would use it, and how would it be used in a specific business process or activity or task?
4. For any BIO under discussion, is the value proposition (investment hypothesis) valid and is the BIO positioned correctly on the Business Impact (vertical) axis? If not, why not?
5. For the various BIOs, does the business unit targeted to use and benefit from the BIO have the bandwidth to participate in the BI application development process and to make the necessary business process changes to adopt the BI application?
6. For the various BIOs, how would realizing them benefit our customers? Our employees? Our suppliers?
7. For the various BIOs and from a business perspective, are they correctly positioned on the Execution Risk (horizontal) axis, and if not, why not? What business risks exist and can they be mitigated?

5.2.2 Some Technical Factors to Consider

1. Where does BI in general fit within the larger information technology (IT) portfolio—is it important, and will the IT organization adapt as needed to take account of the difference between BI projects and traditional IT development projects?
2. Which BIO would be easiest to develop and deploy given our various other business improvement and technical initiatives that require business bandwidth?
3. Do we have the data we need for the various BIOs, and if so what is its quality?
4. For the various BIOs and from a technical perspective, are they correctly positioned on the Execution Risk (horizontal) axis, and if not, why not? What technical risks exist and can they be mitigated?
5. For the various BIOs, are there business system changes planned or underway that would require the BI initiative to change down the road from one or more current data sources that would be used initially for any given BIO—thus causing technical rework?

5.3 APPROACHES TO PRIORITIZING BIOs

The business context in which prioritization of BIOs takes place shapes the approach that a given company may need or want to take.

Typically, there are capital budgeting, IT portfolio planning, and annual operating budgeting processes that govern how capital investments and operating budgets get decided. Accordingly, it is useful to understand those contexts when prioritizing BIOs so that the right considerations are taken into account and so the right documentation is generated by the prioritization process.

From a substantive perspective, there also needs to be a way to prioritize BIOs on their own nonfinancial merits because the BIO with highest ROI might not be the top priority BIO for other valid organizational reasons. For example, a BIO aimed at cross-selling and up-selling a company's products might be the highest ROI, but the marketing and sales organization might be engaged with other priorities that fully absorb bandwidth, such as a reorganization of sales territories or the national launch of a new product line. ROI is always an important factor, but it is not the only relevant factor for prioritizing BIOs.

On the least-formalized end of the spectrum, some companies designate people to read the BIO documentation and then meet to decide the BIO priorities. Using the BI Portfolio Map, they discuss business impact, execution risk, and the specific considerations noted in Section 5.2 and arrive at a consensus about BIO priorities. Other companies prefer more highly structured approaches, such as multiattribute scoring models or formal discounted cash flow analysis. These approaches are not mutually exclusive. For example, one company used a BI Portfolio Map and the attendant business impact and execution risk factors to narrow their portfolio of BIOs from 16 down to 4. They then used a multiattribute scoring model and had their BI steering committee members vote on the BIOs.

5.3.1 Multiattribute Scoring Model With Voting

Table 5.1 is an example multiattribute scoring model for assessing the business impact aspect of BIO prioritization. Each evaluator is asked to score the BIOs across four business impact subfactors, using a scale of 1 to 10, with 10 being the highest. The number of subfactors can be as many as a given company feels are relevant, and weights assigned to subfactors can be customized according to what is most important. In the example, we assume that the evaluators agreed that business impact should be considered from financial, customer, and internal efficiency perspectives. Each evaluator completes his or her scoring

Table 5.1 Using a Multiattribute Utility Model to Quantify the Business Impacts of BIOs				
Business Impact Assessment Worksheet:	The purpose of this worksheet is to promote a structured discussion of BIO priorities. Please use Column 4 to rate the overall business impact of each BIO, using a scale from 1 to 10, where 1 means little business impact and 10 means substantial business impact. This is not a forced ranking, so it is possible to have, for example, three BIOs rated as 9s and the rest rated as 5s. The strategic planning assumption is that somewhere between two and four BIOs can be included in the business case.			
Evaluator Name: Jane Doe	1. Financial Impact (35% Weighting)	2. Customer Impact (45% Weighting)	3. Internal Efficiency Impact (20% Weighting)	4. Overall Business Impact (1 = Little, 10 = Substantial)
BIO 1—Cross-selling	5	9	7	6.27
BIO 2—Customer retention	7	9	7	6.97
BIO 3—Financial analysis	3	2	5	2.28
BIO 4—Workflow analysis	4	5	3	3.85
BIO 5—Executive scorecard	5	5	4	4.27

sheet, as shown in Table 5.1. In this example, Jane Doe (the evaluator) believes the top priority BIO is BIO2—Customer Retention, which has Overall Business Impact Score of 6.97 based on the weighted average factor scores. Once all the evaluators have turned in their scoring sheets, the results can be combined to show the average scores for the group. Multiattribute scoring models have been in use in a wide range of business contexts for decades. There are fairly simple to design and use, especially with the availability of online survey tools such as Survey Monkey.

5.3.2 Discounted Cash Flow ROI Model[1]
Despite the substantial methodological issues that arise from estimating future cash flows, most companies require some form of ROI analysis. Whatever the method of ROI, the ROI model is based on a web of assumptions about future cash flows. For BI, the assumptions need

[1] Adapted from Williams S. BI experts' perspective: projecting ROI for analytics. Bus Intellig J 20(2).

Table 5.2 An ROI Model Can Be Used to Predict the Economic Impact of BIOs

Return-on-Investment Worksheet

Projected Costs and Benefits

		2013	2014	2015	2016	2017	Total
1.0	Costs ($)						
1.1	*BI projects*						
	IT project team labor						
	Business project team labor						
1.2	*Infrastructure*						
	IT project team labor						
	Software						
	Hardware						
	Professional services/external consultants/vendors						
Costs subtotal		$ –	$ –	$ –	$ –	$ –	$ –
2.0	Benefits						
2.1	Supply chain business intelligence						
2.2	Cross-selling business intelligence						
2.3	New product business intelligence						
Benefits subtotal		$ –	$ –	$ –	$ –	$ –	$ –
	NET benefits/costs						
	NET: $ –						
	NPV: $ –						
	Discount rate: 2.0%						

to be about how the particular BIO and associated BI applications are going to improve a specific business process in a way that increases revenue, reduces cost, or both. For example, predictive analytics can increase the acceptance of a marketing offer while reducing the cost of transmitting the offer by narrowing the target list to people or groups who have shown a propensity to accept offers. If you can tie the potential investment in analytics to a specific business process in a way that makes intuitive sense to experienced business leaders, you can generate an ROI model that is as rigorous as possible given the inherent limitations of quantified ROI analysis. Table 5.2 is an example of such a model. As noted earlier, the BIO with the highest ROI might not be selected as the top priority BIO for many good reasons. On the other hand, using the ROI model to prioritize the BIOs is a valid approach as well.

Vignette: Building a Credible ROI Model for a BI Program

A financial services firm uses a standard discounted cash flow (DCF) model to evaluate all of its capital investments. As is often the case with DCF analysis, the capital and operating expense components of the investment are relatively easier to estimate than are the potential incremental revenues, cost reductions, and cash flows—that is, the benefits. To ensure that the assumptions used to project the benefits of the various BIOs were defensible and would make intuitive sense to senior executives, the BI program manager recruited a cross-functional team that included all of the business stakeholders for the BIOs plus a representative from the Chief Financial Officer's organization. Over the course of several weeks, the business stakeholders for each individual BIO developed the assumptions about the economic benefits, and then obtained feedback from within their respective business functions. When the business case was pulled together, the BI program manager could submit it to the executive team with confidence. The DCF model was perceived by the executive team as a big improvement over previous approaches to justify the BI investment, which had relied upon vague assertions from well-known vendors about "customer intimacy" and "enhanced decision-making" and so forth. By tying benefits statements to specific BI process improvements and using defensible, business-driven assumptions about future cash flows, the BI team succeeded in gaining executive approval for the BI program.

5.4 SKILL DEVELOPMENT OPPORTUNITY: DEVELOP AND JUSTIFY A BI PORTFOLIO MAP

5.4.1 Key Objectives
1. Using the BIOs and value propositions summarized below, assign their relative positions on the Business Impact (vertical) axis, ranking them from highest to lowest.
2. Using the Execution Risk assumptions stated below, assign their relative positions on the Execution Risk (horizontal) axis, ranking them from riskiest to least risky.
3. Using the rankings you just assigned, place the BIOs on a BI Portfolio Map and write a short summary of your thinking. A blank BI Portfolio Map is provided as Fig. 5.3.

5.4.2 BIO Summaries
1. *Customer service analysis.* This BIO would deliver customer service scorecards, dashboards, and user-defined queries (pick lists) that

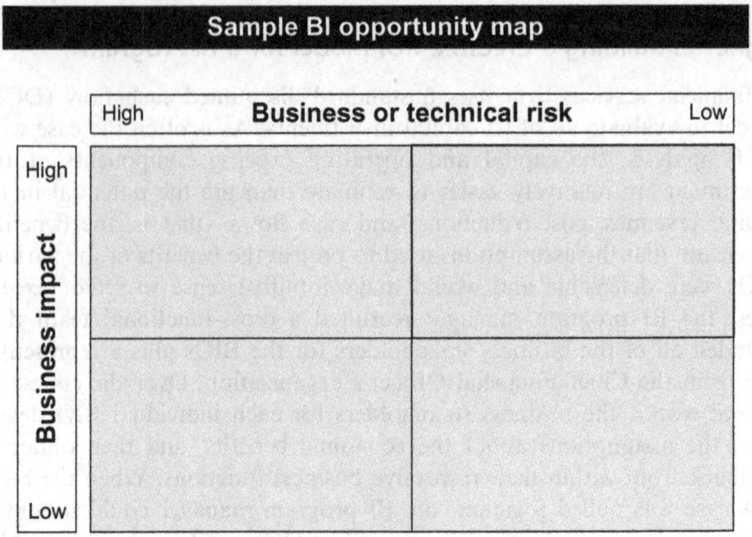

Figure 5.3 Blank BI Portfolio Map.

would enable measuring, monitoring, and improving customer service by customer, channel, distribution center, and product. Assume that the company has benchmarked its performance and is around the industry average. Assume that customer service performance in captured in an overall metric called "% Perfect Orders"—where a perfect order is on time, complete, and billed correctly, and assume that users would be able to drill down to each component of this metric for individual orders.

2. *Revenue analysis.* This BIO would deliver scorecards, dashboards, and user-defined queries (pick lists) that would enable measuring, monitoring, and improving/correcting unfavorable revenue variances against an annual operating plan, against prior-year performance, and against quarterly updates to the annual operating plan. Assume that the company wants to manage revenue attainment by business segment, customer, channel, product, and sales team.

3. *Cost of goods (COGS) analysis.* This BIO would deliver scorecards, dashboards, and user-defined queries (pick lists) that would enable measuring, monitoring, and improving/correcting unfavorable variances to target COGS in relation to an annual operating plan, in relation to prior-year performance, and in relation to quarterly

updates to the annual operating plan. Assume that the company wants to manage the major expenses that drive COGS and evaluate COGS by product, plant, and distribution.

5.4.3 BIO Execution Risk Summaries

1. Assume that there is no difference between the BIOs with respect to the ability of the IT team to do the work needed to design, build, deploy, and support the BI applications needed. Assume that the underlying IT infrastructure (computers, data storage, network bandwidth, development tools, etc.) can support all BIOs for the next 5 years, that is, technology is not a limiting factor.
2. Assume the following about the business systems that are the sources of the data required to realize the BIOs:

   a. *Customer service analysis BIO*. Assume the company has a mature, reliable Order Entry (OE) module within its ERP system, that there is only one ERP system, and that there is only one instance of the ERP system. The OE module is a high-quality source of information about individual orders, order lines, backorders, order request dates, order ship dates, order delivery dates, and order/order line returns. There is also a mature, reliable Accounts Receivable (AR) module within the ERP system that is a high-quality source of information about individual orders, billings, and corrections to orders.

   b. *Revenue analysis BIO*. Assume the company has a mature, reliable Financial Accounting (FA) Module within its ERP system, that there is only one ERP system, and that there is only one instance of the ERP system. Assume that the FA module is a high-quality source of gross revenue and net revenue (sales minus returns and allowances) results at the enterprise and business segment level. Assume that the OE module is a high-quality source of information about individual customer orders and order lines. Assume that the sales, financial accounting, and product management will need to work together to develop business rules that map gross and net revenues reported at the business segment level to gross and net revenues by customer, channel, product, and sales team.

   c. *COGS analysis BIO*. Assume the company has not yet consolidated its manufacturing execution systems (MES) into a single instance within the enterprise ERP system. Assume that the 35 plants collectively use three different brands of MES, that there are multiple instances, and that various MES instances provide information that is complete but whose quality varies from good to poor. Assume that each MES provides information about: (1) production output by product, line, and shift; (2) machine utilization and downtime by line and shift; (3) direct labor by line and shift; and (4) ingredients usage by plant, line, shift, and ingredient. Assume that the FA module is a high-quality source of expense information at the business segment and plant level. Assume that financial accounting and plant management will need to work together to develop business rules that map expenses reported at the business segment level and plant level to products, lines, and shifts.

3. Assume that the business sponsor or sponsors for the BIOs will work effectively with the IT team to design the scorecards, dashboards, and user-defined queries (pick lists) that will deliver the BI and analytics required to realize the BIOs, that is, that business engagement is not a limiting factor.

5.5 SUMMARY OF SOME KEY POINTS

1. Since developing and deploying BI applications and underlying data structures is typically a 3–5 year journey, the BIOs are typically prioritized and managed as a portfolio of investments.
2. The primary BIO prioritization tradeoff is between the potential business impact (ROI) and execution risk of any given BIO.
3. The BI Portfolio Map is a way of depicting the relative positions of the various BIOs with respect to business impact and execution risk so that these characteristics can be discussed as part of the prioritizing process.
4. There are a variety of factors companies can consider when prioritizing BIOs within the BI Portfolio.
5. The factors to be considered vary by company.
6. Companies use different approaches to evaluating and scoring potential capital investments. The requirements for investment justifications need to be considered as BIOs are evaluated and scored.

CHAPTER 6

Leveraging BI for Performance Management, Process Improvement, and Decision Support

Business intelligence (BI) is ultimately about improving business performance. The primary way that BI can increase revenues, reduce costs, or both is by improving the business processes that drive those economic results. Improvements can be in the form of enhanced process efficiency and effectiveness, and/or they can be in the form of more effective, streamlined, and automated decision support. The most relevant business processes to target for improvement generally fall into three broad categories: (1) performance management processes; (2) revenue generating processes; and (3) operating processes. Performance management processes include such activities as planning, budgeting, performance monitoring, variance analysis, scenario analysis, and economic forecasting/modeling. Revenue generating processes include such activities as marketing, sales, product development, product management, and customer service. Operating processes include such activities as purchasing, manufacturing, logistics, demand forecasting, sales and operations planning, order management, human resources development, asset management. Taken collectively, such business processes—under whatever name is used in a given company—are the focal point of BI-enabled business improvement initiatives.

Once the BI strategy has been set, the key BI opportunities (BIOs) have been identified, and actual BI applications have been developed, the only way those BI applications can generate a return-on-investment is if they are effectively integrated with the core business processes that make a difference in business results. Using BI within business performance management (BPM) processes enhances management's ability to plan, measure, monitor, detect variances, assess corrective actions, and improve business performance. Using BI within revenue generating and operating processes enhances management's ability to drive continuous improvement to the processes that drive financial results. Using BI for decision support within any of these processes enables management to bring experience, intuition, and sophisticated decision support techniques to the table for the high-impact decisions companies need to make. With these BIOs in mind, the focus of this chapter is on how BI is used to enhance performance management capabilities, how it used to improve the effectiveness of business processes, and how it can be leveraged for decision support.

6.1 BI AS A KEY ENABLER OF BPM

Managing business performance is a very broad topic, where methods and principles are debated and ideas are drawn from diverse fields. For our purposes, we will focus more narrowly on how BI can be used as the key enabler of a robust and flexible *BPM system*. To avoid confusion, I'll point out right away that we are not talking about packaged software that enables certain aspects of BPM. And we are not going to delve into the various approaches companies use to establish business goals, objectives, financial targets, individual performance plans, and so forth. Rather, our discussion will focus on how a well-designed BI application or set of related BI applications can be used to enhance performance management efficiency and effectiveness. Ultimately, a BI-enabled BPM system should enhance management's ability to drive enterprise performance toward whatever its goals and objectives may be.

To understand the opportunity BI provides for enhancing companies' BPM capabilities, it will be useful to review typical fundamental gaps executives and managers face when it comes to managing business performance. Here are some examples of actual situations encountered at prominent companies in several different industries

- A Vice President for Supply Chain Management at a *manufacturer of consumer packaged goods* (CPG) reported that he lacked timely, accurate performance information and analyses about major aspects of supply chain performance, including customer service metrics, raw material purchase price variances, and distribution center (DC) performance. This performance management gap handcuffed his ability to continuously measure, manage, improve, and control supply chain performance.
- A Chief Financial Officer for a *retail chain* reported that she lacked timely, accurate performance information and analyses about major drivers of financial performance, including store profitability, actual

product gross margins, the components of shrink, and customer life-time value for key customer segments. This performance management gap forced the leadership team to make many decisions based on guesses as to the root causes and optimal solutions to unfavorable variances.

- The Vice President for Customer Services and the Vice President for Lending at a leading *financial services company* reported that they lacked timely, accurate performance information and analyses about major elements of the company's relationship with its customers, including which customers were at risk of leaving and which customers held which of the company's various products. This performance management gap made it difficult to monitor, manage, and improve customer retention performance and cross-selling performance.
- The President of a *freight company* reported that he lacked timely, accurate performance information and analyses about the major factors that drive operational results, including capacity utilization, freight mix, labor productivity, and customer service. This performance management gap made it difficult continuously improve operational productivity and financial performance.
- The leadership team for a *wholesale distributor* reported they lacked timely, accurate performance information and analyses about the drivers of revenue performance, including product movement volumes, purchasing trends for key customers, product margins, DC performance, and store performance. This performance management gap made it difficult to determine the root causes and optimal solutions to unfavorable revenue variances.

All of these companies are successful, well-regarded companies in their industries, and all of them had ready access to timely financial information. *What they lacked was the integrated financial and operational information and analyses needed to monitor, manage, and improve the underlying drivers of performance.* I see this as a fundamental business capability gap—a lack of an efficient, effective BPM system. BI is a multifaceted tool that can deliver custom BPM systems enabled by standard, readily available technical tools.

If we know how we want to measure and manage performance in any given area of a business, we can use BI as a powerful tool to enhance our performance management efficiency and impact. Surveys suggest that many companies spend a lot of effort to manually derive and produce performance management information for use by upper management. This information often takes a week or more after the monthly close to develop, and many companies find it difficult to obtain performance insights on a daily or weekly basis. Further, the information provided tends to be so comprehensive that it is difficult for managers to see the performance variances that are the most important for them to act upon. The general mind-set of both the information producers and management consumers is to provide everything just in case it's needed—which a BI system could do without the clutter, with key performance variances highlighted, and with ready access to underlying information as needed. With BI, performance information can be available as frequently as the underlying source business systems are updated—which might be daily, weekly, biweekly, or monthly.

6.1.1 Characteristics of an Effective, BI-Enabled BPM System

For decades, management teams have been using financial accounting information as the primary tool within top-down performance management and control approaches. Once the accounting books are closed for a given month, the highly aggregated financial accounting information is married up with operational information drawn from enterprise resource planning systems, supply chain planning and execution systems, customer relationship management systems, timekeeping systems, and so forth to glean a picture of business performance. This process is often manually intensive, slow, error-prone, and inflexible. That managers lack the information, analyses, and decision support they need for effective performance management is a reality we have heard expressed over and over again in the course of the dozen or so BI strategy engagements we have conducted over the past 15 years. More broadly, the failings of GAAP-based financial accounting information for managing and improving the underlying business processes that drive the financial numbers has been ably detailed in books such as *Relevance Lost*[1] and *Relevance Regained*.[2] These gaps are business capabilities gaps that can be overcome by leveraging BI to deploy a

---

[1]Johnson HT, Kaplan R. Relevance lost, the rise and fall of management accounting. Boston, MA: Harvard Business School Press; 1987.
[2]Johnson HT. Relevance regained, from top-down control to bottom-up empowerment. New York: The Free Press; 1992.

customized, comprehensive **BPM** system. The key characteristics of an effective **BI**-enabled **BPM** system include the ability to automatically and accurately:

1. *Integrate relevant financial and operational performance information* from multiple sources;
2. *Simultaneously track multiple facets of business performance against multiple and sometime dynamic performance baselines*, for example, versus last year's actual, versus the annual operating budget, versus quarterly updates to the annual operating budget, versus marketing plans, versus production plans, and so forth;
3. *Triage unfavorable business performance variances*—using criteria set by management—in order to quickly call the most adverse variances to the attention of the appropriate manager or managers;
4. Zero in on individual variances and *enable multidimensional analyses of root causes of variances*;
5. Deliver *role-based views of business performance* that are consistent with the scope of executives' and managers' responsibilities, goals, and objectives;
6. Deliver *common, consistent views of business performance* for all executives, managers, and analysts in a given organizational unit, chain of command, and/or business function;
7. Deliver *common, consistent business performance information and analyses* for cross-functional use as needed; and
8. Enable *sophisticated decision support* based on historical business performance information.

A fundamental precept for BPM is comparing actual performance to a performance baseline, triaging the results, and calling management attention to the most impactful unfavorable variances. The performance baseline can be in the form of an operating budget, an annual business plan, a target expressed in relation to the prior year's actual performance, and so forth. The most impactful variances can be measured in ways that are most relevant to a given company and function. Financial variances are ultimately of interest at the enterprise level, but within a given function, there are a range of performance variances that might be relevant. For example, productivity measures are usually of interest to manufacturers and distributors, and customer service measures are usually of interest to a wide range of companies. As a general example, actual performance can be triaged as shown in Fig. 6.1.

General business performance states

	Worse than target	Better than target
Better than last year or trend	④ Target = $10 Actual = $9 Last year = $8	③ Target = $10 Actual = $15
Worse than last year or trend	① Target = $10 Actual = $7 Last year = $8	② Target = $6 Actual = $7 Last year = $8

Figure 6.1 An effective BI-enabled business performance business management system calls attention to the most significant unfavorable performance variances.

The four quadrants reflect different states of business performance, and they are numbered counter-clockwise from the bottom left. Using a simplified example that looks only at financial performance, we see that:

Quadrant 1: Business performance that is worse than target and worse than last year or trend would be a top priority for management attention.

Quadrant 4: Business performance that is better than last year or trend but worse than target could be a second priority for management attention. It may be that the prior years' performance was low for some reason, or it may be that the target is unrealistic. In any event, performance is moving in a positive direction, though not as much as hoped for.

Quadrant 3: Business performance that is better than last year or trend and better than target may be the last priority for management attention—after the unfavorable variances have been addressed. They should not be ignored as they might point to an opportunity that could be further exploited.

Quadrant 2: Business performance that is better than target but worse than last year or trend could occur when business results are expected to decline but do not decline as much as expected, which is reflected by the target being less than last years' actual.

Using this basic framework, companies can design BI-enabled BPM systems that meet all eight of the key characteristics required in order to be an optimally effective tool. In the next section, we will explore how an effective BI-enabled BPM system would work for managing production performance for a manufacturer of packaged food products.

6.1.2 BPM System Example: BI-Enabled Production Performance Management

If we know how we want to measure and manage performance in any given area of a business, we can use BI as a powerful tool to enhance our performance management efficiency and impact. Surveys suggest that many companies spend a lot of effort to manually derive and produce performance management information for use by the various levels of managers and analysts. This information often takes a week or more after the monthly close to develop, and many companies find it difficult to obtain performance insights on a daily or weekly basis. Further, the information provided tends to be so highly aggregated and/or so comprehensive and detailed that it is difficult for managers to see the performance variances that are the most important for them to act upon. A BI-enabled BPM system avoids this problem by highlighting key performance variances, and by providing ready access to underlying information as needed. With BI, performance information can be available as frequently as the underlying source business systems are updated—which might be daily, weekly, biweekly, or monthly. Fig. 6.2 is a hypothetical high-level business architecture diagram for a BI-Enabled Production Performance Management System (PPMS) for a food manufacturing company.

Starting at the top of the figure, the top box indicates that the scope and subject of this BPM system is production performance. Working down through the business architecture diagram and following the circled numbers, we see that the PPMS will leverage BI in a number of significant ways.

1. The enterprise production management function (*Circle 1*) is organized into two sets of production facilities—Plants and Co-Packers for each of two Divisions. These two organizations and their plants are the focal points of the PPMS. The BI component of the PPMS will automatically and accurately perform the eight key characteristics listed in Section 5.1.1. For example, it will integrate relevant

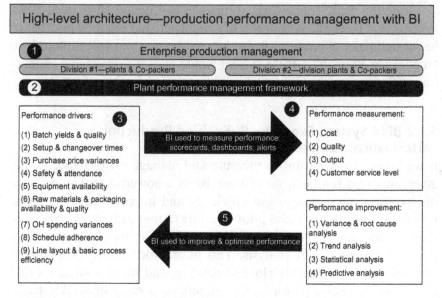

Figure 6.2 A BI-enabled business performance business management system enables impactful management of the underlying business processes that drive successful performance.

and financial and operational information pertaining to all aspects of production management and production performance, and it will be able to produce role-specific, plant-specific, and division-specific views of performance. Basically, the PPMS will leverage BI to provide the information and analyses managers need to drive attainment of performance objectives.

2. There is a performance management framework that is intended to focus plant managers' attention on managing the drivers of successful performance (*Circle 3*) and to provide useful BI-enabled tools to support their performance management efforts (*Circle 4 and Circle 5*). To achieve this, the BI component of the PPMS will leverage a data warehouse or data mart to integrate and store relevant business facts about each plants' performance—using the nine drivers (*Circle 3*) as a guide to what information needs to be available for performance management purposes. The BI component will also produce performance scorecards (*Circle 4*) and enable performance improvement analyses (*Circle 5*).

3. The plant performance management framework is focused on nine fundamental drivers (*Circle 3*) of plant performance and enterprise production performance. These drivers reflect long-understood plant management and production management fundamentals in

practice for decades across almost all manufacturing enterprises. The fundamentals are implemented through policies and business processes that have been adapted to the needs of the food company. The BI component of the PPMS will organize performance information for each of the drivers.

4. BI is used to measure performance (*Circle 4*) in relation to each of the nine drivers and to aggregate the information into scorecards and dashboards using four higher-level performance categories—cost, quality, output, and customer service level. The performance scorecards and dashboards will be updated/refreshed as often as needed to match the operating tempo and control intervals determined by the plant performance management framework. In this hypothetical example, batch yields and quality will be updated upon completion of each batch at each plant so that performance issues can be identified and rectified as quickly as possible. On the other hand, purchase price performance will be updated monthly as part of the financial close. To achieve this alignment between BI, operating tempo, and control intervals, the underlying data sources must be synchronized accordingly, for example, information about batch yields and quality must be pulled from the manufacturing execution system as soon as the batch is completed and sent to the data warehouse and/or data mart.

5. BI is used to analyze performance (*Circle 5*) in relation to the nine drivers. Executives, managers, and analysts can drill down into the underlying causes or sources of unfavorable performance and use various analytical and decision support techniques to inform management decisions and actions aimed at improving and optimizing production performance. We will illustrate this more fully in Section 5.1.4.

The foundation for any BI-Enabled BPM system is a well-structured, integrated repository of relevant business information—typically a data warehouse and/or data mart. The information is drawn from enterprise financial and operational systems. In the case of the BI-Enabled PPMS, that data would come from the enterprise resource planning system, the manufacturing execution system, the timekeeping system, and so forth. With the architecture shown by Fig. 6.2, and with the underlying data warehouse and/or data mart, we would be able to do all of the eight things required of an effective, BI-enabled BPM system (Section 6.1.1). We will illustrate how such a system might be used in the next few sections.

6.1.3 Using a Performance Scorecard to Present Performance Variances

Fig. 6.3 is a high-level wiring diagram of a Production Performance Management Scorecard enabled by the BI-enabled PPMS described above in Section 6.1.2. It is not intended to represent what a business person would see on his or her screen. Rather, it shows the relationships between different levels of performance management views, roughly corresponding to the levels of the organizational hierarchy and the level of detail needed at each level.

In the figure, the numbers in bubbles represent three levels of performance management views. The three views are based on the precept discussed in Section 6.1.1—that is, that actual performance results against baselines should be presented to executives and managers in a way such that their attention is immediately drawn to the most impactful unfavorable variances. That having been said, the views do not limit the ability to drill into any aspect of business performance that an executive, manager, or analyst may wish to examine.

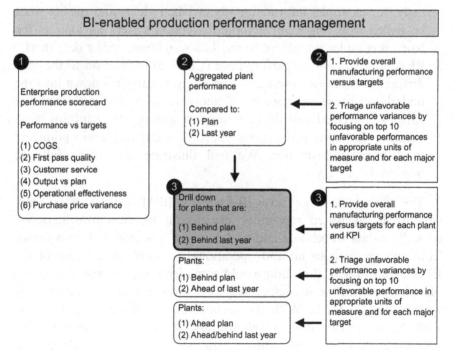

Figure 6.3 A performance scorecard enables executives, managers, and analysts to quickly focus on the most significant performance variances and drill down to the contributing factors.

In our example, View #1 is at the enterprise level, and it could be part of a broader enterprise performance management scorecard that covers other functions such as sales, customer, product management, and so forth. View #1 would enable top executives to monitor enterprise-wide production performance on a regular basis, and it would highlight if there are materially unfavorable variances. View #2 could be used by the entire executive management team if they chose to drill down from View #1, but it is intended for the top operations and/or production executives and their people. This view provides an aggregate view of production performance against the KPIs for the nine drivers of production performance shown in Fig. 6.2. Most importantly, it triages performance information by identifying, for example, the plants with the most negative cost of goods sold (COGS) performance in dollars—on cumulative and current period bases. View #2 enables the responsible managers to know almost immediately where to focus management attention. They can then drill down to View #3, which provides plant level details. This approach would put information at the fingertips of production executives and managers who are charged with meeting key cost, quality, output, and customer service targets.

To further illustrate the drill-down component of the example BI-enabled Production Performance Management scorecard, Table 6.1 displays a hypothetical view of unfavorable production performance variances for a single month.

There are five performance measurement criteria shown across the columns, and there are five plants within each of the two divisions. The BI-enabled scorecard has triaged unfavorable variances and deployed them in the scorecard using appropriate units of measures. For example, the first column shows unfavorable variances in COGS in thousands of dollars. We see that Plant 2 within Division 1 had an unfavorable COGS variance of $201,000. Also, note that some of the units of measure are additive and some are nonadditive. The total of unfavorable COGS variances is additive, whereas First Pass Quality Percentage is nonadditive. Using this type of performance scorecard enhances managerial productivity and effectiveness by eliminating the need to look through page after page and spreadsheet after spreadsheet in order to try to figure out where the performance problems are. In comparison, Table 6.2 shows a typical spreadsheet presentation of sales

Table 6.1 A Performance Scorecard Enables Executives, Managers, and Analysts to Quickly Focus on the Most Significant Performance Variances and Drill Down to the Contributing Factors

Manufacturing Scorecard May 2012—Unfavorable Variances

	Cost of Goods Sold ($000)	Conversion Cost ($/unit)	First Pass Quality Percentage	Plant Asset Effectiveness	Purchase Price Variance ($000)
Divison #1					
Plant 1					−128
Plant 2	−201	−0.405			
Plant 3			97.2		−37
Plant 4	−522	−0.009			−350
Plant 5	−28			67.2	
Total	−751	−0.414			−515
Division #2					
Plant 6					−228
Plant 7	−101	−0.505			
Plant 8			94.6		−57
Plant 9	−622	−0.012			−350
Plant 10	−38			74.4	
Total	−761	−0.517			−635

performance, with actual customer names omitted. When faced with this type of report, where does a manager focus his or her attention? Which sales index is the most material in terms of actual unfavorable revenue dollar variance?

6.1.4 Using BI to Analyze Unfavorable Performance Variances

Once the most adverse unfavorable performance variances have been identified, a robust BI-enabled BPM system would enable executives, managers, and analysts to easily drill down to identify root causes or sources of the variances. Further, it would enable a variety of standard analytical techniques aimed at informing management decisions about the optimal corrective action or actions needed to improve a given aspect of business performance. To illustrate this component of an effective BI-enabled BPM, we will examine how a manufacturing company might analyze unfavorable variance in its order fulfillment process—a process defined to include product production, inventory management, order management, and so forth.

Table 6.2 Typical Performance Reports at Major Companies Have Poor "Signal-to-Noise" Ratios

Division Sales Summary—May

Customer	Index YTD Vol Vs YA	Index YTD Sales $ Vs YA	Index YTD Spend LE Vs YA	Index YTD CPSC Vs YA	Index YTG Sales $ Vs YA	Index YTG Spend Vs YA	Index YTG CPSC Vs YA	Index F12 Vol Vs YA	Index F12 Sales $ Vs YA	Index F12 Spend Vs YA	Index F12 CPSC Vs YA	Index YTD Sales $ Vs OBJ	Index F12 Sales $ Vs OBJ	Index F12 Sales $ OBJ Attainment	Index F12 Spend LE Vs Budget LE
1	99	105	76	77	97	108	113	96	98	105	109	N/A	N/A	N/A	N/A
2	91	92	88	96	98	93	98	95	98	93	97	N/A	N/A	N/A	N/A
3	68	81	37	55	94	102	114	88	93	92	105	N/A	N/A	N/A	N/A
4	89	90	97	109	110	107	101	105	108	106	101	N/A	N/A	N/A	N/A
6	96	99	103	106	98	97	101	96	99	97	101	N/A	N/A	N/A	N/A
7	47	54	41	85	111	111	105	100	105	102	102	N/A	N/A	N/A	N/A
8	79	82	117	149	115	87	76	109	110	90	83	N/A	N/A	N/A	N/A
9	122	123	110	90	109	114	110	106	110	114	108	N/A	N/A	N/A	N/A
10	93	102	123	132	96	84	89	95	96	88	93	N/A	N/A	N/A	N/A
11	82	84	110	134	103	108	108	98	101	108	110	N/A	N/A	N/A	N/A
12	181	156	199	110	93	96	105	96	96	101	104	N/A	N/A	N/A	N/A
13	81	84	48	59	103	108	108	98	101	101	103	N/A	N/A	N/A	N/A
14	64	69	70	109	112	98	89	106	108	96	90	N/A	N/A	N/A	N/A
15	116	135	65	56	111	109	102	107	113	106	99	N/A	N/A	N/A	N/A
16	104	108	123	118	109	102	94	108	109	104	96	N/A	N/A	N/A	N/A
17	76	83	78	103	101	103	105	96	100	99	103	N/A	N/A	N/A	N/A

(Continued)

Table 6.2 (Continued)

Division Sales Summary—May

Customer	Index YTD Vol Vs YA	Index YTD Sales $ Vs YA	Index YTD Spend LE Vs YA	Index YTD CPSC Vs YA	Index YTG Sales $ Vs YA	Index YTG Spend Vs YA	Index YTG CPSC Vs YA	Index F12 Vol Vs YA	Index F12 Sales $ Vs YA	Index F12 Spend Vs YA	Index F12 CPSC Vs YA	Index YTD Sales $ Vs OBJ	Index F12 Sales $ Vs OBJ	Index F12 Sales $ OBJ Attainment	Index F12 Spend LE Vs Budget LE
18	203	173	137	67	117	114	104	113	119	115	102	N/A	N/A	N/A	N/A
19	47	48	66	140	105	103	103	95	100	100	105	N/A	N/A	N/A	N/A
20	69	73	52	75	106	104	102	100	104	101	101	N/A	N/A	N/A	N/A
21	73	78	83	113	107	93	89	102	104	92	91	N/A	N/A	N/A	N/A
23			0			0				0					
24	24	11	109	462	39	104	147	66	34	104	159	N/A	N/A	N/A	N/A
25	98	98	105	108	78	54	73	75	80	56	75	N/A	N/A	N/A	N/A

In Fig. 6.4, the order fulfillment performance drivers are shown to the left, and the BI-enabled performance measurement framework is shown at the upper right. We'll assume that there is an unfavorable variance in customer service—indicated by large bold letters at the upper right. Assuming we have a well-architected data integration environment and appropriate BI applications, we can use BI to help address the customer service variance and improve customer service performance.

In order to understand and correct the variance, some BI-enabled analyses we could do include:

1. *Drilling down* into customer orders to identify all orders delivered late, and/or delivered incomplete, and/or invoiced incorrectly. This would help bound the scope of the problem, and then we could do a *Pareto analysis* to see which products accounted for 80% of the late and/or incomplete orders.
2. Using *statistical analysis*, we could then calculate the Mean Average Percentage Error (MAPE) of the demand forecasts for the products that accounted for 80% of the late and/or incomplete orders. The hypothesis we would be exploring is whether demand

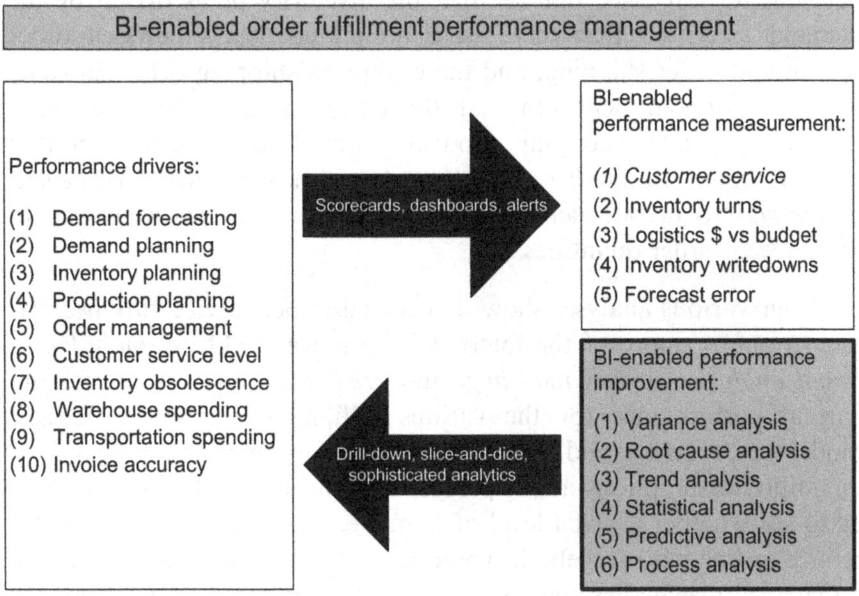

Figure 6.4 Once key unfavorable variances are identified, BI can be leveraged to drill down to root causes and to evaluate options for corrective action and performance improvement.

forecasts that were too low caused production operations to make fewer finished products than actual demand required. As part of this analysis, we would need a *trend analysis* of demand for the relevant products.

3. Using *variance analysis*, we could evaluate planned versus actual production and planned versus actual finished goods inventory for the relevant products—the hypotheses being that we didn't make enough and/or didn't have what we expected to have in inventory.

4. We could use *multidimensional analysis* to analyze the cycle times between receiving each of the customer orders and when the order was scheduled to be picked in the DC—the hypothesis being that perhaps for some reason the late orders did not move fast enough between order entry and when the order was released to the DC.

5. We could use *multidimensional analysis* to analyze the cycle times between when the orders shipped, when the trucks arrived at the customer DCs, and when the orders were received, the hypotheses being that late deliveries might be attributable to a particular third party trucking company and/or due to customer DCs not honoring appointment times.

If our various analyses show that we produced to the relevant product demand forecasts, that we met the inventory plans driven by the demand forecasts, that there were no undue delays between order receipt and order shipping, and there were no shipping delays in route or unmet appointment times at the customer end, then we might hypothesize that underlying product demand has changed. In that case, we could use *predictive analytics* (eg, *time series with exponential smoothing*) to update demand forecasts, giving heavier weighting to more recent order quantities.

If our various analyses show that the customer service variance was due to one or more of the internal factors, we could use *multidimensional analysis, process modeling*, and *predictive analytics* to measure current performance for the various fulfillment business processes, model the processes, and simulate future performance under a range of quantified assumptions about process improvement. This would allow us to see whether a given level of improvement would bring customer service in line with targets. It would also allow us to gage whether the targets are reasonable given current assets, processes, and systems or whether changes would be needed to hit the target.

6.1.5 BI-Enabled BPM: A Tool for Decision Support

Since the 1980s, the idea of technology-enabled decision support for executives and managers has been a topic in business management and information technology circles. The idea has been to design management information systems for executives needs and/or to leverage sophisticated data-intensive operations research, management science, and industrial engineering analyses. A related idea is that management accounting—initially created by industrial engineers—should deliver the kind of information and analyses companies need to drive productivity and profitability. Arguably, the seminal thinking in these areas has led to what is now known as BI. Unfortunately, it has been well-documented that there are still substantial gaps in the financial and nonfinancial information and analyses companies need to better drive and optimize profitability. As we saw in Section 6.1, business people sometimes have to guess at the root causes of performance variances, guess at the economic impact of various options, and guess at what the optimal solution might be. Or if they don't have to guess, it is often because they have commissioned a special analysis of a problem area—which: (1) may not be timely; (2) may be difficult to regularly replicate; (3) may be manually intensive; and/or (4) may be costly.

An effective BI-Enabled BPM system can overcome these gaps by delivering timely and accurate performance information and analyses. *In many cases, the kind of decision support needed by executives and managers does not require supersophisticated analytical techniques or big data or cognitive business techniques.* Rather, the business people charged with driving performance need fundamental BI that: (1) allows them to quickly spot performance problems; (2) assist them in identifying and analyzing the sources or root causes of those problems; (3) allows them to easily predict the economic and operational impact of various corrective actions; (4) enables them to track the results of the decisions they make and the actions they take; and (5) promotes learning. In today's world there is no reason for executives and managers to guess as much as they report that they have to do, a situation that results from fundamental gaps in BPM capabilities. A better way would be to leverage *BI-Enabled BPM that enhances management control and provides decision support.* Fig. 6.5 is a conceptual architecture showing how a BI-Enabled BPM system can serve as a decision support tool for executives and managers. We'll used the circled numbers to elaborate.

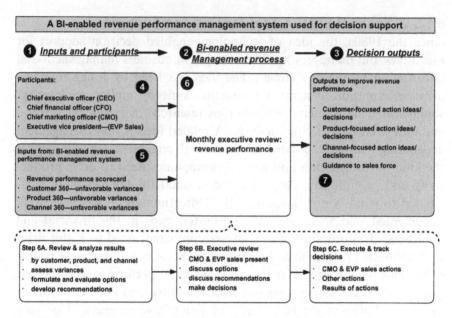

Figure 6.5 Companies can leverage BI for decision support within structured decision-making processes.

1. As with any business process, our hypothetical BI-enabled revenue performance management process has inputs and participants (*Circle 1*), the process itself (*Circle 2*), and process outputs (*Circle 3*). In the case of this management process, the outputs are decisions and action ideas. Collectively, Circles 1, 2, and 3 represent the basic flow of the company's revenue performance management process.

2. The people who participate in the process (*Circle 4*) would have specific roles in the process. For example, the Chief Marketing Officer (CMO) might be responsible for reviewing, analyzing, formulating options, and making recommendations about unfavorable product performance and channel performance variance, using the product and channel scorecards and analyses provided by the BI-Enabled BPM (*Circle 5*). This does not mean that he or she literally have to use the BPM—many times such executives will have analysts do that work. That said, the executive participants have to own what gets presented during the Monthly Revenue Performance Review.

3. The inputs (*Circle 5*) generated by the BI-Enabled BPM system would be designed to meet the needs of a given company. In our hypothetical example, they include an enterprise-level Revenue

Performance Scorecard that focuses management attention on the most impactful unfavorable performance variances. Since the focus here is on revenue, unfavorable variances involve: (1) customers not buying as much as assumed in performance baselines; (2) products not selling at the same price and/or volume as assumed; and (3) sales not occurring within certain channels at the same level assumed. Accordingly, the BI-Enabled BPM generates 360° views for the Customers, Products, and Channels with the most impactful unfavorable variances.

4. The Monthly Executive Review process (*Circle 6*) consists of three defined steps (*6A, 6B, and 6C*) that leverage the BI-Enabled BPM— mainly at Step 6A. The BPM system is used to identify and put a spotlight on unfavorable revenue variances and to drill down to understand root causes, for example, which customers are buying as much of our products as expected, which products are those same customers not buying as much of, which products overall are not moving as fast as expected, and which channels are not delivering as much revenue as expected. Step 6A is also where options and their economic implications would be assessed and recommendations would be formulated. By leveraging a BI-Enabled BPM, executives and managers would be able to overcome many of the information and analyses gaps they routinely face and bring more facts and better analyses into the decision processes (Step 6B) that will occur during the Monthly Executive Review. The result will hopefully be more impactful business decisions and actions (*Circle 7* and *Step 6C*).

In addition to illustrating how BI can enhance decision support in a meaningful way, Fig. 6.5 also demonstrates that we can think of decision-making as a process—and as such it can be specified, managed and improved, just like any other process. We can think of this as *decision process engineering*, and we can apply process engineering approaches to any or all recurring decisions that have substantial financial import and for which we want to apply human business judgement. Basically, some decisions can be automated and trusted to so-called "decision engines" and others require judgments based on experience and intuition. In Fig. 6.5, we assume that the company wants to leverage BI in support of business judgment, and we have applied decision process engineering to specify a repeatable decision process.

6.1.6 BI Enhances Close-Looped BPM

The examples we've used in Section 6.1 and its subsections demonstrate how BI can be a key enabler of BPM. In effect, BI can be used to create a closed-loop system of performance measurement, performance analysis, process analysis, business action, back to performance measurement, and then the cycle repeats. During annual business planning efforts, business results captured by the BI-enabled performance management system can be leveraged in adjusting business goals, budgets, targets, and so forth—along with external information, management experience, customer business plans, and other influences on business performance expectations. Fig. 6.6 shows the step-by-step flow of a closed-loop BI-enabled performance management framework.

6.1.7 Summary: BI Enables Efficient and Effective BPM

In many companies, the primary standard performance management information is the financial accounting system. While high-quality financial accounting information is essential, it provides very little

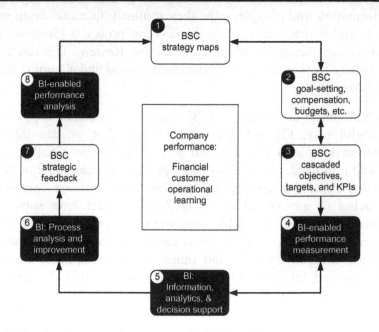

A performance management framework that integrates the use of BI provides more robust capabilities for strategic and operational performance measurement and performance improvement.

Figure 6.6 BI can be used to automate key components of a closed-loop BPM system.

relevant information for managing and improving performance by managing the underlying drivers of performance. As a result of the limitations of financial accounting information, management teams are often limited to reports—rather than having a robust BI-Enabled BPM System. This Section 6.1 was developed to show what is possible by leveraging proven BI capabilities to improve performance management capabilities and processes—and to thereby increase the impact executives and managers can have on the key drivers of business performance—whichever those may be for a given company, function, or industry.

6.2 BI AS A KEY ENABLER OF BUSINESS PROCESS IMPROVEMENT

Business processes are the means by which companies operate and their business strategies are realized—or not realized, as the case may be. Accordingly, we are interested in how they perform and in improving them. The subject of how to go about systematically improving business processes has been around for a long time, dating back to the scientific management school of thought. Disciplines such as industrial engineering, logistics, supply chain management, process engineering, operations research, systems engineering, and human factors engineering have all made substantial and highly relevant contributions to the body of knowledge available to executives and managers who seek to improve the core business processes that drive their companies' results. Further, approaches such as Six Sigma and packaged Business Process Management software have provided proven tools, and modern enterprise software applications use software-encapsulated business process workflows based on alleged "best practices."

So there is no lack of knowledge, methods, and tools for business process improvement. That having been said, our work with executives and managers in many different successful companies has made it clear to me that they still lack the information, analyses, and decision support needed to systematically and continuously improve the core business processes that make a difference in the results they achieve for their customers, their stakeholders, and their shareholders. The breadth of this "BI gap" is shown by Table 6.3, wherein we show the areas where companies say they need better BI. By extension, if they need better BI then they have a BI gap, which as we've said is actually a

Table 6.3 Successful Companies Across Industries Experience BI Gaps Across Their Enterprises

BI Opportunities Identified Via Structured Interviews—By Industry and Function

Industry	Revenues	Enterprise Performance Management	Sales	Marketing/Product Management/Category Management	Manufacturing/ Operations	Supply Chain	Inventory Management	Financial Management	Workforce Management
CPG/retail									
Company A	$2.8 B	X	X	X	X	X	X	X	X
Company B	$2.4 B		X			X	X	X	
Company C	$440 MM	X	X	X	X	X	X	X	X
Company D	$4.5 B		X	X		X	X	X	
Financial services									
Company E	$3 B	X	X	X	X			X	X
Company F	$1 B		X	X	X			X	X
Company G	$22 B		X	X	X				X
Company H	$10 B		X	X	X			X	
Distribution									
Company I	$2.9 B		X	X	X	X	X	X	
Other verticals									
Company J (hospitality industry)	$11 B		X	X	X				
Company K (public utility)	$2 B	X			X	X	X	X	X
Company L (investor-owned utility)	$2 B	X			X	X	X	X	X
Government Agency A	n/a	X			X			X	X
Government Agency B	n/a	X			X			X	

business capabilities gap. With this gap in mind, this section will focus on how BI can be used to help enable business process improvement.

6.2.1 BI Is a Key Tool in the Business Process Improvement Toolkit

Many of the process improvement methods available to executives and managers are analytical frameworks that require information (data) in order to understand current process performance characteristics and model/simulate the impact of potential future-state process. To meet these needs, relevant data needs to be integrated, processed, and made available as information about costs, quality, cycle times, productivity, and/or asset utilization—depending on the type of process being targeted for improvement. Often, the data needed is acquired on a one-off, ad hoc basis by business analysts who know their way around the various data sources available to them. While this can work, it may not be an efficient or effective way to enable continuous process improvement. BI can be a key tool for business process improvement by delivering information, analyses, and decision support that fall within two general types:

1. *BI About a Process*

   BI about a process is basically BPM BI, which we discussed in Section 6.1. Many books have been written about performance measures, which give companies many choices. The art is to select the performance measures that are most relevant, actionable, and congruent for a given company and circumstance. In trying to improve process performance, companies need performance measures that BI can deliver, such as information about process costs, quality, cycle times, and so forth. Process costs, process cycle times, process output, and process quality are examples of *BI about a process*.

   Financial accounting systems capture expenses, which generally are then mapped into a cost accounting system that may or may not be a process cost system. The type of cost accounting system in use depends on the industry and company. Process manufacturers will typically have good information about process costs, but companies in other industries often do not. Standard costs, product costs, and project costs are common cost systems and they do not provide process costs. *BI enables automated determination and delivery of standardized process costs, and these can be analyzed from multiple perspectives over time.*

Various operational systems contain information that can be used to determine process cycle times, process output, and process quality. While the information exists, it may not be readily available for continuous tracking and improvement purposes. For example, a plant maintenance system has machine utilization and downtime information, a scheduling system has information about work orders, a manufacturing executive system has cycle time, quality, and output information, and an order entry system has information about when orders were placed and shipped. *BI can integrate this information from multiple sources and automate delivery of standardized process cycle time, output, and quality measures that can be analyzed from multiple perspectives over time.*

2. *BI Within a Process*

For business processes that are data intensive, BI can automate how data is leveraged and thereby reduce the cost and the cycle time of the process. For example, marketing departments generally need to segment their customers or prospects and then deliver an outbound communication of some sort—like e-mailing an offer. This requires combing through data to select people based on various characteristics and then generating lists. BI is a tool that can do these things more efficiently than manually intensive approaches whereby analysts have to use Excel, Access, and multiple SQL-generated file extracts to get the job done.

Another example of BI within a process is consumer lending by retail banks and credit unions. When a customer or member applies for an auto loan, the lender typically wants to know as much as possible about the person seeking a loan. In addition to standard loan application information and credit agency reports, the lender wants to be able to see the entirety of any existing business relationship with the applicant. This might require searching through several product-oriented business systems, such as the credit card system, the home equity system, and the demand deposit system, to determine if the applicant has such accounts and if so what is the status of the accounts. BI is a tool that can consolidate customer information, improve the quality of the information, and make it readily available to a structured lending underwriting process.

When we talk about business process improvement, the assumption is that the process is not performing as it should or as it might or as it needs to. We need BI about a process to understand how the process is performing today so that we can tell going forward whether our efforts to improve the process are working. From that perspective, *BI about a process* is about the results of the process, whereas *BI within a process* is a method for improving the results of the process. Leveraging BI within a process is not the only way to improve a process—other approaches could include training, employee selection, incentive systems, and implementing better business systems. That being said, BI is underutilized for process improvement, and more and more companies are looking to make better use of it. Given the essential role of business processes in achieving business strategies, goals, and objectives, companies that seek to systematically improve their business processes can use BI as a powerful tool. Table 6.4 provides some further examples of BI about a process and BI within a process, mapping them to performance management processes, revenue generating processes, and operating processes.

In the next subsection, we'll demonstrate how to identify specific ways that BI can help enable executives and managers to improve the key processes for which they are responsible.

6.2.2 Determining How to Leverage BI for Business Process Improvement

There are a number of proven frameworks for business process analysis and mapping. One that works well for identifying and aligning BIOs to leverage BI for business process improvement is shown in Fig. 6.7.

1. The top portion of the business process map (*Circle 1*) is a BI-focused adaptation of a process audit framework developed by Michael Hammer.[3] Hammer describes five process enablers, which we can relate to BI as follows:
   a. *Process Design (inputs, participants, outputs, customers, process steps)*
      BI can be an input to many different processes. Some examples include: (1) scorecards and dashboards used within company performance management processes; (2) multidimensional analysis used to segment customers in support of marketing and sales processes; and (3) predictive analytics used within demand forecasting processes.

[3]Hammer M. The process audit. Harvard Business Review, April 2007.

Table 6.4 BI Is Robust Tool for Business Process Improvement

Types of Processes	Types of BI	
	Examples—BI About a Process: • Scorecards, Dashboards, Alerts • Measures, Metrics, Performance Indicators • Process Characteristics	Examples—BI Within a Process: • Decision Support (Models, Simulations) • Advanced and Predictive Analytics • Cognitive Business, Analysis of Unstructured Data
Performance management processes, eg, planning, forecasting, budgeting, monitoring, variance analysis, scenario analysis	BI about a company's Performance Management Processes could include measures like forecast accuracy, the cycle times for various types of variance analyses, or the cycle time for running economic scenarios—all measures of the performance of performance management processes themselves.	BI within a company's Performance Management Processes—as discussed in Section 5.1—might include BI applications such as demand forecasts, financial forecasting models, performance scorecards, analytical scorecards, automated variance analyses, cost analysis models, econometric models, and capital project prioritization models. BI within Performance Management Processes is essentially decision support.
Revenue generating processes, eg, sales, marketing, product development, product management, customer service	BI about a company's Revenue Generating Processes would typically be tailored to the industry in which the company competes. There are a multitude of performance measures for each of the specific processes—examples include such measures as revenues versus plan, market share growth, new product time to market, and customer service level.	BI within a company's Revenue Generating Processes would be used to make the process more effective and efficient. There are a multitude of possibilities within each of the specific business processes. Examples include such BI applications as customer segmentation models, customer propensity models, customer lifetime value models, sales forecasts, automated loan underwriting, fraud detection models, pretransaction analysis of shoppers' social media and web engagement, sentiment analysis, and many more.
Operating processes, eg, purchasing, manufacturing, service delivery, logistics, demand forecasting, order management, sales, and operations planning	BI about a company's Operating Processes would typically be tailored to the industry in which the company competes. There are a multitude of performance measures for each of the specific processes—examples include such measures as purchase price variances, manufacturing productivity, percentage of perfect orders, supplier inbound schedule adherence, and customer satisfaction ratings.	BI within a company's Operating Processes would be used to make the processes more effective and efficient. There are many possibilities within each of the specific business processes—examples include such potential BI applications as supply network optimization models, vendor scorecards, inventory optimization models, capacity planning models, demand forecasts, staffing level optimization models, and many more.

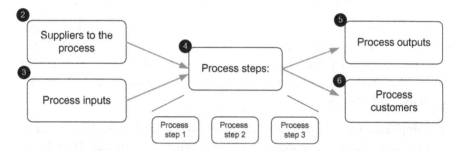

Figure 6.7 Process mapping can be used to identify opportunities to leverage BI for process improvement.

b. *Process Performers (people)*

BI can substantially improve the productivity and effectiveness of people in their jobs. For example, business analysts with good BI at their fingertips can spend much less time collecting and managing data and far more time analyzing the information BI delivers, becoming more future-oriented and decision-support oriented and less reporting-oriented.

c. *Process Owner (executive or manager with responsibility for process results)*

As people who are accountable for process results, having good BI at their fingertips provides executives and managers with a clearer picture of where things stand and an enhanced ability to drive the business and economic results for which they are accountable.

d. *Process Infrastructure (information and management systems)*

BI applications are a key part of many process infrastructures across many business functions and in many industries.

e. *Process Metrics (the measures used to track process performance)*

Process performance is typically measured by cost, cycle time, service level, quality, output, and asset utilization. These measures usually need to be generated by a management accounting system or by management accountants and business analysts. BI can automate, speed up, and expand the universe of measures that are readily available and enable shorter control intervals.

By systematically thinking through how BI in its various forms can be aligned and leveraged for the five business process enablers, companies can identify and document BIOs, as we discussed in chapter "BI Opportunity Analysis."

To complement the BI-focused process audit framework, we can also use a SIPOC diagram, which is shown at the bottom of Fig. 6.7 and represented by *Circles 2 through 7*. The SIPOC diagram comes from the Six Sigma method of business process improvement. Basically, all processes have:

a. *S*uppliers: The people and companies who participate in a process, providing time, resources, and/or goods and services (*Circle 2*). Examples are many, such as a vendor who provides raw material for a manufacturing process or a functional vice-president who owns a customer service process. In the BI world, a supplier might be a business analyst who leverages BI to provide information and analyses to executives and managers.

b. *I*nputs: The actual tangible and intangible resources provided to the process. Examples are many, such as a trucking service that delivers finished goods from a plant to a DC as part of a larger distribution process (*Circle 3*). In the BI world, an input could be any of the various types of BI, from advanced and predictive analytics to multidimensional analysis of the root cause of unfavorable variances.

c. *P*rocess: The actual steps, activities, and workflows used to perform a process. Examples are many, such as production planning, customer segmentation, customer service, sales force management and so forth (*Circle 4*). For BI, the goal is to leverage BI within the scope of a business process that makes a difference to profitability.

d. *O*utput: The result of a process that hopefully meets the need of an external and/or internal customer (*Circle 5*). Examples are many, such as a finished product, a successful call center interaction with a customer, or a management decision and corresponding action. For

BI, the goal is to enable a more-effective process and thereby achieve a required, expected, and/or improved output or rate of output.

e. Customer: the external and/or internal person, group, or company that is the intended beneficiary of the process, such as the person who buys a product or another company unit that requires the output as an input to a different downstream process (*Circle 6*).

Using the SIPOC Framework as shown in Fig. 6.7, we can systematically examine how BI can be leveraged to improve a process. Ideally, any business process is designed to meet the needs of an internal and/or external customer. In an actual process design or improvement context, we would look at all SIPOC aspects, not just the opportunities to leverage BI enablement. For our purposes here, we'll focus just on the BI aspects—again using the numbers in the picture.

2. We can specify which person or persons who are suppliers (*Circle 2*) to the process are to provide *BI about the process* and/or *BI to be used within the process*.
3. We can identify ways to improve the process by using BI as an input (*Circle 3*).
4. We can examine how BI can be used within or about the process and at which step or steps (*Circle 4*).
5. We can determine whether BI in some form should be the output of the process (*Circle 5*).
6. We can determine whether an internal or external customer would benefit from BI as an output of the process (*Circle 6*).

The business process map depicted by Fig. 6.7 is not a deterministic model. Rather, it is a useful and structured way for companies to look at their opportunities to leverage BI to improve processes of interest. It is designed as a conversation starter among the executives, managers, and analysts who are charged with driving company results. As such, it fits well as a means of BI Opportunity Analysis, as we described in chapter "BI Opportunity Analysis."

6.2.3 Leveraging BI for Improving Performance Management Processes

Perhaps the most critical task for most companies is managing enterprise performance. This encompasses such activities as planning, forecasting, budgeting, controlling, variance analysis, scenario analysis, communicating goals and results, and decision support. Over the years and still today, many companies approach performance management with tools that are inefficient and ineffective. Their approaches are inefficient because they are slow, manually intensive, and make use of nonstandardized approaches to obtaining, integrating, and managing financial and operational performance data. Their approaches are ineffective because they fail to provide executives and managers with detailed, integrated, high-quality information about how core business processes are performing. I've seen this repeatedly in practice, and academics have treated the subject in depth.[4] Fortunately, BI can be leveraged to overcome these gaps in efficiency and effectiveness—and thereby improve enterprise performance management processes.

The kind of information and analyses frontline business people say they need to drive the results for which they are responsible and accountable is what used to be called management accounting information, that is, information about process costs, quality, cycle times, service levels, productivity, and asset utilization. Providing this information and related analyses is typically the job of management accountants, financial analysts, and business analysts—whose efficacy has been hampered to a meaningful degree by: (1) the lack of fully automated access to high-quality business information and (2) the lack of advanced tools for analyzing such information. While spreadsheets have been a huge advance and will continue to be widely used, modern BI and analytics represent the next generation of BPM tools. Here are two high-level examples of how BI can enhance BPM processes:

1. *Common, standardized business information for planning, forecasting, budgeting, modeling, and scenario analysis.* Done well, BI is based on an underlying data warehouse and/or data mart, and thus it delivers common multidimensional views of business transactions, trends, events, and performance. Planning, forecasting, and budgeting almost always start by looking at past performance to derive assumptions about future performance. BI eliminates much of the arduous data discovery work needed to develop and justify those assumptions. The same underlying data is also an input to models and scenario analyses, which basically predict and evaluate what might happen in the future under various assumed conditions.

---

[4]The shortcomings of management accounting with respect to providing relevant performance management information are the subject of two excellent books: *Relevance lost* (Johnson and Kaplan, 1987) and *Relevance regained* (Johnson, 1992).

A well-structured BI environment provides the same facts to everyone who needs them to perform their parts of the BPM process.

2. *Standard scorecards and dashboards for variance analysis, performance control, and communicating strategic and operational results.* Companies today often spend considerable manual effort to generate monthly scorecards and dashboards by extracting bits of information a piece at a time from standard reports or report data files, dropping the information into spreadsheets, and then copying the spreadsheets into presentation decks for upper management. One study revealed that many companies invest over $100,000 per year in labor costs to produce such manual scorecards and dashboards. BI automates such work, and it provides a robust platform for drilling down to root causes of variances, as we illustrated in Section 6.1.

While BI has tremendous potential for improving enterprise performance management processes, capitalizing on this potential generally takes time. The reason for this is the scope of the endeavor. In order for enterprise performance management processes to fully leverage scorecards and dashboards for variance analysis, performance control, and communicating results (#2 above), common standardized business information must be in place (#1 above). The typical company has lots of business systems and lots of data, and it takes time to integrate and ensure the quality of all that data. For that reason, companies often choose to build underlying data warehouses and/or data marts in business-focused increments, for example, an increment for operations performance management or for revenue performance management. So when it comes to leveraging BI to improve BPM processes at the enterprise level, a useful strategy is to leverage BI to improve the Revenue Generation Processes and the Operating Processes that drive performance. In doing so, BI about those processes—that is, performance management information—will be developed and delivered.

Over time as specific BIOs are delivered, a by-product is that enterprise performance management processes are also improved. For example, in Section 6.1.5 we demonstrated how BI could be used for enterprise revenue performance management. The example assumes the existence of the following revenue management BI applications:

- a Revenue Performance Scorecard;
- a Customer 360° View for customers with unfavorable revenue variances;

- a Product 360° View for products with unfavorable revenue variances; and
- a Channel 360° View for channels with unfavorable variances.

The revenue management BI applications would have come about by virtue of the company having defined a BIO for revenue management and developed the associated BI applications. Once delivered, the company's performance management processes would have been improved. As subsequent BIOs are realized, enterprise performance management processes can be further enriched.

Because of this linkage between BIOs and enterprise performance management processes, it is important that the opportunities for improved performance management processes be evaluated as part of the process of identifying and defining BIOs. In the context of any particular BIO, we can ask the following:

- What planning, forecasting, and/or budgeting data is needed for this BIO, if any?
- What variance analysis capabilities are needed for this BIO, if any?
- What data are needed for modeling and simulation, if any?
- What performance analysis drilldowns are needed, if any?

Since most BIOs are about performance management and process improvement, the linkages are often already established. For example, a production management BIO will often be defined in terms of needing to deliver the information, analyses, and decision support required to: (1) understand and predict performance; (2) monitor the underlying processes that are the drivers of performance; and (3) analyze and improve those underlying processes.

In summary, this section has described how BI can be used to improve a company's performance management processes. To capitalize on this potential, companies may wish to prioritize BIOs that are related to the most urgent business areas for improvement. If revenue attainment has been a challenge, then prioritize a BIO that enhances revenue performance management capabilities and simultaneously delivers the information, analyses, and decision support needed to improve the underlying revenue generation processes. If improving margins or profitability has been a challenge, then prioritize a BIO that enhances operational performance management capabilities and enables improvement of the underlying operating processes that drive productivity. Most companies have practical opportunities to leverage BI to improve the efficiency and effectiveness of their enterprise performance management processes.

6.2.4 Leveraging BI to Improve Revenue Generation Processes

In Sections 6.1 and 6.2.3, we discussed leveraging BI for performance management and improving performance management processes. Those principles and methods apply equally to revenue generation processes in that we need to measure, manage, and improve attainment of revenue targets. Since we have already talked about performance management in some depth (*BI about a process*), this section will focus on how *BI within* revenue generating processes can improve the effectiveness and efficiency of such processes. The opportunities for leveraging BI within revenue generating processes are often based on advanced analytics, predictive analytics, data-centric market segmentation techniques, multidimensional analysis, big data analytics, and cognitive business techniques. The range of these BIOs is quite broad, and the techniques themselves have been well-described by their specialized practitioners. Our focus here will be to provide examples of how BI—which encompasses these techniques—can be used to enhance the efficiency and effectiveness of revenue generation processes. As an overview, Table 6.5 shows that different companies across several major industries have identified similar opportunities to leverage BI to improve fundamental revenue-generation processes.

While the specific BI applications and uses vary by company and industry, we have seen a large degree of commonality between companies with respect to the fact that they want to leverage BI to enhance their sales and marketing processes. We will highlight three examples to illustrate the BI-related thought processes of the executives, managers, and analysts we interviewed.

6.2.4.1 Leveraging BI for Enhanced Revenue Generation in the Financial Services Industry

Companies in the financial services industry generally have more individual customers than with which they can build personalized relationships. Whether we consider large financial conglomerates or more focused companies in retail banking/credit unions, investment

Table 6.5 Sales and Marketing People in Several Different Industries Have Identified Many Ways for Using BI to Improve Their Revenue Generation Processes

Cross-Industry View of BI/Analytics Opportunities for Sales and Marketing

Industry	Segmentation	CRM— Personalization	Advanced Analytics	Predictive Analytics	Revenue Management	Pricing and Promotion	Cross-Sell, Up-Sell, Retain	Product or Category Management
CPG/retail								
Company A			X	X	X	X	X	X
Company B			X	X	X	X		X
Company C	X	X	X	X	X	X	X	X
Company D					X	X		X
Financial services								
Company E	X	X	X	X	X	X	X	X
Company F	X	X	X	X	X	X	X	X
Company G	X		X	X			X	X
Company H	X	X	X	X	X	X	X	X
Distribution/logistics								
Company I	X	X	X	X	X	X	X	X
Company J	X	X	X	X	X	X	X	
Other								
Company K (hospitality industry)	X	X	X	X	X	X	X	X

management, life insurance, property and casual insurance, consumer lending, or whatever, these companies often have hundreds of thousands or millions of individual customers. To grow revenues, these companies need to do such things as:

- segment their customers,
- estimate customer lifetime values,
- personalize interactions with customers,
- understand price elasticity of demand for their products or services,
- identify cross-selling and/or up-selling opportunities,
- determine which customers are likely to take advantage of promotional offers,
- determine which promotions have the most resonance with which customers,
- determine which promotional campaigns generate the highest return on investment,
- identify customers at risk of defecting,
- take actions to retain at-risk customers, and
- reward loyal customers.

Given the large number of customers these companies serve, all of the above tasks are data-intensive, which makes the tasks ideal opportunities for leveraging BI in various forms. To capitalize on these opportunities, many companies want to create the so-called "360° View of the Customer"—which consists of transaction histories for each customer, so-called "reference data" for each customer (name, age, address, etc.), and sometimes customer-related data purchased from outside market research firms. In essence, the collection of 360° views provides a comprehensive database of customer information upon which to build BI applications that enhance the efficiency and effectiveness of revenue generation processes.

6.2.4.2 Leveraging BI for Enhanced Revenue Generation in the Consumer Packed Goods Industry

Business-to-business companies that manufacture and/or distribute CPG may not have as many individual customers as financial services companies have, but they need to do many of the same things. A company that makes CPG products may sell to several hundred grocery chains, a number of national drug store chains, a few warehouse clubs, and a couple dozen food service distributors. At the same time, CPG manufacturers and distributors have to understand the end consumers for their products and which channels are the most important for reaching them. All this adds up to the fact that there are many opportunities for companies in the CPG value chain to leverage BI to enhance their revenue generating processes. To capitalize on these opportunities, many of these companies want to create an integrated view of customers, products, and channels. Having such a view enables them to have a deeper, more specific understanding of which products are being purchased by which customers and through which channels. Armed with a comprehensive view of revenue drivers, manufacturers and distributors can leverage BI to:

- understand price elasticity of demand for their products,
- identify cross-selling and/or up-selling opportunities,
- determine which customers are likely to take advantage of trade promotion offers,
- determine which promotions have the most resonance with which customers,
- determine which promotional campaigns generate the highest return on investment, and
- identify products that are at risk of losing shelf space at retail.

At a more specific level, having comprehensive information about customers, products, and channels can be leveraged by manufacturers to guide product research and development, and by distributors to guide the range of products they offer to retailers. While the specifics will vary, there are many opportunities for manufacturers, distributors, and retailers to leverage BI to enhance revenue generation processes.

6.2.4.3 Leveraging Big Data and Cognitive Business Techniques for Shopper Marketing in the Retail Industry

One of the arguments of big data analytics and cognitive business proponents is that the vast trove of social media data, consumer search histories, and consumers' click streams at retailers' web sites can provide valuable clues as to individual shoppers' purchase intentions. This "pretransaction" data can be leveraged to influence the shopper's "path to purchase." Since much of this pretransaction data is unstructured data, and because there is so much of it, those who would capitalize on it need to employ advanced forms of BI—such as sentiment analysis, text disambiguation, pattern recognition, and other forms of cognitive business. This approach to enhancing the revenue generation processes of retailers is relatively unproven as this book is being written in 2015, but it deserves mention because if the potential of this idea were actually to realized, retailers would ignore it at their peril.

More broadly, the sales, marketing, and product development functions at companies with large numbers of customers, products or services, channels, and/or markets have been early adopters of BI as a valuable and flexible tool for enhancing revenue generation processes. BI can make these processes more efficient by automating most of the fundamental data acquisition, integration, management, and analysis processes required for enabling sophisticated marketing, sales, and product development techniques. BI can make revenue generation processes more effective through such approaches as enabling more actionable and specific customer and market segmentations, delivering comprehensive views of the total relationship with customers, enabling more personalized and timely interactions with customers, focusing promotional and advertising investments where they have the highest potential return, identifying customers at risk, and modeling how much it is reasonable to spend to retain customers. When it comes to the use of BI to enhance revenue generation processes, BI is a double threat—it can enhance top line growth, and it can enhance the productivity of investments in sales, marketing, and product development.

6.2.5 Leveraging BI to Improve Operating Processes

Since we have already talked about BI for performance management (*BI about a process*), this section will focus on how *BI within* operating processes can improve the effectiveness and efficiency of such processes. The opportunities for leveraging BI within operating processes are generally based on advanced analytics, predictive analytics, optimization, simulation and modeling, multidimensional analysis, and process control techniques. The range of these BIOs is quite broad, and the techniques themselves have been well-described by their specialized practitioners. As an overview, Table 6.6 shows that different companies across several major industries have identified similar opportunities to leverage BI to improve fundamental operating processes.

While the specific BI applications and uses vary by company and industry, we have seen a large degree of commonality between companies with respect to the fact that they want to leverage BI to enhance fundamental operating processes. We will highlight examples to illustrate the BI-related thought processes of the executives, managers, and analysts we interviewed.

Table 6.6 Operations People in Several Different Industries Have Identified Many Ways for Using BI to Improve Operational Performance

Cross-Industry View of BI/Analytics Opportunities for Operations Functions

Industry	Demand Analysis	Inventory Management	Customer Service	Supply Chain and Distribution	Manufacturing or Service Execution	Sales and Operations Planning	Cost and Financial Management
CPG/retail							
Company A	X	X	X	X	X	X	X
Company B	X	X	X	X		X	X
Company C	X	X	X	X	X	X	X
Company D	X	X	X	X		X	X
Financial services							
Company E	X		X	X			X
Company F	X		X	X			X
Company G			X	X			
Company H		X	X	X	X		X
Distribution/logistics							
Company I	X	X	X	X	X	X	X
Company J	X	X	X		X	X	X
Other							
Company K (hospitality industry)			X	X			X
Company L (public utility)	X	X	X	X	X	X	X
Company M (investor-owned utility)	X	X	X	X	X	X	X
Government agency A	X		X		X	X	X
Government agency B					X	X	X

6.2.5.1 Leveraging BI to Enhance Operating Processes in the CPG Industry

In chapter "The Strategic Importance of Business Intelligence," we put forth the idea that the strategic importance of BI is related to the complexity of the industry. The CPG industry is complex from a value chain and operational perspective. Even a modest-size CPG manufacturer makes hundreds of products and product variations that need to reach potentially millions of end consumers via several distinct distribution channels.

Having the right product on the right shelf at the right time is a challenging task that necessitates holding inventory in order to provide responsive customer service and avoid stockouts. It also requires an effective and efficient distribution approach to customers in different channels—customers who each have their own way of doing business and who can often dictate business practices around replenishment, order-processing, delivery, invoicing, and so forth. To further complicate matters, many mass-market CPG products are subject to highly variable demand based on the season and/or on specific events, and fashion products are subject to demand uncertainty based on changing consumer preferences. To cope with the complexity of the industry, companies need to do such things as:

- analyze historical product sales volume history by customer, channel, and time of year to develop a demand trend baseline;
- predict demand for every product based on prior trends, known changes to customer buying patterns, known changes to customer order patterns, planned pricing and promotion actions, and plans for introducing new products;
- build production plans and schedules based on predicted demand and inventory strategy;
- build distribution plans and schedules based on production plans;
- adjust production, distribution, and inventory plans based on actual demand and changing company financial goals;
- employ customer service/order management processes that are efficient from an internal operations perspective and effective from customers' perspectives;
- engage in strategic cost modeling and supply network optimization to achieve margin and operating profit objectives; and

- continuously improve manufacturing and distribution processes to offset margin pressures coming from large retailers and private label products.

Given the large number of products, and the many possible permutations of which products are sold in what quantities to which customers and customer locations via which DCs and channels, the CPG industry is data-intensive. Accordingly, BI can enhance the efficiency and effectiveness with which these tasks are accomplished. Since operations are driven by the level and pattern of demand, many CPG manufacturers and distributors want to create what is often called a "demand signal repository." This is a specialized name for a standard data warehouse and/or data mart that integrates product unit sales volume and pricing history with customer and channel information in order to make demand forecasting more efficient. When demand history is merged with historical data about plant production, inventory, customer service performance, DC performance, supplier performance, and other operational and financial information, companies can readily develop and deploy BI applications that perform or help perform the various operations management and operations improvement processes listed above. Done well, such BI applications can improve the efficiency and effectiveness of many fundamental operational processes.

6.2.5.2 Leveraging BI to Enhance Operating Processes in the Grocery Industry

The typical grocery store carries some 40,000 products to meet the needs of consumers. How, when, and in what quantities those products get to the retail shelf is complex operationally. Consumer demand for individual products is variable by season, day of the week, holiday event, and the idiosyncratic behavior of individual shoppers. Demand is made even more variable by the many trade promotions offered by CPG manufacturers, which result in frequent price changes that spur pantry by deal-conscious shoppers, that is, buying more product than would typically be consumed by their household during the period between shopping trips. Further, some products are subject to inventory shrink from various causes—such as product spoilage, theft, store use (think cleaning supplies), or going past their code date (shelf life). Since product purchases and demand patterns drive stock replenishment, the entire upstream value chain is subject to fluctuations in order patterns and quantities from individual stores. Combine demand variability with the large number of products to be replenished and the large number of vendors from which they are obtained, and you have a complex operation. As a result, grocers have been focusing on improving their operating processes, and in a slow-growth, slim-margin business like the grocery business there is not a lot of room for inefficient and ineffective operating processes. With all these complexities in play, grocers typically need to:

- predict and shape demand to the extent they can so that their replenishment processes help them avoid stockouts—which have been shown to aggravate consumers and cause lost sales;
- avoid or identify and correct operational performance issues at stores to ensure customer satisfaction;
- manage the root causes of inventory shrink, such as overordering, insufficient inventory coverage, and ineffective management of perishables;
- achieve targeted product margins;
- execute effective purchasing practices, balancing acceptance of trade promotions, forward buying, inventory carrying costs, and shrink;
- monitor, measure, and improve store ordering processes to balance stockouts, shrink, and inventory holding costs; and
- monitor, measure, and improve the operational aspects of product replenishment, such as inventory levels, direct store deliveries, inbound product deliveries to company-operated DCs, DC operations, contract manufacturing of private label products, and any company-operated central manufacturing operations.

Given the large number of products to be stocked, and the fact that most grocery operators have at least several stores and in some cases thousands of stores and multiple DCs, grocery operations is data-intensive. Accordingly, BI can enhance the efficiency and effectiveness with which these tasks are accomplished. One advantage that grocers have is that they have immediate access to actual demand data, as captured by their point-of-sale (POS) terminals at the checkout stands. This means that they can leverage POS data as inputs to BI-enabled predictive analytics as an efficient and effective way to predict future demand at a very granular level, that is, by product, product-family, promotion group, store, and store department, time of day, time of the week, time of year, event, market, and product category. Such BI-enabled demand predictions are a key input to operational processes—such as ordering, purchasing, inventory replenishment, central manufacturing, and labor scheduling.

In addition to leveraging BI to enable demand forecasts, grocery chains (and other retailer chains) can leverage well-designed data warehouses and/or data marts to provide financial and operational data for a range of other BI-enabled approaches to improving operating processes. For example, optimization models have long been used for decision support within supply chain and logistics processes to achieve targeted balances between service levels and costs. For a grocery chain, BI-enabled optimization models aimed at minimizing stockouts could be used to set inventory targets and required production plans. Within the purchasing function, sophisticated BI-enabled margin models and cost models could be used to help make optimal decisions regarding whether or not to accept trade deals, which is basically a tradeoff between lower per-unit purchase price versus inventory holding costs and the risk of spoilage. More broadly, grocers can help offset the inherent complexity of their industry by leveraging BI to improve the efficiency and effectiveness of their operating processes.

More broadly, the operating processes in many companies are often complex. This is most pronounced in data-intensive industries that operate under material degrees of demand variability and uncertainty. To cope with this complexity, many companies use spreadsheet and ad hoc data management techniques for such critical operating processes as demand forecasting, demand planning, inventory optimization, service level optimization, operations planning, and so forth. While sophisticated analytical techniques have been available for decades, they have often been applied inefficiently or foregone altogether due to the difficulty of acquiring and leveraging the data needed to apply the techniques. A well-designed BI environment provides a robust platform for BI applications that can make fundamental operating processes more efficient and effective.

6.2.6 Summary—Leveraging BI for Business Process Improvement

Section 6.2 has looked at BI from the perspective of how it can be leveraged to improve business processes. A key opportunity lies in the power of BI to augment typical top-down financial views focused on reductions to chart-of-account line item expenses. By providing companies with a practical tool for business process improvement, BI enables executives and managers to optimize costs while also achieving other important related business objectives, such as providing good service to customers, making quality products, and being able to sell products and services at a price customers are willing to pay. By focusing BI applications on improving core business processes designed to meet customers' needs, companies can move beyond blunt-force approaches to improved profitability to laser-focused approaches that optimize across multiple business objective. This is more of a bottom-up approach whereby we improve the underlying core business processes that generate business results. As such, it represents an important advance beyond top-down approaches driven by income statement and balance sheet numbers that have been shown to be insufficient for driving improvement processes. The opportunities for BI-enabled process improvements are many, and companies can identify such opportunities by using a method like the high-level process map provided in Section 6.2.2. The combination of BI about process performance and BI used within processes enables systemic improvement of performance management processes, revenue generation processes, and operating processes.

6.3 BI AS A KEY ENABLER OF HIGH-IMPACT BUSINESS DECISIONS

Since the term "BI" was first coined in the mid-1990s, its value proposition has often been framed by marketers and industry analysts by phrases like "enables better decisions" and "helps outsmart the competition." What has often been left unexamined is the exact mechanism by which such value propositions are realized. What I have seen in practice, and what has been discovered by academic research, is fairly obvious: *in order for BI to have value as a decision support tool it has to be used in the context of business processes that make a difference in revenue growth, productivity, or both.*

In Section 6.1, we discussed how BI can be leveraged within BPM processes, which would certainly focus on revenue growth, among other goals and objectives. We argued there that BI about various aspects of company performance constituted decision support, and that such support need not be in the form of highly sophisticated analytical techniques. Simply being able to quickly identify the most significant performance issues, analyze their roots causes, and evaluate the economic impact of decision options would be a substantial advance in the BI-enabled decision support capabilities of many successful companies.

In Section 6.2, we discussed how BI about a process and BI within a process can be used to improve process efficiency and effectiveness. BI about a process is used to evaluate how a process is performing today—it is a diagnostic tool that helps executives and managers decide where to focus business process improvement efforts. BI within a process is aimed at efficiency and effectiveness. Efficiency generally comes from using BI to automate manually intensive data analysis tasks, standardize information and analyses, and provide all decision-makers with the same information and analyses at the same time. Effectiveness generally comes from using BI to inject decision support techniques into revenue generation processes and/or operating processes so that key decisions made within such processes leverage the best available information and analyses to evaluate a richer set of options for which the economic outcomes can be reasonably estimated. Examples of such decision support uses for BI are many, including:

- using clustering to group customers based on their purchase behaviors, which enables finer-grained segments and more personalized marketing and customer service interactions;
- using customer lifetime value models to enable differentiation in customer service, tailored and economically sensible loyalty rewards, and economically sensible retention strategies for at-risk customers;
- using decision engines for applications such as automated underwriting, fraud detection, and risk analysis;
- using supply network optimization models to decide where to locate plants, service centers, DCs, maintenance depots, and the like; and
- using reliability models to decide on asset maintenance and repair strategies.

All of the above decision support uses of BI are intended to enhance the effectiveness of the business processes in the context of which they are applied. While BI has always been marketed as a decision support tool, recent attention has been given to big data analytics and cognitive business, which are essentially opportunities to leverage newer kinds of data and digital content using newer analytical and decisions support techniques. As companies formulate BI strategies, it is important to understand where big data analytics and cognitive business fit in the evolution of computerized decision support. That is our next topic.

6.3.1 The Evolution of Computer-Assisted Decision Support Systems

The subject of decision support systems has been around for decades. As computers first started to be widely used in business, early adopters started to look beyond their capabilities for automating day-to-day tasks and business processes, and more toward potential uses to support decision-making. A central challenge was to determine which decisions were most appropriate for computerized decision support techniques. Due to the high cost of computing power and data storage at the time, decision support was only practical for decisions that would have a high economic impact on the company, that were complex, and that could not be adequately informed by less expensive manually intensive analytical methods.

As computing and storage costs came down, the range of business decisions that could be informed by decision support methods expanded. This opened the door for creative application of well-established statistical analysis, operations research, and applied mathematics methods to an ever-widening range of business situations. Collectively, these methods comprise the most part of what have traditionally been called "analytics." By the mid-1970s, there emerged what we now call "analytics platforms" or "analytics toolkits." These are software packages that bundled a software development environment, a run-time environment, and collections of precoded analytical methods. An analytics platform enabled a small team comprised of business experts and software application developers to quickly assemble and test decision support applications—without having to code the complex underlying analytics. For example, a company looking to forecast demand could put together a data set of past sales transactions and then apply different precoded time series forecasting methods to the data. More broadly, the advent of analytics platforms stimulated a push toward greater acceptance of sophisticated analytical methods to support complex, high-impact business decisions. The degree to which any given company embraced decision support systems varied, in part due to cultural resistance among executives who did not understand the underlying math, and in part due to the challenge of acquiring and managing the data sets required as inputs to the analytical techniques.

Despite the barriers, the ease with which analytical applications—a subset of BI—could be developed, tested, and deployed spurred their use across a wide range of business functions. People in the supply chain, logistics, manufacturing, and operations worlds applied standard precoded analytical methods in the context of complex, recurring business situations that required decisions that could have substantial economic impacts on their companies—favorable or unfavorable. People in the sales and marketing world applied techniques such as clustering, collaborative filtering, and customer lifetime value models to generate more fine-grained behavioral segmentations of customers, to profile the segments, to predict what product/service promotional offers to make, to determine the economics of trying to retain customers at risk of taking their business elsewhere. People in the asset maintenance world used predictive analytics and cost models to forecast when equipment would fail, to predict how long it would take to repair, and to optimize maintenance strategies. Other examples abound.

Fast forward to today, and we see that a new class of analytics is being promoted as "big data analytics" and "cognitive business." Big data analytics proponents argue that the vast and rapidly growing quantities of unstructured data, such as texts, tweets, photos, video clips, and social media interactions, must have value and it is simply a matter of "monetizing" the data. Accordingly, unstructured big data (indexed digital content really) is stored in low-cost database clusters while "data scientists" try to figure out ways that such digital content can be leveraged to create business value. Cognitive business proponents argue that techniques for analyzing unstructured data can inform business decisions, and that machine-learning programs can finally realize the long-sought promise of artificial intelligence and computers that think and learn like humans.

As has always been the case with BI in general and other decision support techniques in particular, the potential business value of big data analytics and cognitive business techniques lies in their potential use in the context of business processes that make a difference to profitability and business results. In that sense, the use of these newer techniques needs to be linked to decisions made in the context of performance management processes, revenue generation processes, and operational processes. This argues for explicitly considering big data analytics and cognitive business opportunities when we do BIO analyses and business process mapping to identify and align potential BI investments with core business processes.

6.3.2 BI as a Decision Support Tool

Our primary focus up to this point has been on BI as a strategically important capability that is leveraged to enhance the efficiency and effectiveness of critical business processes. While we have mentioned that BI is a decision support tool used within those business processes, we have not explicitly looked at how BI works in the context of business decision-making. Since business people make all kinds of decisions every day, and since our focus is on business performance and business processes, we'll narrow our focus to the use of BI to support business decisions about how best to respond to performance issues. As we discussed early on, BI is an umbrella term that encompasses several different styles of BI. These range from static reports to highly sophisticated analytics, and their uses for decision support vary—as shown by Table 6.7.

While there are many models of human decision-making, Table 6.7 reflects a simple framework of decision stages—a framework that will be useful for showing how BI can be used to support decisions for resolving business performance issues. The model assumes the following decision stages:

1. *Recognition* that there is a performance issue that needs to be resolved—whether through a regular periodic business performance review process or through ongoing performance monitoring;
2. Determination of the *Importance* of the performance issue, whether that is characterized in terms of financial impact, customer service impact, or other relevant performance measure—so as to focus managerial bandwidth and attention appropriately;
3. Developing an understanding of *Causal Factors* of the performance issues;
4. Formulation and evaluation of *Options*; and
5. Putting forth a *Recommendation*.

For each of the decision stages, we see that various styles of BI can be useful. The old standby for most companies is the static report, which has utility but does not capitalize on modern BI-enabled decision support capabilities. Most executives and managers want to understand

Table 6.7 BI Can Be Used Across the Stages of Business Decision-Making					
Style of BI	Stage of Decision-Making				
	Recognition	Importance	Causal Factors	Options	Recommendation
	"We Need to Make a Decision About…"	"This Is a High/ Medium/Low Value Decision"	"The Need for This Decision Is Driven By…."	"We Have These Options With These Potential Impacts"	"We Recommend Option…"
Static report	Good for identifying performance issues if reader understands the report	Depending on report, it may highlight economic issue and magnitude			
Alert	Targeted business rules that call attention to performance issues	An alert can be set based on business-defined thresholds of importance			
Ad hoc analysis		Can be used to analyze the economic impact of a performance issue	Good for drilling down to causal factors	Good for backward-looking analysis to generate assumptions for options analysis	
Scorecard/ dashboard	Good for triaging performance issues to focus management attention	Good for ranking performance issues based on economic impact	Good for delivering prepackaged drilldowns to causal factors		
Multidimensional analysis	Prepackaged, drillable multidimensional analyses can be used to recognize performance problems, assess their economic or business magnitude, used to trigger decision processes, and used to drill down to causal factors			Good for backward-looking analysis to generate assumptions for options analysis	
Advanced analytics	Can enable statistical process control to identify		Good for backward-looking analysis of		

(Continued)

Style of BI	Stage of Decision-Making				
	Recognition	Importance	Causal Factors	Options	Recommendation
	"We Need to Make a Decision About…"	"This Is a High/Medium/Low Value Decision"	"The Need for This Decision Is Driven By…."	"We Have These Options With These Potential Impacts"	"We Recommend Option…"
	performance issues		trends and causal factors		
Predictive analytics		Can be used to predict the economic impact of a performance issue			Good for modeling the economic results of various options as the basis for a recommendation
Simulation					Good for applying probabilities to the options and running predictive models enough times to generate risk-adjusted economic results of various options as the basis for a recommendation
Prescriptive model					Good for generating rankings or recommendations based on optimization techniques
Big data analytics and cognitive business					Combines other forms of analytics with the ability to analyze unstructured data to offer the ability to look backward, look forward, simulate, and recommend or decide

Table 6.7 (Continued)

what happened in the past, but they are far more interested in being able to predict the future, assess their options, and deal with the complexities of the decisions to be made. Leveraging the right BI tools provides the kinds of decision support that executives, managers, and analysts say they need to make more impactful and timely decisions.

6.4 SKILL DEVELOPMENT OPPORTUNITY

6.4.1 Insert BI Into a Business Process
6.4.1.1 Key Objectives
1. Using Fig. 6.8, draw a high-level SIPOC diagram for a business process with which you are familiar. It can be related to your current

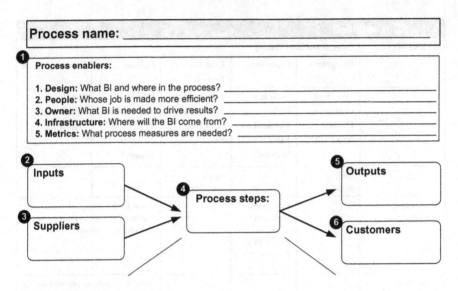

Figure 6.8 Blank process map.

job, a prior job, or any process that you know well enough to do a SIPOC diagram for. Fill in the name of the process in the top box.

2. As you fill in your SIPOC diagram (boxes 2 through 6), think about the styles of BI that are used or could be used to enhance one or more aspects of process performance—like cost, cycle time, quality, customer service, and so forth.

3. In box 1, answer the questions posed.

6.4.2 Design a Performance Scorecard
6.4.2.1 Key Objectives

1. Fig. 6.9 is a high-level view of core business processes for a building products distributor that sells to building contractors through a network of local branches. Based on the identified processes, identify one BIO and define it in a sentence or two.

2. For your BIO, identify at least one performance driver and performance indicator.

3. Assume that your company has great BI. For your BIO, briefly describe a performance scorecard based on BI, how the scorecard would help managers focus where they need to, and how you would use BI for variance analysis and performance analysis.

4. Think through your BI-enabled performance management system and what it could be worth to your company.

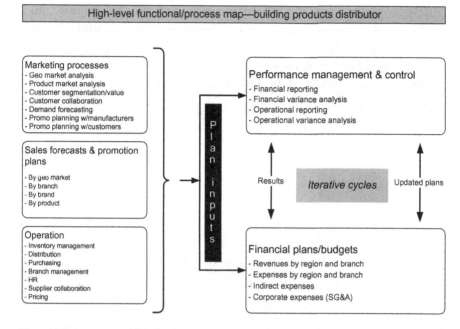

Figure 6.9 Business processes for a distributor.

6.5 SUMMARY OF SOME KEY POINTS

1. BPM is largely about achieving targeted business and economic strategies, objectives, and performance standards and is typically monitored as continuously as company performance information flows allow.

2. Business performance is measured, monitored, assessed, and managed from multiple perspectives—that is, at the enterprise level, by business units, by product, by customer, by channel, by employee, and so forth.

3. Business performance is also analyzed, forecast, simulated, and hopefully improved.

4. All of these aspects of BPM require regular access to transactional business data, derived business facts, and analytical perspectives—which BI delivers.

5. Business process reengineering/process improvement principles, methods, and techniques have been around for decades.

6. BI is a flexible, multifaceted tool that complements business process improvement techniques.

7. BI *about a process* is used to measure process performance and identify performance variances for use in gap analysis and continuous improvement.
8. BI *within a process* is used to improve the effectiveness and/or efficiency of one or more steps within the process.

CHAPTER 7

Meeting the Challenges of Enterprise BI

As we discussed in chapter "Leveraging BI for Performance Management, Process Improvement, and Decision Support", business intelligence is ultimately about improving business performance. While the concept of leveraging BI for improving business processes and enhancing business performance management capabilities is straightforward, the journey from concept to reality is complicated. There are a substantial number of predictable execution challenges to meet—some that cross organizational boundaries, some that business units must meet, and some that fall squarely in the lap of the information technology unit. From an enterprise perspective, achieving BI success is essentially a general management challenge, one that requires effective adaptation, synchronization, and cross-unit execution of six major workflows:

- BI Strategy, Organization, and Management
- Iterative BI Development
- Business Process Improvement
- Technical Infrastructure and Operations
- Change Management
- Data Governance

More broadly, achieving BI success as an enterprise requires strong business leadership and an ability to balance BI activities with the many other business improvement activities that are always underway at most companies. While the information technology unit plays a critical role, the business units are the only units who can actually leverage BI to achieve the return-on-investment associated with a targeted BI opportunity (BIO). Accordingly, there is a strong argument that an enterprise BI initiative should be business-led, and that predictable risks and barriers to success should be aggressively managed. Meeting the typical challenges of enterprise BI is the subject of this chapter.

7.1 A GENERAL MANAGEMENT VIEW ABOUT BI SUCCESS

Every company is different, so the specific general management challenges to achieving BI success on the scale of an enterprise or substantial business unit will vary. And of course much has been written about leadership, general management, program management, information technology strategy, and other topics that bear on the ability of companies to adapt to new opportunities, meet new challenges, and change the way they do business. Since this is a book about BI strategy and successful execution, my focus is on applying what has been learned over time about those subjects to the particular challenges of leveraging BI so that it enhances execution of business strategies and achieves a desired level of competitive parity or differentiation. From a general management perspective, there are six major workstreams that need to be planned, coordinated, resourced, synchronized, and executed. There are also several often-encountered obstacles to BI success—situations that I have observed during the course of developing twelve custom BI strategies and program plans for companies in several different industries.

7.1.1 Major Workstreams Required for Enterprise BI Success

We've talked so far about identifying a portfolio of BI opportunities (BIOs), prioritizing the BIOs, and leveraging BI within the core business processes that impact profitability. Getting from vision and potential to a return on BI investment involves leading and managing a group of business and technical activities that entails cross-unit collaboration and cooperation—mainly between sponsoring business units and the information technology (IT) teams charged with building BI applications that meet the intent of the BIOs. Experience has shown that this is often easier said than done, for a variety of understandable reasons which we will explore later. That having been said, we can group these activities into six major workstreams, as shown in Fig. 7.1 and about which it is useful to make a few key points.

1. While these workstreams are collectively important, that does not mean that they are equally important. Some of the workstreams consist of activities that are directly related to creating business value, and others make an indirect, enabling contribution. This is shown on the left side of Fig. 7.1, where we group value creation activities and enabling activities separately. The general management challenge is to make sure that the enabling activities are done in a balanced and appropriate way that does not impede progress, as opposed to becoming ends in themselves, which is too often the case.

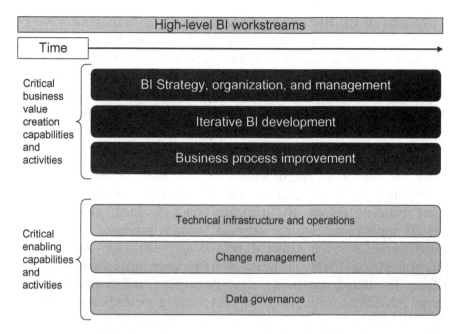

Figure 7.1 Value is created through Iterative BI Development and Business Process Improvement; the other workstreams are not ends in themselves.

2. Each workstream is about a management and/or technical topic that has been written about extensively, that has an associated body of knowledge, that employs proven methods and tools, and that is the purview of specialists who tend to see the world through their particular lens. The general management challenge is to ensure coordination and cooperation among these specialists in order to keep the primary objective front-and-center: develop BI applications quickly and get them in the hands of the business people so they can start generating a return on investment. For example, a successful BI initiative does not need "world class" data governance, it just needs data governance that is good enough for BI purposes.
3. Each workstream has a defined purpose, stated objectives, specified deliverables, and primary activities. These are the building blocks for a synchronized BI program plan and schedule. The activities and deliverables should be tailored to meet the exact needs of the company, its BI strategy, and the specific BI application. For example, a BI application that would be used by five analysts would probably require less change management than an application to be used by 500 customer service representatives in a call center.

As part of the BI Strategy, Organization, and Management workstream, a major goal would be to tailor all of the workstream activities and deliverables to the BI program scope and objectives and to synchronize them appropriately. An example of this is provided as Fig. 7.2, which is a simplified and high-level representation of the work that needs to be accomplished in order to have a successful BI program.

While the graphic depicts parallel efforts among the workstreams, there are numerous interdependencies that need to be understood, highlighted, and managed so as to maintain schedule integrity, meet budgets, deliver BI applications as designed, and integrate the BI applications into the targeted business processes. Two of the interdependencies are explored below, and there are many more. Accordingly, a primary challenge of BI program management is identifying the interdependencies, managing them, and resolving differences between organizational units involved in the end-to-end process

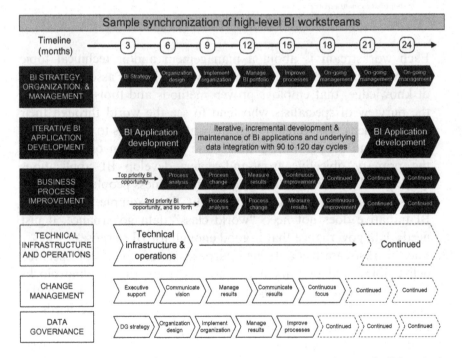

Figure 7.2 The BI Application Development and Business Process Improvement workstreams should determine the scope, timing, and approach for the other workstreams.

of developing and deploying BI applications. In large companies this is easier said than done.

1. Companies often need to establish or revise their organizational approach to BI. This generally requires change management in the form of executive support, and the selected BI organizational design generally needs to be coordinated with the organizational design for data governance.
2. The initial BI application development project cannot be fully launched until an appropriate technical infrastructure is in place. After companies have formulated a BI strategy, they often have to establish or augment their technical infrastructure. Establishing the infrastructure involves acquisition of technical gear, and company purchasing processes have their own logic, timetables, and processes. Accordingly, a BI project cannot really get much done until at least a development environment with the right tools has been established.

7.1.2 Workstream Details

This section is comprised of six graphics—one for each of the six major workstreams. The goal of including these graphics in this section about general management of BI initiatives is to provide leaders and managers with a top-down view of the building blocks of BI success. We would assume that day-to-day leadership and management of an enterprise BI initiative would be entrusted to an experienced, business-oriented BI program manager. That having been said, executive leadership and BI governance is still required, and these graphics provide a view into the kind of activities that should be found in a BI program plan and schedule. Further, they provide a handy list of topics that should be probed during periodic BI program reviews. The objectives, deliverables, and activities of each workstream are intended to guide and ensure effective completion of work that contributes to the overall success of an enterprise BI program. The graphics are Figs. 7.3a–7.3f.

7.1.3 Identifying Risks and Barriers to Success

Risk management is a key component of any significant business improvement program. From a general management perspective, it is important to manage: (1) the cost, schedule, and technical risks that are inherent in any program or project; and (2) the specific risks attendant to the nature of the business improvement program itself.

(a)

Workstream details: BI strategy, organization, and management

OVERVIEW

Description:	Objectives:	Key deliverables:
Set the stage for BI success by systematically determining how BI can be used to improve profitability and performance, identifying business and technical risks to BI success, and then organizing and managing BI to overcome risks and capitalize on major opportunities.	Determine strategic importance of BI, analytics, and big data to company. Identify top BI opportunities and the business strategies they support and the business processes that can be improved by leveraging BI. Determine and mitigate risks. Identify and evaluate organizational and BI management options and implement most appropriate.	· BI Opportunity portfolio & business case · BI Requirements document · BI Readiness assessment · BI Data architecture & technical strategy · BI Program plan · BI Organization design & implementation plan · BI Portfolio management process

Activities:

Activity BI#1. BI strategy → Activity BI#2. organizational design → Activity BI#3. implement organization → Activity BI#4. BI portfolio management → Activity BI#5. continuous improvement → Activity BI#5. continued

Activity BI#1	Activity BI#2	Activity BI#3	Activity BI#4	Activity BI#5
1. Identify strategic importance of BI and barriers to success. 2. Identify key BI Opportunities (BIOs) & Requirements. 3. Determine current BI technical state and barriers to success. 4. Identify/evaluate data architecture and technical strategy options. 5. Develop comprehensive program plan (roadmap), data architecture, and technical strategy.	1. Identify current enterprise and business unit goals, objectives, and performance measures. 2. Identify BI organizational design options, advantages, and tradeoffs. 3. Select preferred BI organizational design option. 4. Develop comprehensive implementation plan.	1. Conduct business unit briefings and training. 2. Monitor business unit execution of agreed-upon BI organization responsibilities. 3. Provide business unit feedback. 4. Monitor and adjust organization as needed.	1. Conduct monthly BI performance reviews. 2. Identify and rectify performance issues. 3. Provide record of monthly issues and actions. 4. Conduct post-audit of executed technical and BI applications development projects. 5. Conduct annual BI portfolio priority review as part of budget process. Adjust as needed.	1. Use information from activities BI#3 and BI#4 to drive continuous improvements in such areas as: · Business unit adherence to agreed-upon BI organization, processes, and activities · BI application development methods and results · BI project performance · BI team skills · Business user adoption

(b)

Workstream details: Technical execution – iterative BI development

OVERVIEW

Description:	Objectives:	Key deliverables:
Perform all of the technical activities required for rigorous design, development, testing, deployment, and maintenance of high-quality BI applications that meet documented business requirements. Provide cost-effective user training and support.	1. End-to-end traceability between business requirements for BI and analytics and the deployed applications. 2. Application of proven, rigorous, BI-specific life-cycle development methods to reduce risk. 3. Strong user training and support that promotes user adoption and business impact.	· BI application documentation · BI applications & data marts · Data warehouse increments · Testing plans, test data sets and test reports · User training materials · BI application maintenance/enhancement · Meet project cost, schedule, and technical goals

Activities:

Activity DEV#1 BI application development → Iterative, incremental development & maintenance of BI applications and underlying data integration with 90 to 120 day cycles → Activity DEV#N BI application development

↓

Activity DEV#1A. BI application design & modeling → Activity DEV#1B. ETL development data integration → Activity DEV#1C. BI application development → Activity DEV#1D. End-to-end testing & migration to production → Activity DEV#1E. user training, support, & BI maintenance → Activity DEV#1E. continued

Activity DEV#1A	Activity DEV#1B	Activity DEV#1C	Activity DEV#1D	Activity DEV#1E
1. Refine BI application requirements. 2. Develop logical data model. 3. Document BI application use cases.	1. Develop physical schema and instantiate in the database. 2. Develop source-to-target mappings. 3. Develop ETL strategy. 4. Develop and test ETL code.	1. Define user screens based on use cases and BI tool options. 2. Develop metadata and connections to underlying database. 3. Develop user screens.	1. Define end-to-end test streams and test data sets. 2. Conduct testing and correct bugs, if any. 3. Migrate to production.	1. Develop business user and tool training based on use cases. 2. Deploy application to users and provide training. 3. Respond to user questions. 4. Track and resolve application bugs and enhancement requests using established prioritization approach.

Figure 7.3 The BI Workstreams are the building blocks of BI success.

(c)

Workstream details: Business process improvement

OVERVIEW:

Description:	Objectives:	Key deliverables:
Create business value with BI, analytics, and big data by leveraging these tools to improve core businesses processes. Increase revenues and/or reduce costs by leveraging BI and analytics.	For business processes targeted for BI-enabled improvement: 1. Assess process maturity and gaps 2. Model current-state & future state 3. Identify training/change management needs 4. Identify KPIs 5. Implement, measure, refine, measure, etc.	• Business process maturity assessment • Business process model (SIPOC) • BI Use cases within business process • Business process KPIs (before and after) • Business process training/change plan • Monthly process performance measurement • Monthly process performance review

Activities:

Activity BP#1. process analysis | Activity BP#2. process change | Activity BP#3 measure results | Activity BP#4. continuous improvement | Activity BP#4 continued | Activity BP#4. continued

1. Administer process maturity assessment. 2. Conduct process analysis, modeling, and visioning sessions. 3. Develop BI use cases for the process. 4. Identify process KPIs and current values. 5. Refine and finalize business case for BI-enabled process change. Gain executive support.	1. Conduct stakeholder analysis. 2. Develop communication themes, plans, and materials. 3. Develop training plans and materials. 4. Execute communications and training plans. 5. Conduct post-training audience survey to identify gaps in communication and/or understanding to guide on-going management efforts.	1. Use BI application to measure process performance monthly using established KPIs. 2. Review process performance with process owner and business unit process participants. 3. Identify root causes of process performance gaps. 4. Obtain corrective action plans when needed and follow up on progress.	1. Publicize wins in such areas as BI enabled: • Revenue increases • Cost reductions • Market wins • Process improvements. 2. Share process improvement lessons learned and best practices. 3. Publicize awards and top performers.

(d)

Workstream details: Technical execution – technical infrastructure & operations

OVERVIEW:

Description:	Objectives:	Key deliverables:
Provide on-going technical management and continuous improvement of all aspects of technical infrastructure and technical operations established to enable first-rate BI and analytics for the enterprise. These are separate activities from Iterative BI Development Workstream, but must enable both development and operations.	1. Provision IT resources and tools to enable BI and analytics across the enterprise or business unit, whether from a shared services unit, from outside vendors, via a dedicated asset, or a via a mixed model. 2. Operate and optimize the technical infrastructure to balance cost, quality, & service	• Service level performance • Targeted asset utilization • Targeted cost structure • User satisfaction

Activities:

Activity tech#2 technical infrastructure & operations | Activity tech#2 continued | Activity tech#2 continued | Activity tech#2 continued | Activity tech#2 continued | Activity tech#2 continued

1. Provide on-going management of all non-development technical activities required to support the BI program.

2. Migrate to or instantiate the BI data architecture.

3. Execute the BI technical strategy.

4. Acquire IT assets and BI tools and/or shared services and/or cloud services to enable the technical strategy.

5. Rationalize BI toolsets to balance licensing costs, tool support costs, and responsiveness to business user needs.

6. Conduct appropriate capacity planning and planning for growth in users.

7. Manage licensing costs.

8. Administer all systems.

9. Conduct planned maintenance.

Figure 7.3 (Continued)

(e)

Workstream Details: Change Management

OVERVIEW:

Description:	Objectives:	Key deliverables:
Change the corporate culture to better exploit information, sophisticated analytical tools, and advanced/predictive analytics to drive business success. Proven change management techniques provide the essential ingredient for BI success.	Create a comprehensive, multi-level, multi-unit communication plan to explain BI vision and strategy and discuss "burning platform" that demands change. Integrate BI objectives into individual performance plans. Conduct "BI Roadshow" via in-person meetings and videoconferences. Monitor, review, and communicate business unit BI performance.	• BI vision & mission statement • BI communication plan • BI change management plan • BI roadshow materials • Monthly BI performance conversations • Monthly BI success stories

Activities:

Activity C#1. executive support	Activity C#2. communicate vision	Activity C#3. manage results	Activity C#4. communicate results	Activity C#5 continuous focus	Activity C#5. continued

1. Conduct stakeholder analysis. 2. Present draft BI vision and BI strategy. 3. Brief executives about key findings from BI readiness assessment. 4. Conduct organizational design workshop. 5. Develop approach to integrate BI and data governance goals with individual and organizational goals. See also activities BI#2, DG#2 & BP#1.	1. Develop enterprise and business unit communication themes. 2. Develop BI Roadshow plans, schedules, roles, and materials. 3. Execute BI roadshow. 4. Conduct post-roadshow audience survey to identify gaps in communication and/or understanding to guide on-going management efforts.	1. Establish business unit BI performance as a standing agenda item for monthly review. 2. Review business unit adoption of developed BI applications. 3. Review key performance indicators of business processes targeted for BI-enabled improvement. 4. Obtain corrective action plans when needed and follow up on progress.	1. Publicize business unit BI wins in such areas as BI enabled: • Revenue increases • Cost reductions • Market wins • Process Improvements 2. Share BI lessons learned and best practices. 3. Publicize BI awards and BI top performers.	1. Use information from activities BI#3 and BI#4 to drive continuous improvements in such areas as: • Business unit adherence to agreed-upon BI organization, processes, and activities • BI application development methods and results • BI project performance • BI team skills • Business user adoption	

(f)

Workstream Details: Data Governance

OVERVIEW:

Description:	Objectives:	Key deliverables:
Create a common view of customers, products and/or services, channels, geographies/markets, and organizational performance -which is critical for successful enterprise BI and analytics. Appropriate data governance enables common views by managing data an enterprise asset while also retaining appropriate business unit autonomy.	Create a tailored data governance organization with defined processes, tools, methods, and staffing approaches that are consistent with the strategic importance of BI to the business. Align the data governance plan with broader enterprise and business unit strategies, goals, and objectives. Implement and monitor.	• Data governance vision & mission statement • Data governance organization • Data governance implementation plan • Data stewardship plan • Data stewardship implementation plan • Data quality plan • Data quality implementation plan

Activities:

Activity DG#1. DG strategy	Activity DG#2. organizational design	Activity DG#3. implement organization	Activity DG#4. manage results	Activity DG#5. continuous improvement	Activity DG#5. continued

1. Assess current data governance, including data stewardship, & data quality. 2. Identify gaps in relation to best practices and in relation to enterprise BI strategy. 3. Survey executive awareness of and attitudes. 4. Educate executives. 5. Develop DG strategy with vision and mission statement for executive approval.	1. Identify current enterprise and business unit goals, objectives, and performance measures. 2. Identify DG organizational design options, advantages, and tradeoffs. 3. Select preferred DG organizational design option. 4. Develop comprehensive implementation plan.	1. Conduct business unit briefings and training. 2. Monitor business unit execution of agreed-upon DG organization responsibilities. 3. Provide business unit feedback. 4. Monitor and adjust organization as needed.	1. Conduct monthly DG performance reviews. 2. Identify and rectify performance issues. 3. Provide record of monthly issues and actions. 4. Share DG lessons learned and best practices. 5. Publicize DG awards and DG top performers.	1. Use information from Activities DG#3 and DG#4 to drive continuous improvements in such areas as: • Business unit adherence to agreed-upon DG organization, processes, and activities • DG methods and results • Data stewardship methods and results • Data quality methods and results • DG project performance • DG skills	

Figure 7.3 (Continued)

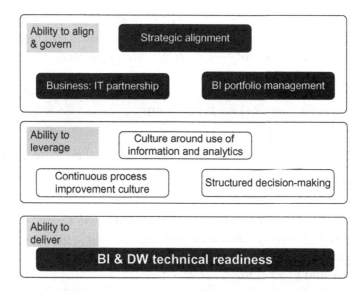

Figure 7.4 A key to managing risk is to assess and address the known risks to BI success.

For example, building and launching a new production plant has the inherent risks of any construction project, and it has specific risks— such as the risk that the manufacturing execution system will not correctly interface with the enterprise resource planning system. Our focus in this section is on the specific risks that are common to BI programs and that have been experienced by many companies over the past 15 years or so. As with any risk management approach, the first step is to identify the relevant risks, and the second step is to mitigate them or plan to mitigate them. While there are different BI readiness assessment and BI maturity models that have put forth over the years, there is no "one right way" to go about risk assessment for a BI program. That having been said, I believe that the framework depicted in Fig. 7.4 is a useful general management tool for developing an enterprise view of BI program risk.

7.1.3.1 Risk Factor #1—Ability to Align and Govern
The ability to align and govern determines whether a company has a reasonable chance to execute a multiyear effort whereby BI is systematically deployed.

1. *Strategic Alignment*—the extent to which the company has invested in, or is it willing to invest in, a BI-oriented strategic planning effort to identify BIOs that would create business value.

2. *BI Portfolio Management*—the extent to which the company has a portfolio management approach that can be used to manage the BI initiative with constancy of purpose and consistency of funding over time.
3. *Business-IT Partnership*—the degree to which business units and IT can forge effective working relationships.

7.1.3.2 Risk Factor #2—Ability to Leverage
The ability of business units to leverage BI in their core processes determines whether a company has a reasonable chance to make effective use of BI applications that get developed.

4. *Culture Around Use of Information and Analytics*—the degree to which the company embraces moving beyond simple reports to leverage BI as an additional valuable input for performance management and process improvement.
5. *Continuous Process Improvement Culture*—the extent to which the company values or prioritizes process improvement and is adept at making the improvements.
6. *Structured Decision-Making*—the degree to which the company values moving beyond traditional gut-feel or personality-driven decision processes for deciding upon business courses of action.

7.1.3.3 Risk Factor #3—Ability to Execute
The ability to perform the necessary technical work determines whether a company has a reasonable chance to design, build, deploy, and support BI applications of suitable fitness for use—at a reasonable cost and within a reasonable timetable.

7. *BI and DW Technical Readiness*—the degree to which the company has the technical infrastructure, BI technical skills, and BI-focused technical policies, processes, and methods that are critical to BI success.

By systematically evaluating BI-specific risks using a suitable framework, companies can anticipate and avoid the common risks that have derailed BI programs in the past. The above framework is one tool, and there are others—and there is no reason that more than one tool cannot be used. That having been said, there is one caveat worth considering: risk management is a specialty, and it is possible to go overboard and get too detailed with the risk mitigation approach embedded in the BI program plan. Risk and uncertainty are part of all business situations and business improvement programs, and the key from a general management perspective is to focus on the main risks and not create unnecessary overhead. As with data governance and change management, risk management is an enabler, not an end in itself.

7.1.4 Summary: General Management for BI Success

In many respects, general management of an enterprise BI initiative is just like managing any other significant business improvement program. It requires leadership, managing the interfaces across organizational units, building buy-in and cooperation between key executives and managers, ensuring accountability for progress and results, and highlighting successes. At the same time, a successful enterprise BI initiative requires oversight of specific activities and mitigation of specific risks. This section has introduced the major workflows and key risks that must be led and managed. How this gets done in any given company is situation-specific, but the fundamentals are well-known. The road from BI vision and strategy to the point where business leaders, managers, and analysts have the timely, high-quality information, analyses, and decision support they need is challenging, but the journey has been shown to be worth it. In the next section, I will discuss some of the most common BI-related challenges with which I've seen companies struggle.

7.2 CHALLENGES FOR BI SUCCESS

As with any major business improvement program, an enterprise BI initiative faces challenges. Over the past fifteen years, I've come to believe that primary challenges boil down to two: (1) the need for business people to think about BI as more than reports and see its full potential; and (2) the need for IT to adapt so that BI projects can go faster. The actual manifestations of the challenges are generally specific to particular companies, and we won't deal with those. Rather, what follows is a discussion of the challenges I've seen across companies and industries. The challenges occur to different degrees in different companies, and not all of the challenges occur everywhere. That being said, these are challenges that impact the prospects for BI success, and I believe companies can use this discussion to inform their thinking about their own challenges—and hopefully avoid them.

7.2.1 Challenge: Lack of a Business-Driven BI Strategy

A common and flawed approach to BI strategy is to let technology and data be the primary focus. An analogy would be to build a manufacturing plant first—and wait until after the plant is finished to decide what products to make for whom. With such a strategy, you wouldn't know who your customers really are, what product they need, what the best equipment would be for making the product, how they would use the product, what they would be willing to pay for it, and whether you could earn a return on your investment in the plant. In the BI world, it has been shown to be more effective to figure out a *business strategy for leveraging BI* first, and then use this business-driven BI strategy to drive the entire BI program, including technology selection and timing. In addition to identifying and prioritizing BI opportunities (BIOs) that are explicitly linked to business performance management and business process improvement opportunities, a business-driven BI strategy addresses the key topics discussed below.

7.2.1.1 BI Mission

Successful companies tend to do a pretty good job of focusing on the things they really need to do well. Their business strategies drive their functional strategies, and their functional strategies drive whatever business improvement initiatives are needed—including business process improvement initiatives. When it comes to BI, companies often suboptimize the value of BI because they have not decided at the top about the degree to which BI is strategically important. Absent of such a determination, the BI mission is unclear—are we trying to exceed the competition, match the competition, enhance the execution of our business strategy, or simply avoid hindering our business strategy? Do we need to go fast, or is slow and steady sufficient? What proportion of our IT budget should be spent on BI? *If the mission and strategic importance of BI have not been determined and communicated across the enterprise, then BI tends to command less management bandwidth and attention, which hinders realization of the BI Strategy.* A business-driven BI strategy overcomes this problem.

7.2.1.2 Link Between BIOs, Business Performance, and Business Process Improvement

A BI strategy is based on identifying opportunities to enhance business performance by enabling business process improvements (BIOs). In many cases, however, the link between potential investment in BI and business value creation has not been articulated in a way that business leaders and managers find compelling. Confusing terminology is one part of the problem. Vague value propositions—such as "enabling better business decisions" or "enhancing business agility" or "monetizing big data"—or "out think the competition"—are difficult for business leaders to embrace. *Most business leaders and managers have very specific performance objectives to meet in very specific timeframes. To invest in BI, they need to see in very practical terms how specific BI applications would help them be successful.* A business-driven BI strategy overcomes this problem.

7.2.1.3 BI Barriers and Risks

There are a number of barriers and risks that get in the way of BI success. Some of the BI-specific barriers have to do with the business units who must leverage BI in order to realize a given BIO. Some of the barriers have to do with how BI initiatives are approached within a broader enterprise IT context. And some of the barriers have to do with how well business units and IT units get along. *Successful BI initiatives require identification and dynamic management of a range of BI success factors.* A business-driven BI strategy anticipates and avoids well-known BI barriers and risks.

7.2.2 Challenge: Higher IT Priorities Slow BI Deployment

While BI has been shown to be strategic in many instances, and while it is a powerful performance management and process improvement tool, it is seldom the top priority of Chief Information Officers (CIOs)—despite what they say in surveys. As shown in Fig. 7.5, BI is but one part of the IT portfolio.

From an enterprise perspective, it makes sense that keeping vital customer-facing and mission critical internal business systems up and running is the top priority (the bottom two layers of the graphic). Minimizing IT operating costs and the labor costs of the many IT projects also makes sense if cost minimization is a central focus of the enterprise IT strategy, which is not always appropriate. And standardizing polices, processes, and methods is an important way to attempt to balance cost, quality, security, maintainability, and other system characteristics. That having been said, using a "one size fits all" approach to BI development and operations has a cost that is sometimes steep. Specifically, BI projects take longer and cost more than

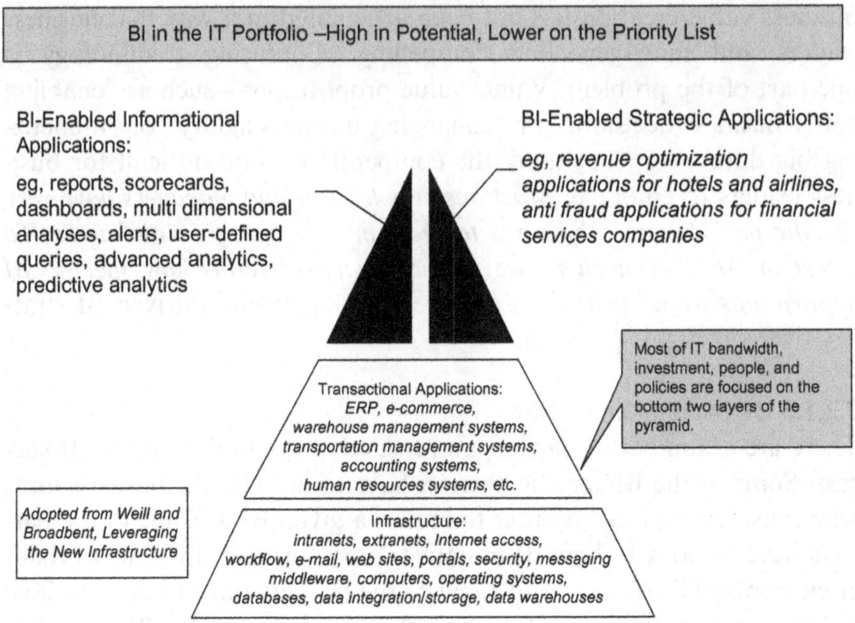

Figure 7.5 *IT organizations have to optimize for the entire IT portfolio; BI is generally a small part of the portfolio.*

they should, which often leads business sponsors to lose confidence in the BI team and sometimes leads to withdrawal or curtailment of funding for the BI initiative. *This challenge can be avoided by empowering the BI team—letting it have its own IT assets, policies, methods, and dedicated capabilities.*

7.2.3 Challenge: Higher Priorities Impede Business Engagement

Even when a business-driven BI strategy has been developed, there is no guarantee that the business people who would benefit from the identified BI opportunities will engage sufficiently to help ensure BI success. Looked at objectively, formulating a BI strategy only requires any given individual leader or manager to engage for somewhere between 30 and 90 minutes. Executing a BI strategy may require several person-months of effort from several business people during development and testing of a single BI application. That is why determining the strategic importance of BI is so important. We'll use a mini-case to illustrate the challenge of competing business priorities.

The situation involved a company that had created a business-driven BI strategy. The BIOs had been aligned to company business strategies, which included an objective to provide performance scorecards that would help the company cope with the complexity of its industry. However, when it came time to start executing, the BI team rean into the challenges below.

- An SVP responsible for financial management for the operations function was too busy to engage. He was assigned 20 hours per week to three projects, plus he had to do his regular job—a job that would have been made markedly easier by BI applications he had helped define.
- An EVP and General Manager of a $1 + billion division stated that having better BI for managing revenue attainment was "not in the top ten of her marketing VP's objectives for the year"—even though identified BIOs that her people helped define supported attainment of stated performance objectives, such enhancing their ability to actively manage the mix of brands, segments, and customers and improve the efficiency and effectiveness of sales and marketing planning.
- A handful of VPs in such areas as sales reporting, supply chain, customer services, and inventory management did not have the time to review BIO descriptions and prototypes of scorecards and dashboards—even when it was made clear that the scorecards and dashboards were part of the company's approved business strategy.

While this example may be an extreme case of bandwidth issues impacting business engagement, lack of effective engagement is a big challenge for successful BI initiatives. On the one hand, this is understandable given the demands on business leaders, managers, and their staffs in this age of lean operations. It is further understandable given that many companies have hundreds of capital projects underway in any given year, and the business people assigned to those projects are spread thin. On the other hand, if business people cannot or will not engage effectively on BI projects, then what gets built may not meet business needs as the BI team would be left to guess at BI requirements. Some of the implications of less than ideal levels of business engagement may include:

1. The BI opportunities (BIOs) and the associated business cases may be too generic, vague, or tool-centric to obtain executive buy-in and the required capital investments. This delays or forecloses the launch of an enterprise BI program.

2. The BI requirements may not be suitably specific to support realization of the BIOs. Without good requirements, IT may deliver the wrong data, which often taints a BI application so that it is not adopted by the target user community.
3. User acceptance testing of developed BI applications may not be sufficiently rigorous, potentially resulting in applications being deployed and then found wanting.

Ultimately, BI is a business improvement tool, but if business units cannot or will not engage effectively it becomes a challenge to deliver BI applications that are suitable for intended business purposes.

7.2.4 Challenge: BI Enveloped by a Broader Data Management Initiative

Data management is a specialty within the IT world. Its practitioners have developed a huge "body of knowledge" that guides what they try to accomplish through enterprise, top-down data governance initiatives. As with other specialties, such as Six Sigma or Total Quality Management (TQM), data management offers benefits up to a point. What I've often observed though, is that after a point the methods of the specialty become an end unto themselves—regardless of the consequences for other business objectives. This is an important point to understand because data management is always is part of the context in which enterprise BI initiatives are executed. We'll examine the potential challenge of balancing BI and data management by discussing Fig. 7.6, which is the lens through which data management practitioners see the world of data.

The basic precept of data management is that data is an enterprise asset and needs to be managed as such. To accomplish this, data management focuses on the subjects shown in Fig. 7.6, such as Data Architecture, Data Quality, and so forth around the circle. In this framework, BI is only one of the subjects, shown as "Data Warehousing & Business Intelligence." As you might expect, each subject is a specialty in its own right, with its own methods, practices, tools, books, articles, conferences, educational opportunities, and so forth. On the surface, this framework is eminently reasonable. For example, data security is certainly important, and who can argue against the need for data quality? From a BI perspective, the challenge is how to achieve the optimal balance between getting BI applications developed quickly and

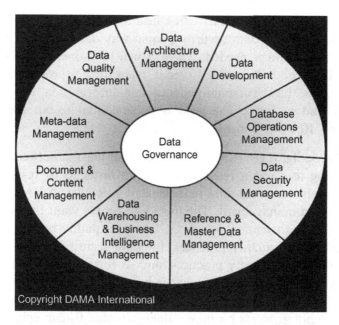

Copyright DAMA International

Figure 7.6 Data management initiatives look at enterprise data broadly and try to perfect it all, whereas BI looks only at the data needed for BI-enabled returns on investment.

effectively and doing enough with respect to the other data management subjects. We'll use two examples to illustrate the tradeoffs:

1. BI initiatives need to be based on a data architecture that is suitable for realizing BI opportunities. They also need to use suitable data models and business-driven designs. On the other hand, data architects and data modelers may seek ideal or theoretical conceptions of "the best way" to model any particular data warehouse, data mart, or BI application. This can lead to protracted discussions and acrimonious meetings about the supposed best architecture or best data model—and slow BI development to the point where deadlines are missed and/or the scope of what is delivered does not meet business sponsors' expectations. This is a case where the pursuit of the "perfect" is at the expense of the "good-enough."

2. Data security is critical in many situations. On the other hand, BI applications need data created by enterprise applications. Because of the importance of data security, which no one would argue, companies place limits on whether, when, and how data can be replicated (copied) and moved within the organization.

The complication that this can cause a BI initiative lies with the need to justify to data security people why data needs to be replicated, what data is needed, where it will be moved, how it will be protected, who will be able to see it, what further processing will be done to it, how personally-identifiable information will be protected, and so forth. The need is understandable, but the process can slow BI development.

More broadly, there can be a fundamental tension between BI projects needing to go at a reasonable pace in order to be responsive to business needs and what data management specialists believe constitutes sound data management. The metadata people want the best possible metadata management practices, the data quality people want the best possible data quality practices, the data security people want the best possible data security practices, and so forth. From a BI strategy perspective, it is a question of what is being optimized—data management or BI delivery. The argument we favor is that data management, per se, does not generate business value—whereas BI can enhance business performance and profitability. Data management is about the quality and protection of the data assets; BI is about leveraging the asset to create value. This is not to say that data management is not needed; rather, we see it as a question of balance. Achieving that balance can be a challenge, depending on company-specific factors.

Vignette: How Data Management Best Practices Can Impede BI Success

A large multiyear program to leverage a company's data assets was launched on the strength of the projected return-on-investment, which was 100% dependent on the BI applications that were to be built based on prioritized BIOs. In addition to executing BI projects, the company also sought to stand up and build best practices data management services units in such disciplines as data governance, requirements, data modeling, and data analysis. As the initial BI project moved forward, it encountered typical challenges—such a substantial increase in the scope of data to be made available for the BI applications and a lack of focus on delivering a BI application quickly to show top management and thereby maintain executive support. The project also encountered an instance where the focus on data management best practices severely impacted timely completion. Specifically, the lead data modeler insisted on using what he believed was a best practices approach to data modeling—regardless of the impact it would have on the BI development effort. Essentially, the type of data modeling used tripled the number of database tables that would need to be built, which tripled the programming workload of the Extract, Transformation, and Load (ETL) team. Further, any changes to the data model also increased the number of ETL program changes that were required. All this could have been avoided had a proven, cost-effective approach to data modeling been used. Unfortunately, optimizing for what were supposedly data modeling best practices—at the expense of timely BI delivery within budget—caused the project to be severely late and over budget. This then caused withdrawal of executive support—at least temporarily—for the BI portion of the larger data management initiative.

7.2.5 Challenge: BI Managed Under Typical IT Policies and Methods

7.2.5.1 The IT Shared Services Mindset

ITIL is a set of practices for IT service management (ITSM) that focuses on aligning IT services with the needs of business. ITIL describes processes, procedures, tasks, and checklists which are not organization-specific, but can be applied by an organization for establishing integration with the organization's strategy, delivering value, and maintaining a minimum level of competency.

Wikipedia.

Managing IT is a complex endeavor that encompasses asset management, operations management, planned maintenance, reactive maintenance, program and project management, and resource management. The ITIL approach is a shared services approach to delivering IT services across multiple IT projects, including BI projects. In a steady state world, an IT organization could be staffed to meet known plus reasonably predictable operations and maintenance needs. In a dynamic world where IT has to adapt to business competition, technological innovation, and evolving business operations, a primary challenge is to staff dozens if not hundreds of IT projects. These projects require a diverse set of technical skills that must be available in the right quantity at the right time so that all projects have the skills needed to accomplish the technical work.

One approach would be for every project to staff just for its own needs, but that would create idle capacity at various points in a system development lifecycle. In order to minimize the costs of excess resources, many IT organizations have adopted an IT shared services model, which is essentially a matrix management approach applied to IT. Organizational design experts have known for years that matrix management is the most complicated form of organization to manage—due to resource scheduling complexity and resource availability conflicts between projects. *In a shared services world, there is also a conflict between: (1) IT service standards and policies intended to optimize service excellence; and (2) the more delivery-oriented world of project managers and the business units they serve. One result is that IT project managers cannot truly control schedule performance or the technical methods used. Another result is that the IT people have to serve more than one supervisor—the manager of the particular shared service and the project manager or managers for the project to which they are assigned.*

We'll use Table 7.1 to illustrate the relationship between available IT services under the shared services approach and a theoretical portfolio of projects.

Table 7.1 Scheduling IT People Under the Shared Services Approach Can Be Complex, Time-Consuming, Subject to the Difficulties of Estimating Required Work Efforts By Job Type, and Prone to Resource Schedule Conflicts				
Company IT Projects	**Project 1**	**Project 2**	**Project 3....**	**.....Project N**
Enterprise IT Services (Representative Subset)				
Information Needs Identification and Refinement				
Source System Reverse Engineering				
Data Model Development (logical and physical)	▲1	▲1	▲1	
Data Architecture Assessment				
Data Integration Design and Development	△2	△2		
BI/Analytics Application Design and Development				
Data Governance Policy Adherence				
Data Dictionary and Meta Data Management				
Master Data Identification and Management				
Data Provisioning				
Data Connectivity				
End to End Support for SDLC for DW/BI Projects				
Disaster Recovery Design for Data Warehouse/ Other Data Stores				
Archiving for Data Warehousing				

The left-hand column lists all the different types of IT services available for IT projects, including BI projects. The triangles are used to denote two IT resources; #1 is a data modeler and #2 a data integration designer. We see that the data modeler is assigned to three projects, and the data integration designer is assigned to two projects. If it were to turn out that the data modeler is spread across too many projects, or if his or her skills are required at the same time for two or more different projects, then the data model deliverables will be delayed for one or more projects. There is a dependency between data models and data integration designs, so if the data model is delayed, the data integration designer may not be able to start or complete his or her work on time. That delay then cascades through the rest or the project lifecycle. More broadly, there are many such dependencies between the various IT services during a typical project lifecycle, so if any one or more service does not have adequate capacity, or if the services are being optimized for their own sakes, or if the people providing the services are not solid performers, then projects get delayed. To further complicate matters, the number of people needed by a given project would vary according to the project, and the services needed would also vary by project. These factors make for scheduling challenges and inhibit the ability of project managers to control the resources they need to get the work done.

The example we used is a simple one. Imagine the complexity of trying to align IT resources across dozens or hundreds of projects. Under the shared services approach, a BI initiative and its projects would be one customer among many. Accordingly, the pace at which the BI project can proceed hinges on the availability of the right IT people, who might be simultaneously serving multiple projects. The pace would also depend on how the various people approach their jobs. For example, the manager of Data Model Development may aspire to building a "world class data modeling organization" and not be willing to have data modelers adopt the 80–20 rule for the BI project. More broadly, all of the IT service managers may be trying to optimize their function, as opposed to optimizing schedule or technical performance on any given project. It is akin to all teachers giving big homework assignments because they each think their subject is the most important and they don't coordinate/don't care to coordinate to avoid an unfairly adverse impact on the students.

We can think of an IT shared services organization as a job shop. In a job shop form of product manufacturing, different machines are used in different mixes to make a large variety of possible end products in response to order flows that are highly variable. This type of manufacturing is the most complex from an order sequencing and machine scheduling perspective. In an IT services organization, different IT people with different skills and skill levels are used in different mixes across multiple projects. As a job shop, an IT services organization has to grapple with the challenge of managing the mix and quantity of skills it has available for the various projects it has to execute. While bottom-up labor estimates for each project are developed as part of the IT capital planning process, there is substantial variability in how long the IT people will have to take to perform their services. For example, how long should it take to develop a data model? And what happens to a BI project schedule that assumed an IT resource would be available half-time and that resource is not as available or is not available at the right times? There are also factors outside the control of the IT service provider, and there are variations in performance between service providers. Arguably, resource planning in the IT world is even more complex that in the high-mix, low-volume manufacturing world, and the result is that schedule adherence and quality are hard to meet at the same time. This ends up slowing down BI application development projects unless scope is allowed to be reduced.

7.2.5.2 Best Practices Development Methodologies for IT Projects and BI Projects are Different

Given the complexity of IT, companies have to employ rigorous development methods. This ensures that systems work as required by the business, that they don't break anything that is already working, that they can be maintained, that they are well-documented, and that new systems or applications work in the existing technical environment. Accordingly, companies tend to standardize a system development lifecycle methodology (SDLC) and use it on all IT projects. This also ensures that all IT people use a common approach, which allows any given person to be used on any given project. Additionally, many companies also have a formal project management methodology with its own set of deliverables.

While there is no doubt that an SDLC is necessary, there are technically and organizationally valid reasons why a standard IT SDLC should be substantially modified and streamlined in the case of enterprise BI initiatives. Basically, the impacts of using an inappropriate SDLC for BI projects include:

- excess costs incurred for work that is not needed for effective, high-quality BI development results;
- schedule delays due to stage gates and documentation reviews that are not aligned with best practices BI stage gates and documentation types;
- excess costs associated with having to justify exceptions to IT managers who are not BI people and who may have legitimate but conflicting organizational objectives; and
- excess costs and schedule delays due to having to conform the BI project to the "best practices" goals of managers of IT shared services.

Our point here is that in using a standard IT SDLC, it makes sense to tailor it for BI initiatives because some of the standard IT SDLC activities or deliverables do not add value and are not required to develop and deploy a BI application or data environment of suitable quality. That said, there seems to be an organizational bias in many organizations to avoid asking for exceptions to the SDLC. This slows BI application development and adds cost.

7.2.5.3 What is Being Optimized?

One of the biggest criticisms of BI initiatives is that BI projects take too long and cost too much. The criticisms come from business sponsors who are frustrated because what should be simple from a technical perspective is made slow and difficult because the processes for BI development and delivery are not being optimized. *The fundamental issue with managing a BI initiative using standard IT policies and methods is lack of goal congruence between how IT needs to operate and how BI projects can be executed most effectively. IT is optimized for control, risk minimization, and cost minimization—a careful, deliberate, and time-consuming mode of operation. BI is optimized for speed of delivery and business-driven value creation.* Within such an environment, BI projects can only go as fast as broader IT policies, practices, and procedures permit.

From a general management perspective, the most straightforward way to resolve this inherent conflict of interests would be to create an autonomous BI organization with its own policies, people, and IT assets—hardware, software, and tools. The only truly necessary interface between a BI unit and the IT organization is around acquiring data needed for BI purposes, subject to appropriate security measures. Once a BI unit has the data it needs, its designers, developers, analysts, and so forth can execute BI projects quickly and effectively in concert with the business people sponsoring the project. All this is not to say that the BI unit can be allowed to operate as a "rogue unit." BI and data warehousing are mature technical fields with proven methods, and the BI unit needs to be held to the highest professional standards.

7.2.6 Challenge: Barriers to Data Access

There are a number of challenges associated with obtaining the business data needed for BI purposes. Some of the most common are listed below.

1. For security and/or privacy reasons, some companies have policies against replicating data (copying and moving) to databases outside the system of origin (the system that created the data).
2. Companies with mainframe-based applications have business applications that may have been created many years ago. Understanding the structure and meaning of such data requires knowledge of COBOL plus time from the IT people who maintain the system and/or from business analysts who may work with the data.
3. Some companies have existing data warehouses from which data of interest to BI might be gotten. The challenge that is sometimes encountered is that it is not always clear where the data originally came from and how it might have been altered before being stored in the data warehouse. Therefore, its true meaning may be unknown.
4. Some BI systems are poorly documented and may have undergone many changes since originally designed and deployed. Without good documentation about the data structure, understanding the structure and meaning of such data requires time from the IT people who maintain the system and/or from business analysts who may work with the data.
5. Data about customers or products may exist in multiple systems, and thus a determination about which system should be the "system of record" for given data elements needs to be made. This often requires time from business analysts or business users who work with such data regularly.

Ultimately, obtaining access to data and understanding its business meaning is almost always a challenge that is time-consuming to overcome.

7.2.7 Summary—Challenges for BI Success

In addition to my own direct experience, I've served as a judge for an annual BI and data warehousing best practices competition since 2001. In that capacity, I've reviewed hundreds of case study submissions and help pick best practices winners. The companies who win these competitions recognize the substantial business impact that BI can have, they integrate BI into strategically important business process, and they adapt their IT policies and practices so that BI projects are not impeded. While weak business sponsorship and/or lack of business engagement can be barriers to success, I have reluctantly concluded that managing BI as an IT initiative is the far larger barrier to BI success. From a general management perspective, this is an organizational design problem, which is the subject of the next section.

7.3 ORGANIZATIONAL DESIGN FOR BI SUCCESS

When a company launches a major BI initiative, it is rarely the case that it is starting from scratch. At the very least, most companies make extensive use of static reports—sometimes thousands of them, and sometimes so many that no one has a good handle on how many are still used. Companies also make extensive use of spreadsheets as reporting tools. Beyond these fairly common starting points for BI initiatives, there are a variety of other possible current-state factors that may be part of the organizational context that is the starting point for designing a BI organization for success.

1. *Impetus for BI.* At some companies, key leaders and managers have concluded that they need better BI in order to be successful. At other companies, the impetus could be as casual as a leader read or heard something about BI, big data, or cognitive business and decided that the company needs a BI strategy. For yet other companies, it could be that the CIO is pushing for BI because he or she has many peers at other companies who are doing it, or because the CIO is an innovator. *The strength of the impetus for BI affects how a company is willing to organize for BI.*

2. *Conception of BI.* At many companies, BI is thought of as reports, and that is as far as it goes. At others, the limitations of reports are well-understood and there is a desire for more forward-looking information and analyses. At still others, there is an analytical culture already in place and a desire to leverage BI more extensively. *How key people think about BI affects how the company is willing to organize for BI.*

3. *Extent of "Shadow IT."* At some companies, business units have purchased and deployed their own BI tools and databases. This is particularly common at companies that have grown by acquisition yet maintained some degree of decentralized operations, but it is also common at large companies where business units feel that IT has not been responsive to their BI needs. The existence of shadow IT often results in different tools being used within the various business units, and the BI developed with the different tools is often extensive and/or integral to their operations. *The extent of shadow IT affects organizational design choices around centralization versus decentralization of various aspect of BI governance, funding, infrastructure, design, development, operations, maintenance, licensing, and user support.*

4. *Existing Data Warehouses, Data Marts, and/or Reporting Environments.* At many companies there may be existing data environments that are used for BI and reporting. It is not uncommon to find what might be called a "data warehouse" but that is not actually a data warehouse. It is also not uncommon to find older data warehouses that perform poorly, that are prone to crashing under existing workloads, and that are not suitably-designed to perform future workloads. Further, shadow IT within business units often relies on desktop relational databases in which various data extracts are stored. *The nature of existing data environments and the requirements for future BI impacts organizational design choices around architecture and tools, which impacts the work to be done, the skill sets needed, and the organizational placement of people.*

5. *Existing BI Team or Teams.* Many companies have reporting or BI teams that have been operating for some time. These teams may be located in the IT unit and/or in one or more business units. The team or teams may be using desktop tools or the simpler features of a BI tool. In some cases, there may be a group of power analysts using more advanced analytics software. *The nature, organizational location, and capabilities of any such teams affects organizational design choices around centralization versus decentralization, training, and methodology.*

6. *Existing Tool Sets.* Companies that have established data environments for enabling BI and/or reporting have tool sets for acquiring data from source systems, moving it into a data warehouse and/or data mart and/or reporting database, developing BI applications and/or reports, and getting the BI and/or reports out to users. *The nature, organizational locations, functionality, and suitability of existing tool sets affects organizational design choices around future-state tool sets, training, and skill sets.*

To further complicate the organizational design task, the exact nature of the current state may not be well-known in large companies. Absent a good understanding of the current state, it is possible that the organizational design for BI may not be suitable for the BI mission.

7.3.1 Organizational Approaches to BI

Assuming that the current state of BI *is* well understood, the key inputs to the organizational design task include:

1. the current organizational structure of the company;
2. the BI strategy and BI mission;
3. known plans for changes to the current organizational structure; and
4. the major workflows for the BI initiative.

The central challenge is marshalling and focusing the right business and technical resources at the right time so that BI projects can be executed efficiently and effectively and so that the supporting technical infrastructure can be well-managed and administered.

As a means of doing so, the concepts of BI Competency Centers (BICC) and BI Centers of Excellence (BICOE) have been widely written about and promoted. There are differences between the two concepts, but the basic idea is to ensure that the expertise, methods, policies, incentives, and tools needed to do BI projects well is available to a degree that is necessary to achieve the BI mission and realize the BI strategy. From an organizational design perspective, the BICC and the BICOE can be seen as specialized instances for achieving cross-functional coordination, cooperation, and focus. They are organizational design templates, which can be adapted as needed to a company's specific BI mission and strategy. There is utility in understanding the BICC and BICOE thinking because their proponents have done a good job of identifying the design choices companies need to make in order to devise a suitable organizational approach to BI. That having been said, there is no reason to try to graft either approach onto an existing organizational structure if a more customized approach to organizational design is preferred. Some of the important design choices to be made when designing an organization for BI success are shown in Table 7.2. When making these choices, I strongly recommend that the key business leaders and IT leaders work together to develop a consensus approach based on a sensible migration from the current state of BI to the desired end state.

To illustrate the need for a consensus approach, consider a company that consists of a central headquarters unit and four wholly-owned operating units. Each of the operating units is at a different stage of BI maturity, two of the operating units have their own IT and BI teams, and the other two units share IT and BI resources with the corporate headquarters unit. Because the company grew by acquisition, the various units use different tools, and there are three distinct data warehouses. None of the data warehouses is particularly advanced, and the BI delivery tools have limitations in relation to the desired BI strategy. All of the units have strong reporting capabilities, but more advanced BI styles are needed.

From a BI organizational design perspective, this situation requires careful attention to what aspects of BI should be centralized and shared, and what aspects should remain with the operating units. Because each operating unit is a profit center, and because each operating unit is in a different business, the company is highly dependent on the executives and managers in the operating units for delivery of business results. An attempt to overcentralize BI would not be well-received because the two units with their own IT and BI teams are in a fast-paced, high-growth mode and they can't wait for a centralized BI team to develop their BI applications for them. On the other hand, if there were to be a way to share some of the cost of data warehousing and data mart physical and software assets, that might be attractive. So in this case, it might make sense to centralize the BI infrastructure but have the responsibility for BI application development rest with the operating units. As to BI methods, it might make sense for the headquarters unit to sponsor development of a standard, agile BI life-cycle method, provide training, and provide incentives to the operating units to adopt the method. To arrive at these various design choices, it

Table 7.2 Achieving a Successful Approach to Cross-Functional Coordination, Cooperation, and Focus for BI Requires Careful Company-Appropriate Organizational Design Choices

BI Organizational Design Choices	Factors	Importance
Choice of customer	Is the customer the entire company, a business unit, or some combination of units?	Determines organizational scope and focus for BI requirements
Organizational placement of BI unit(s)	Locate within a business unit or units, or within IT, or within both?	Determines whether BI performance is IT-driven or business-driven; influences whether BI is a "poor relative" within IT or a customer of IT
Dedicated people, shared resources, and/or virtual team	How much BI work needs to be done, how quickly, and at what cost?	Strong influence on BI development schedule adherence and actual realized cost
Where BI is developed	Centralized within BI unit, decentralized out to business units, or mix that varies by type of BI or customer for given BI application?	Impacts speed and quality of BI delivery, BI maintainability
Location of BI and BI-related skills	Within the BI unit only, within business units, or mix?	Has to be consistent with where BI is developed
Standardization of BI methods	Standardization promotes quality and maintainability, ad hoc may speed delivery	If standardized, need training and enforcement; if ad hoc there is potential adverse impact on speed and quality of BI development
Accountability for BI deployment, that is, rolling out BI apps regularly	What degree of assurance of progress is required by BI strategy and mission?	If high degree of assurance is required, need performance management and control processes of appropriate scope
Pace of BI delivery	How fast do we need to go, what should be the pace and scope of what gets delivered?	Drives tradeoffs between staff levels, BI project scope, BI project execution capacity, cost, and time to delivery
Level of assurance regarding business adoption of deployed BI	Strategic importance of BI, degree of business unit BI maturity and autonomy	Drives need for performance management and control processes of appropriate scope
BI tools supported by BI unit	Current state tool sets, switching costs, politics of forcing tool changes, skill/headcount requirements	Impacts total costs of tools across the company and the amount of BI development rework and training required to switch tools, if any
Skill development approach	Degree of assurance needed about pace of development of BI skills across the company, degree of business unit BI maturity and autonomy	Impacts training costs, speed of BI capability development, and potentially speed and quality of BI development
Approach to BI quality	Centralized versus decentralized, quality assurance or quality control	Impacts aspects of lifecycle development and project management, may impact speed of development
Approach to BI performance measures and metrics	Traditional cost, schedule, and technical performance measures, business adoption metrics, business value creation metrics?	If high degree of rigor is required, need performance management and control processes of appropriate scope

would be helpful for such a company to use a consensus-building approach, rather than try to drive the organizational design from a top-down perspective.

More broadly, the choices and decision factors listed in Table 7.2 can form a solid starting point for designing an organizational approach to BI success. That is not to say that they are the only considerations. Ideally, the organizational design would also be aligned with business unit performance objectives, individual performance plans, span of control considerations, market compensation conditions, appropriate decision authority considerations, and so forth. Further, if the BI unit is comprised of more than a few people, it may be necessary to provide for financial management, administration, and people development. Also meriting consideration is the pace at which the BI unit is built. It may be that a small nucleus can get the ball rolling, with the size and formality of the unit evolving at a manageable pace consistent with the degree of urgency for getting BI applications built and deployed. Ultimately, organizational design for BI success is part art, part science. The science is around applying well-understood organizational design levers, such as choice of customer, span of control, degree of autonomy, location of value creation, and so forth. The art lies in weaving and institutionalizing a BI organizational approach that achieves a productive working relationship between business people, IT people, and the BI team. That takes much more than an organization chart and some position descriptions.

7.3.2 Organizational Experimentation and Exploitation of Big Data and Cognitive Business Techniques

When it comes to big data and cognitive business, companies can exercise a choice between business-driven, discovery-based, or hybrid strategies. With a business-driven strategy, we figure out ahead of time how leveraging unstructured data and cognitive business techniques can improve profitability. With a discovery-based strategy, we employ a research and development (R&D) approach that seeks to uncover profit improvement opportunities through exploration of unstructured data and possibly structured data. With a hybrid approach, we do both.

Under either approach, companies would need to make organizational provisions for the people and technologies that are specific to big data and cognitive business. From a technology perspective, the tools of big data and cognitive business are different from the proven tools for BI and data warehousing. This includes the Hadoop ecosystem of tools, plus a variety of newer techniques for large-scale storage and management of data that are not based on SQL and well-established relational database management system techniques. From a people perspective, companies would need people who know the new tools. They would also need so-called "data scientists"—people with the skills to figure out how to leverage unstructured data or combinations of unstructured and structured data, to make an economic difference for their companies. In addition to traditional statistical analysis skills, it has been argued that data scientists should be Ph.D. scientists from diverse fields who can think outside the box.

From an organizational design perspective, the typical professional R&D model is very useful for companies that exploit big data and cognitive business. Companies where R&D is crucial to their business model establish an orderly, repeatable process for managing a portfolio of research projects. The projects move from a basic research to applied research to commercial exploitation. Such companies deploy R&D assets specific to their field, research scientists, and appropriate management and administrative processes. Applying this model to big data and cognitive business, we can anticipate that companies would need to:

- Acquire, install, and manage the big data and cognitive business technologies needed to create what has traditionally been called a "sandbox"—a place for experimental analysis of data;
- Hire data scientists and appropriate administrative support staff;
- Depending on scope, hire a manager or managers with professional R&D management experience;
- Establish a process for identifying and resourcing research projects;
- Establish a stage-gate process for moving projects through to commercialization;
- Acquire, install, and manage a big data and cognitive business production environment for applications that succeed in proving they can enhance profitability.

In adopting this R&D model, companies may also wish to avail themselves of the lesson-learned by professional R&D organizations. One inherent challenge lies comes from the nature of basic research—while it can be purposeful, one also hears that "creativity can't be rushed." In contrast to that view is the maxim that one should "fail early and fail often." Ultimately, it is up to each company to decide how much of a leash to allow when it comes to a discovery-based strategy for big data and cognitive business.

7.4 SKILL DEVELOPMENT OPPORTUNITY: ASSESS BI CHALLENGES, RISKS, AND BARRIERS

7.4.1 Key Objectives

1. Apply the analytical frameworks presented in this chapter to your company. Feel free to deviate from the topic list below if you wish.
2. Evaluate how your company can organize BI so as to address the key challenges, risks, and barriers you've identified.

7.4.2 Topic List: BI Challenges, Risks, and Barriers

1. The strategic importance of BI and the BI mission—are they articulated at our company?
2. Is the value proposition of BI captured by BIOs and understood by executives and managers?
3. Do we face any of the following challenges:
   a. Relative priority of BI within IT
   b. Relative priority of BI to business leaders and managers
   c. BI enveloped by broader data governance initiative
   d. BI managed as IT initiative
   e. Barriers to data access
4. Have we achieved strategic alignment between our BIOs, our business strategies, and our core business processes?
5. Do we have an effective business–IT partnership?
6. Can we manage a BI portfolio?
7. Will our culture embrace the use of information and analytics?
8. Do we have a culture of continuous process improvement and are we good at it?
9. Do we use structured decision-making for complex decisions that have a big economic impact?
10. Are we ready and able to execute BI and DW technical projects?
11. How would we synchronize and execute the six major workstreams?
12. Do we have an effective organizational approach to enterprise BI?

7.5 SUMMARY OF SOME KEY POINTS

1. Nearly two decades of cumulative experience with BI and data warehousing has shown that there are several major workstreams that must be considered when undertaking an enterprise BI initiative. These workstreams often need to be coordinated and synchronized across a company's business unit boundaries. Accordingly, both general management and program management perspectives and skills are needed.

2. BI and data warehousing have been around since the mid-1990s and have been adopted by companies of all types across most industries. There are a lot of cumulative lessons learned that enable us to anticipate risks and barriers to success—and hopefully overcome them. There are a number of BI readiness assessments (aka BI Maturity Models) that companies can used to identify risks and barriers. Challenges and risks that are specific to BI need to be managed—and managed in a way that they do not hold up rapid, sustainable progress in getting BI applications deployed to business users.

3. Because BI involves information technology and data, it is often managed as an IT initiative. This means that an enterprise BI initiative is likely to be managed in accordance with policies, resource strategies, and methods intended to optimize control, minimize excess resource capacity, and optimize capacity utilization of multipurpose IT infrastructure. From a business perspective, the primary objective of an enterprise BI initiative should be to develop and deploy BI applications as quickly as possible so they can be used to increase revenues, reduce costs, or both. The independent variable to be optimized is time to market—where the "market" is the business unit sponsoring a given BIO. Optimizing time to market also speeds up time to value. In most companies, there is a basic lack of goal congruence between business units that want to leverage BI and IT units who are not incentivized to adapt to best practices BI methods. As a result, BI initiatives are often executed in an IT policy context that slows development and deployment of BI applications and undermines the credibility of BI in general.

4. The data of interest for BI may be on a mainframe, on a company web server, within a proprietary business application, within a client server system, within a legacy data warehouse, within departmental databases, within departmental Excel spreadsheets, within a customer

or supplier system, in the Cloud, or provided by a third-party data provider. The net effect is that access to the business data needed for BI purposes is often much more difficult than implied by data architecture drawings, and a lot of "data archeology" work is often required to determine whether data is available and suitable for realizing a given BIO.

5. Senior business leaders generally have demanding performance objectives which require them to focus much of their leadership attention and management bandwidth on areas other than BI. Many successful companies run lean—business subject matter experts who are needed to help design BI applications and help ensure they are adopted may not have the time to effectively engage. Lack of effective business engagement substantially increases the risk that developed BI applications will not match true business requirements and/or will not be adopted.

6. Data is ubiquitous, dynamic, error-prone, and highly complex to standardize across an enterprise of any size. Companies embark on enterprise data management and master data management initiatives aimed at "managing data as an asset" and creating a "golden record" about key business subjects like customers and products. If BI priorities are subjugated to broader data management initiatives, the pace of BI development and deployment is often much slower, even though BI is often one of the highest and best uses of company data.

CHAPTER 8

General Management Perspectives on Technical Topics

While investments in BI need to be business-driven in order to deliver a return on investment, there are a number of important technical topics that come into play and affect BI program performance. These topics are more strategic than the choices of which particular technology products are most suitable. From a general management perspective, making effective technical choices demands solid business and technical thinking. On the business side, a key determination is how best to provide the technical infrastructure needed for BI execution. There are options, and each choice has pros and cons. It is also important to take a business-driven perspective on the data flow value chain whereby by data is converted into business information, business analyses, and decision support. There are cost implications to the choices, and there is a balance to be achieved between enabling and promoting fast self-service access to data and driving enterprise and business unit adoption of structured BI uses for performance management and process improvement. On the technical side, a key challenge for CIOs is resolving often-encountered differences in goals, methods, and incentives between mainstream IT best practices and BI best practices. CIOs also face the challenge of a rapidly-evolving BI technical landscape, which may demand investment in new technologies for managing big data and in new types of database management systems optimized for particular analytical tasks. From both perspectives, the choices are important because they affect investment levels, total cost of ownership of BI infrastructure, ability to execute, switching costs, pace of adoption, ability to differentiate, and the return on BI investment.

8.1 THE TECHNICAL LANDSCAPE FOR BI PROGRAM EXECUTION

While some or most of what follows in the next few paragraphs may be known by business leaders and managers, the discussion to come will be helped by having a common working understanding of the technical landscape for BI execution. Toward that end, we'll start by stating that the technical landscape in which BI programs are executed is dominated by what we'll call "Big IT." Most of the history of business uses of IT has been about investment in automating and improving the effectiveness of day-to-day business tasks. Initially this was done via custom-developed business software programs. Later the focus was on installing preprogrammed packaged enterprise software applications, often costing tens of millions of dollars or more. Big IT is the world of large data centers, enterprise software, outsourced IT, dominant hardware vendors, mature database technology, Cloud, and large IT consultancies. It is also where the lion's share of IT capital and operating budgets is spent. The Big IT world is the context within which BI programs generally have to operate, and it has characteristics that are important to understand for BI purposes. To aid this discussion, Fig. 8.1 presents a generalized technical landscape, geared toward a business audience. We'll key our remarks to the numbered circles in Fig. 8.1.

As a framework for understanding the implications of Big IT for BI success, we'll make a distinction between technical infrastructure (bottom half of the graphic) and data infrastructure (top half of the

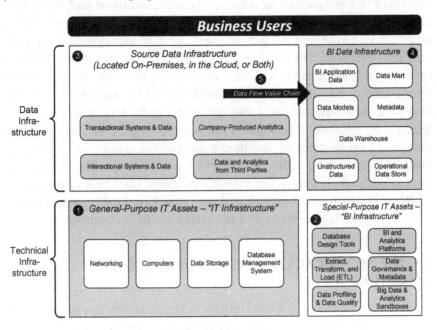

Figure 8.1 The technical environment for BI program execution has to provide the tools for BI success.

graphic). When we use the word "infrastructure" we mean the IT assets that are integral to the systems companies use to do their business. Both the technical infrastructure and the data infrastructure consist of general-purpose components and BI-related components, where the components are IT assets.

The technical infrastructure consists of:

1. *IT Infrastructure*—general-purpose IT assets that comprise the "IT Infrastructure" (Circle 1); and
2. *BI Infrastructure*—special-purpose IT assets that comprise the "BI Infrastructure" (Circle 2). The IT infrastructure consists mainly of networks for moving data around, computing power to process the data for business applications, data storage capacity, database management software, web servers, and business applications. The IT infrastructure must be augmented for BI purposes by the addition of BI infrastructure, which consists of special-purpose tools for BI and its enablers, such as data warehouses and data quality tools.

The data infrastructure consists of:

1. *Source Data Infrastructure*—data generated by and used by various company business systems—which from a BI perspective is considered "source data;" and
2. *BI Data Infrastructure*—source data that is further processed for BI purposes and stored in databases created to enable BI applications.

The source data infrastructure (Circle 3) consists of transactional systems data, interactional systems data, company-produced analytics, and third party data and analytics. By "transactional systems" we mean the business systems companies use to run their day-to-day business, typified by enterprise resource planning systems, human resources information systems, the financial record-keeping systems of financial institutions, the point-of-sale and inventory systems of retailers, and so forth. By "interactional systems" we mean web sites and mobile applications that enable companies to interact with prospective customers, suppliers, and business partners. By "company-produced analytics" we mean calculated numeric values or qualitative values such as vendor reliability scores, customer lifetime value scores, customer propensities to accept marketing offers, and so forth. Such values are calculated by using transactional and/or interactional data and the results may then be migrated forward into the BI Data Infrastructure. In practice, such customer-produced analytics may be both a source of data to the BI Data Infrastructure and a customer for data from the BI Data Infrastructure. That core data may be augmented by data and/or analytics purchased from or otherwise provided by third parties, such as market research firms or suppliers. More broadly, the data infrastructure may encompass data that is located in company data centers, in a Cloud or Clouds, or both.

The Source Data Infrastructure provides for creation, movement, processing, and storage of data so that it can be retrieved and used as needed to run the business. The data infrastructure must be augmented for BI purposes by adding special-purpose data structures (databases) that are optimized for BI/analytical applications, that is, the BI Data Infrastructure. Taken as a whole, the data infrastructure enables a data flow value chain (Circle 5)—whereby data is initially used for day-to-day operational and analytical purposes (Circle 3) and then later used for broader BI and analytical purposes (Circle 4).

Among other things, a successful BI program requires IT Infrastructure (Circle 1), BI Infrastructure (Circle 2), and an orderly and reliable flow of source data (Circles 3 and 5) into the BI Data Infrastructure (Circle 4). Accordingly, companies have options in three general areas:

- *IT Infrastructure for BI*: (1) Shared service provided by company data center; (2) Dedicated IT assets for BI; (3) Cloud service; (4) Mixed model.
- *BI Infrastructure*: choice of tools for each category of special-purpose BI assets, for example, choice of ETL tool.
- *BI Data Infrastructure*: data architecture, data flows, database structures, business user access to BI applications, business user access to data for exploratory analysis (sandbox), and big data research and development.

The choices to be made are important because they have a material impact on BI program performance. Making balanced and effective choices requires a general management perspective—one that blends managerial economics with: (1) business-driven views of the strategic importance of BI; and (2) seasoned, BI-aware technical strategy perspectives. These general management choices are made more confusing by evolutions within the world of Big IT—which now encompasses Cloud offerings, big data storage and retrieval technologies, more sophisticated data storage technologies, and the emergence of special-purpose database management systems that supplement or replace relational database management systems in certain circumstances.

8.2 TECHNICAL INFRASTRUCTURE FOR BI

In many companies, general-purpose IT assets that arc functionally-suitable for BI purposes are already in place. Whether these assets are the optimal assets to use for BI is a question companies need to con-sider, which we'll do in this section. Given that BI has been around for well over a decade, it is also likely that a given company will have some or all of the special-purpose IT assets needed for BI. Sometimes these assets may be technically dated, or if not they may have limita-tions with respect to achieving the BI mission and realizing the BIOs. We'll explore this subject as well.

8.2.1 IT Infrastructure for BI

The tradeoffs in this area of the technical landscape involve considera-tions of asset ownership, operating costs, control, and accountability for BI program performance. From a general management perspective, a given company can leverage its IT infrastructure across multiple sys-tems activities, including the workloads for transactional systems, interactional systems, and BI/analytical applications. Because the IT infrastructure offers few or no opportunities for differentiation, and because it is a significant committed cost, companies have an economic motivation to leverage the IT infrastructure across as many business applications as possible—BI included. This "shared service" tactic avoids (or more likely postpones) needing to add additional infrastruc-ture and cost. So if the IT infrastructure needs of the BI program can be accommodated without adding infrastructure capacity, why wouldn't a company want to leverage its existing infrastructure to serve the BI program?

8.2.1.1 The Challenge of IT Infrastructure as a Shared Service to the BI Program

Setting aside for the moment the fact that BI technical processes can be resource-intensive and thus likely to require incremental IT infra-structure, there are tradeoffs to be made between the goal of avoiding incremental IT infrastructure costs for BI purposes, and the goal of delivering BI applications to the business users on a fast-cycle, iterative basis. Over the past 15 years or so, many companies have succeeded with the objective of delivering meaningful BI applications very 60, 90, or 120 days. If the BI program has to share IT infrastructure with transactional systems and interactional systems, it becomes one "customer" among many for IT shared services—and in many cases a minor one at that.

Experience has shown that if the BI program has to operate in the world of Big IT, there are a range of challenges that might otherwise be avoided. The challenges stem from the fact that best practices for data center operations and IT systems development are not necessarily best practices for BI, though there are overlaps. This causes friction in that the BI development is slowed, and may cause interpersonal friction if the BI team can't meet schedule objectives and takes heat from business sponsors for delays cause by data center practices and policies. To the extent that these challenges arise, they are likely to have an adverse impact on cost, schedule, and quality performance for any given BI application development project. The BI team often has to incur costs and take time for work and/or documentation that is not needed for BI. The alternative is to try to justify an exception, which can be hard to do in many company IT environments. The BI program may also have to navigate what can be a labyrinth of procedures to get things done, and it can have progress held up due to resource conflicts with the needs of other IT projects. The net effect is that the BI program may not control the IT assets and resources it needs to meet its delivery commitments. This creates an unfavorable organizational dynamic where the BI team gets blamed for delivery delays that are beyond its control.

From a general management perspective, choosing to provide IT infrastructure as a shared service to the BI program is essentially a decision to optimize IT infrastructure costs over BI delivery performance. If this is done explicitly, then it may be fair game for the BI program to report instances where delivery performance has been adversely impacted as a result of the decision to optimize IT costs. In many companies, doing so would be risky because the people who drive such decisions do not tend to like being reminded when an unfavorable outcome results from their decisions. To avoid that risk, the

BI program could choose to be a "good corporate citizen" and keep quiet—preferring instead to make up lost time by other means, such as by reducing the scope of the BI application to be delivered or cutting back on testing or both. None of this is to say that optimizing IT infrastructure costs is the wrong decision. Rather, the point is that all choices have costs, and in this case the cost could be subpar BI delivery performance.

8.2.1.2 Providing Autonomous and Dedicated IT Infrastructure Assets to the BI Program

A way to avoid the risk that the shared service IT infrastructure poses to BI delivery performance is to provide separate IT infrastructure assets to the BI program and let the program manage those assets autonomously. A central consideration in deciding between the shared service approach and the autonomous dedicated IT assets approach is the economics of the options. The starting point for economic analysis is determining the BI-driven incremental cost of IT infrastructure, that is, network bandwidth, computing power, data storage, and database management system licensing. In arriving at the incremental cost, it is important to take account of costs that would be incurred under both options. For example, BI data architectures store large amounts of data, so it is likely that added storage capacity would be required under either approach. Further, the special-purpose IT assets for BI— the BI infrastructure—would be required in any event, so those costs can be ignored for now. Once a realistic determination of the incremental cost of dedicated IT infrastructure for BI has been made, companies can trade off that cost versus the risk of potential delays to BI delivery—or even failure of the BI program if the delays extend into a year or more.

In considering the autonomous dedicated assets approach, it is also useful to understand that the assets needed for BI are different than the typical shared assets companies have in place, as discussed below.

Different System Reliability Requirements. BI systems generally do not have to achieve the very high levels of system reliability and availability that transactional and interactional systems that run on shared assets have to achieve. For example, if a BI application is unavailable, in many cases that would not impede the ability to take and process a customer order. Technically-speaking, BI systems do not require hot failover to a remote data center, they do not need 99.9999...% uptime, and targeted disaster recovery can be in days rather than hours or less. In effect, this means that the functionality and costs of existing shared general-purpose IT assets are likely to exceed that which the BI program needs.

Different General-Purpose Infrastructure Requirements. The hardware and systems software for computing and data storage required for a Big IT (data center) operation is often overkill even for a substantial BI program. If the BI program is required to be a tenant in such an environment, it will "overpay" for the services it needs in relation to what it could pay under an autonomous dedicated assets approach. If the data center has excess capacity that the BI program then absorbs, the BI program is likely to be charged a transfer price that exceeds the market price for assets that better match its actual requirements. If the data center has to add capacity on behalf of the BI program, existing business arrangement and switching costs make it likely that the incremental capacity will be of the same type as the existing capacity, and thus overkill for the BI program. If the data center were to add incremental capacity of a type more suitable for the BI program, then the economic argument for shared infrastructure would go away.

In addition to the above considerations, deciding whether to provide autonomous dedicated assets for the BI programs runs into the complications of transfer pricing, absorption of IT fixed costs, IT costing algorithms, sunk costs versus relevant costs, and service level agreements. How these subjects are thought about and the resultant policies impact the organizational dynamics of the decision.

8.2.1.3 Considering Cloud-Based IT Infrastructure for BI

IT outsourcing has been a part of the Big IT landscape for decades. The central strategic argument for doing so is based on the philosophy that companies have core competencies and IT is not one of them, and on the assumption that IT is not a source of competitive differentiation. According to this argument, IT should be a utility—a commodity available to all and neutral with respect to competitive dynamics. Aspects of this argument are certainly debatable given that core business processes of companies across industries rely heavily on information technology. In today's world, not many business processes have not been automated. That aside, outsourcing as a business took off in the late 1990s, led by computer systems integrators and large consulting companies who partnered with hardware and application software vendors. With the advent of commercial exploitation of the Internet in the late 1990s, there arose a new breed of IT outsourcing companies called "application service providers"—companies that established IT infrastructure and hosted business applications such as various modules of enterprise resources planning (ERP) systems. There are still companies that go to market using that term.

The latest form of IT outsourcing is based on offering customers IT assets "in the Cloud."

The term "Cloud" simply means that the IT assets are hosted by a third party and made available to customers via the Internet. There are public and private Clouds, but both types use the Internet as the networking backbone—they simply have different levels of network security and access controls. Under this approach, the company would execute a contract that specifies services, service levels, monthly costs, and business terms that would constitute a lease of IT infrastructure assets. This could establish a predictable level of IT operating expenses, depending on the pricing structure of the deal. Further, it would require no incremental investment in IT assets, which show up on the balance sheet. On the other hand, FASB deliberations in 2015 may result in operating leases having to be shown on the balance sheet, in which case the balance sheet advantage would go away. Lastly, it would avoid the risk that the shared service IT infrastructure poses to BI delivery performance—though at the cost of having less control of the assets and service levels.

In thinking about the Cloud, it is useful to remember that the architecture of the underlying IT assets is no different than what is available to any company that wants to have its own IT assets and leverage the Internet for networking the assets, for example, across multiple geographic locations. Anything that can be done in the Cloud can also be done by any company that wants to. So the argument for leveraging Cloud-based IT assets for a BI program comes down to economics, differentiation, control of sensitive data such as customer data and financial data, startup time, and switching costs.

Regarding economics, it used to be that adding incremental computing power and storage capacity had to be done in big increments, which meant that there were scale advantages to be had. In todays' world, that is less the case once the assets have been put into service.

On the other hand, the Cloud option provides almost instantaneous access to IT infrastructure, so if spending three to six months establishing a company-operated IT infrastructure for BI is too long, then the Cloud could warrant consideration, all other things being equal. Some companies are reluctant to cede control of vital data, and if BI is indeed strategic, then relying on an outside party to provide the foundation for BI success might trouble such companies. Also, it is important to keep in mind that some Cloud deals require multiyear commitments, which creates switching costs. There are also technical aspects to switching costs, in that the database management system used is foundational for BI applications, and thus switching from the Cloud provider would entail rework if the underlying database would need to be changed.

8.2.2 BI Infrastructure for BI Programs

The universe of special-purpose IT assets for BI and its enabling disciplines is largely a world of packaged software. Fig. 8.1 shows six different categories of tool functionality:

- Database design tools—also known as data modeling tools;
- BI and analytics platforms, for example, Microstrategy, Cognos, Business Objects, SAS, QlikView, SPSS, Tableua, and many others;
- Extract, transformation, and load (ETL) tools—also known as data integration tools;
- Big data and analytics sandboxes, that is, special-purpose databases, file management systems, and data management tools;
- Data profiling and data quality tools; and
- Data governance and metadata management tools.

Some of the specific tool offerings span more than one functional category. For example, ETL tools commonly bundle in data profiling and data quality functionality. The subject of how to effectively select and acquire packaged software is well-covered in other quarters, so we'll focus attention on some characteristics of the BI tools world that may be useful to keep in mind, as shown in Table 8.1.

8.2.2.1 Contribution to Competitive Differentiation

Among the categories of tools, the opportunity to create competitive differentiation lies with the BI platforms and tool and with the big data management tools. These are the tools used to build the BI and big data applications via which a company's BI opportunities (BIOs)

Table 8.1 Considerations for Providing a BI Infrastructure for a BI Program

Technical Component—BI Infrastructure	Purpose	Ownership	Contribution to Differentiation	Switching Costs	TCO Impact	Focus of Business Decisions for BI	Focus of Technical Decisions For BI
Extract, Transformation, and Load Tool	Acquire data needed for BI/analytical purposes, prepare it, and put it into data warehouse/data mart	Company licensed	Generally low	High due to investment in ETL programs	Substantial	Business terms, TCO, and ability to meet projected ETL workloads	Selection of best ETL tool for the expected processing workload volumes and types over time, often using a structured competitive proof-of-concept
Data Profiling and Data Quality Tools	Ensure that data needed for BI/analytical purposes conforms to specifications	Company licensed	Generally low	Generally low	Low	Business terms and lowest TCO for reasonably-expected actual workloads. These tools often have features and functions that may never be used, depending on the company.	Often bundled with ETL tool and should be evaluated via ETL proof-of-concept
Data Governance and Metadata Management Tools	Provides the means for business users to understand the lineage and business meaning of data needed for BI/analytical purposes	Company licensed	Generally low	Generally low	Low		These tools serve a mix of technical users and business users. Evaluate technical suitability based on user profiles and use cases.
BI and Analytics Platforms and Tools	Develop and deliver business information, analyses, and decision support to business users via BI applications	Company licensed or Cloud	Substantial opportunity based on business-driven BI strategy	Can be substantial due to investment in BI applications and deployment into business processes	High	Business terms, TCO, styles of BI to be supported, number of actual expected users, ease of use, training, help desk	Evaluate technical suitability based on projected processing workloads and response times, mix of general-purpose and special-purpose tools, expected role of self-service (if any)
Big Data & Analytics Sandboxes	Store and manage user access to big data in various forms, including unstructured data	Company licensed or Cloud	Substantial opportunity based on business-driven strategy for exploiting big data	Can be substantial due to investment in BI applications and deployment into business processes	Moderate to high	Business terms, TCO, styles of BI to be supported, number of actual expected users, ease of use, training, help desk	Evaluate technical suitability based on projected processing workloads and response times, mix of general-purpose and special-purpose tools, expected role of self-service (if any)

are actually realized. Within this category, there are general-purpose tools and special-purpose tools. The general-purpose tools are often called "platforms" and they are typified by products such as Business Objects, Cognos, and Microstrategy. The special-purpose tools are typified by "analytics platforms"—such as SAS and SPSS—and by the open-source tools for big data management—such as Hadoop. *Generally, while there are product-specific pros and cons, it is creative and effective leveraging of the tools that creates competitive differentiation, not the tools themselves.*

8.2.2.2 Switching Costs

There are high switching costs associated with two categories of tools: ETL tools and BI and Analytics Platforms and delivery tools. Both categories encompass tools that are the foundation for building, deploying, maintaining, and managing the BI Data Infrastructure (Fig. 8.1, Circle 4). Once companies start to develop and deploy BI applications based on data in underlying data structures, such as a data warehouse, the cumulative investment grows—and with that comes switching costs. Accordingly, it is very important to make careful choices in selecting these tools.

8.2.2.3 Total Cost of Ownership (TCO)

Because of their central role in realizing BI opportunities, the ETL and the BI and Analytics Platforms and delivery tools can be priced aggressively on a "value-based" model. This pricing power is augmented by a meaningful degree of concentration in product market share within the two categories, though there are certainly options from lesser-known companies. As a result, these two BI Infrastructure asset categories have the most substantial impact on TCO.

8.2.2.4 BI and Data Warehousing Appliances

"Appliances" is a term that is applied to hardware/software bundled offerings that have been developed to meet the needs of BI programs. The hardware component is optimized for the computing workloads that are required for data warehousing and BI. They are intended to eliminate the need for general-purpose computing assets in the IT infrastructure for enabling BI. The software component encompasses ETL capabilities and BI development and delivery capabilities. Accordingly, appliances are relatively expensive and they create switching costs.

8.2.3 Big Data Technical Considerations[1]

Internet-based companies like Google, Facebook, and Yahoo have been at the technology frontier when it comes to managing and monetizing big data content. The sheer volume, velocity, and variety of their content required them to develop situation-specific architectures that enabled low-cost storage and fast content retrieval. The basic three-tier architecture has come to be called the "Hadoop stack"—consisting of:

- Hadoop Distributed File System (HDFS)—a file system
- Hadoop YARN—a job scheduler and resource manager
- Hive or Pig—query specification layers

The Apache Software Foundation has developed Hadoop as an open source technology, and companies like Cloudera and Hortonworks have commercialized Hadoop "distributions"—think packaged software with no license fees but that require sophisticated implementation and operational skills off of which the Hadoop provider earns a fee.

At roughly the same time, the need for large scale storage and management of digital content spawned new approaches that are not based on SQL and well-established relational database management system techniques. A partial list of these different data management approaches includes:

- columnar databases
- document stores
- key value/tuple stores
- graph databases
- multimodal databases
- object databases
- grid and cloud database solutions
- XML databases
- multidimensional databases
- multivalue databases

The proliferation of newer data management approaches evolved with big data in mind has created architectural uncertainty for CIOs in companies who have decided to move forward to leverage big data. And when one throws in the consideration of cloud options versus the

---

[1]This section is excerpted from Williams S. Big data strategy approaches: business-driven or discovery-based? Business Intelligence Journal 19(4).

on premises option, the big data technology situation becomes even more uncertain.

For the companies who deal with big data all the time, they have already made their technology bets and are living with them. For traditional companies who need to make technology choices, it is very important to be careful and to maintain flexibility going forward. Essentially, none of the newer data management approaches/products—many of them open source—have been proven in the marketplace over the long haul. While open source products offer licensing cost advantages over traditional RDBMS products, many are dealing with technical challenges that have been solved in the relational world long ago. Further, parallel RDBMS products processing SQL have been on the market for decades. Given the current state of big data technology, it is important to use a structured evaluation process as part of formulating the technical portion of a big data strategy—with an emphasis on product maturity, performance benchmarking, potential switching costs, and analysis of the financial stability of vendors.

The other technical factor that is important to consider is sourcing of big data content. Simply put, is big data content routinely generated in the normal course of your company's business operations or by virtue of its social media strategy? If not, should it be acquired, in what form, where would it be acquired, and how would it be managed? Companies like Google, Yahoo, Twitter, and Facebook are in the business of both capturing and generating big data content. Your company may not be.

8.2.4 Summary—Technical Infrastructure for BI

An adequate technical infrastructure for BI provides a foundation for program success. It ensures that the BI program has responsive access to required IT infrastructure. To be responsive, the IT infrastructure has to managed in such a way that the legitimate needs of the Big IT world do not work to the detriment of BI and data warehousing technical best practices. If a shared services approach can be effectively adapted, then that approach merits serious consideration. On the other hand, with IT organizational dynamics being biased toward standardization, the shared services approach poses risk to BI program performance, regardless of how well-intentioned efforts to adapt BI-friendly practices might be. To avoid that risk, companies have the option to create a dedicated IT infrastructure for BI, assuming the projected benefits of the BIOs outweigh the incremental costs of added IT infrastructure. Assuming that an adequate IT infrastructure can be provided, sound technology acquisition practices will ensure that the BI infrastructure is also adequate. Those special-purpose IT assets are critical for developing BI applications on time, for ensuring suitable data quality, and for ensuring that deployed BI applications meet the many diverse needs of the business community.

8.3 DATA INFRASTRUCTURE FOR BI

While the technical infrastructure for BI is foundational for success, the data infrastructure is the most crucial and complicated component of the technical landscape for BI program execution. It used to be that almost all of a company's data resided in an IT and data infrastructure owned and operated by the company. Third-party data, if any, was brought into the company in structured ways. Today, more and more of many companies' data is in the Cloud. Some may have originated in Cloud applications like Saleforce or SuccessFactors. Other data might have been originated by a company's vendors and made available via the Cloud. The net effect is that the Source Data Infrastructure has become more fragmented, which only adds to the inherent complexity of acquiring data for BI purposes.

Once source data moves outside of the Source Data Infrastructure, it is generally a free-for-all with respect to how it is used for creating business information, business analyses, and decision analyses. This self-service, artisan-like approach creates many conflicting views of business reality—and it is expensive and error-prone to boot. Under this approach, business people use spreadsheets and desktop databases to hunt down relevant data and use it for reporting and analytical purposes. With the advent of newer self-service BI tools over the past several years—such as QlikView and Tableau—individual users are more empowered to go out and get the data they need. This can be a fast approach and good for ad hoc one-off analyses. It also spawns potentially-conflicting views of business reality more quickly than traditional methods. The self-service artisan approach is likely to continue because of the dynamic nature of business information needs, not all of which can be met on a timely basis while the enterprise data infrastructure for BI is being deployed.

To further complicate matters, even though the source data infrastructure is well-structured for many business applications, in many cases it is a technical and business challenge to ascertain what data is where and whether its quality is sufficient for BI/analytical purposes. Against this backdrop, the data infrastructure for BI attempts to bring order to the data that is to be used to run the company and improve its performance. This concept is depicted in Fig. 8.2.

The journey from ubiquitous ad hoc methods for leveraging information, analyses, and decision support to a more ordered and effective BI Data Infrastructure generally takes several years, during which time the old way and the new business-driven BI approach coexist. Over time, more of the company's use of data is migrated to the BI Data Infrastructure—which enables BI applications that deliver a common view of business facts, a common perspective for business performance management, and a rich source of information and analyses for improving core business processes. From a general management perspective, there are several factors that impact the cost, delivery time, and suitability of the BI data architecture for enabling the BI strategy and realizing the targeted business benefits from a portfolio of BI opportunities.

8.3.1 Establishing the Data Flow Value Chain for BI

Fig. 8.2 depicts a data flow (Circle 2) from a Source Data Infrastructure (Circle 1) to a BI Data Infrastructure (Circle 3). While this looks simple on paper, it is actually one of the riskiest and most complicated factors that impedes BI success. The source data

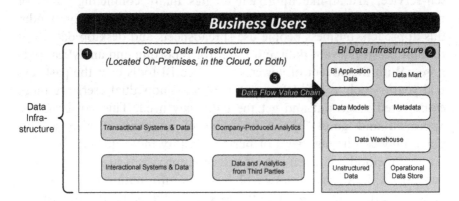

Figure 8.2 A well-designed, well-executed data infrastructure can corral the data needed to realize a BI strategy.

infrastructure generally encompasses dozens of systems, if not more, and these systems rely on hundreds or thousands of data files and/or relational database tables that usually have names that are not comprehensible except to the IT people and business analysts who regularly work with the systems and associated data. Accordingly, finding the right data to bring into the BI data infrastructure in order to enable development of BI applications that realize BI opportunities is a matter of data archeology. It takes an indeterminate amount of time that can only be estimated. This fact, coupled with considerations of data privacy, data security, and potential limitations of data replication, means that establishing the data flow into the BI data architecture is a nontrivial task. It also means that when vendors of BI-as-a-Service say "just give us your data and we'll quickly deliver BI" they are usually deliberately understating the challenge. To further complicate matters, the Source Data Infrastructure itself is evolving. With more and more companies leveraging Cloud platforms and Cloud-based systems, the data of interest for BI purposes does not always exist inside the four walls of the company data center. This situation has spawned new technical approaches to moving data around for operational and BI purposes.

8.3.2 Designing the BI Data Infrastructure

For most of the past 20 years, a BI Data Infrastructure has been thought of as an information and analysis value chain or factory—raw transactional, informational, company-produced analytics, and third-party data is moved downstream through several key technical processes and databases, and then converted to BI applications and/or staged as business information ready for analysis. This has involved designing an orderly arrangement of databases that have assigned roles whereby:

- data from the source data environment flows in and is staged for further processing;
- data is integrated and data quality rules are applied;
- data is stored in ways that enables multiple downstream business uses of common business facts;
- data is organized for common, business-defined informational, analytical, and decision-support uses;
- data about where the data came from, how it is logically organized, and what it means is kept on hand for quality, adaptability, data management/governance, and database maintenance purposes; and

- data—including unstructured data—is made available for data exploration and experimental purposes.

Collectively, these various databases constitute what is known as a "data architecture." With recent technical advances, some of the processes and tools for moving data along the value chain have changed, but there still needs to be an engineered and transparent data architecture. Nobody likes a black box when it comes to information and analyses used for important business decisions, and traditional BI Data Infrastructures are still widely used. Historically, the optimal data architecture has always been subject to debate and to what amounts to religion-like differences of expert option. As with any architectural choice, there are pros and cons, and many books have been written on this topic. Some of the significant factors to consider are highlighted below.

8.3.2.1 Business-Driven Data Architecture

BI is all about information and analyses, and thus the BI data architecture is crucial to business utility. A business-driven, purpose-built BI data architecture is based on tight coupling between business processes, the BIOs intended to enhance process performance and profit improvement, and business data that enables BI applications. Under such an approach, the BI data architecture is designed as depicted in Fig. 8.3, which promotes a common view of business facts for all business functions to leverage through BI applications developed using the common data.

This is different from an approach that simply stages lots of data in a common location—often as a collection of data files and relational tables that business analysts can use as they see fit. This latter approach is common among older data architectures that support the self-service, artisan-like approach that creates many conflicting views of business reality.

There are two traditional options for bringing about a business-driven data architecture. Under a so-called Three-Tier Data Architecture, a central data warehouse is built, and then data marts designed for specific informational, analytical, and decision support uses are built and they get their data from the data warehouse. Under a Two-Tier Data Architecture, there is no central data warehouse. Rather, a series of subject-oriented data marts are built, and over time

Figure 8.3 A business-driven data architecture provides a common view of business information for enterprise analytical and decision support purposes.

they come to be considered a data warehouse. A newer approach to business-driven data architecture is to use sophisticated software to create what amounts to a virtual data warehouse or data mart. With this approach, the source data of interest is not physically stored in a data warehouse and/or data mart. Rather, it is called up from various systems within the Source Data Infrastructure and used to create business-defined views of business information—"on the fly" in technical jargon. All of these approaches work if done correctly, and a full treatment of the pros and cons is beyond the scope of this discussion. That having been said, the choice does impact development costs and database maintenance costs because of the difference in the number of databases to be built and their structure. From a general management perspective, there are well-established and generally-accepted criteria for evaluating BI data architecture options.

8.3.2.2 Methods for Providing BI to Business Users

It has been customary for years to talk about how BI gets to business users by using a framework similar to the one depicted by Fig. 8.4.

On the left are the sources of data, such as an ERP system and a call center system. On the right are methods by which data and/or BI applications are provided to business users—including tablets and mobile devices. In the middle are three basic data architecture templates. Starting at the top, the one-tier data architecture is almost always to be found—it is the basis for the self-service, artisan-like approach to reporting and business analysis. It has been in use since before data warehousing and BI were in play, and it has been the mainstay for enterprise reporting for decades. It has the disadvantages we've previously noted—disadvantages that data warehousing and BI are intended to overcome. Next are the two-tier and three-tier data architectures, the main technical difference being whether or not a central data warehouse is built.

It is important to note that these are basic templates that are generally adapted as needed in practice. For example, the one-tier data architecture will generally coexist for a time with one of the other data

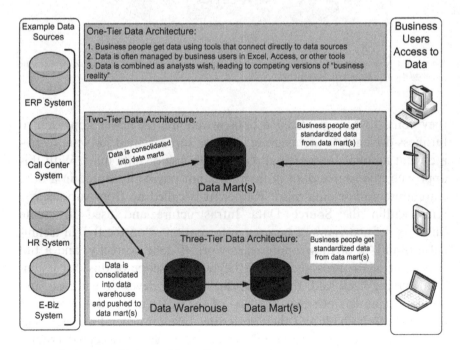

Figure 8.4 Traditional simplified views of data architectures.

architectures because the data files available from the source systems have become integral to producing the hundreds or thousands of standard reports that companies use to run their business. The newer virtual data architectures we discussed are also in effect one-tier data architectures because they get data directly from source systems. There are also situations where one company may have more than one data warehouse—such as when a company grows by acquisition. This can result in what is called a federated data architecture, whereby various data is moved around among data warehouses, data marts, and possibly other data repositories and subsequently used for BI purposes. Lastly, a variant of the one-tier data architecture is when data—structured and unstructured—is moved from the sources into a data repository (a "sandbox") where power users and data scientists can use it for ad hoc analyses and discovery activities. There are no right answers when it comes to BI data architecture, only useful approaches. From a business perspective, some factors to consider when working with the BI team to design a BI Data Infrastructure are shown in Table 8.2.

8.4 BI AND THE CLOUD

These days, just about anything a company wants to do with IT can be done in the cloud. From a BI perspective, the cloud can be a source of IT infrastructure, of BI infrastructure, and of BI applications.

Cloud computing is the latest version of outsourcing, and we previously related the argument that IT is not a core competency nor a source of competitive advantage. According to that line of thinking, IT should be thought of as a utility and a candidate for outsourcing. Let's revisit this argument from a BI strategy perspective.

The basic core competencies argument holds that companies compete based on certain capabilities through which they create differentiated products and/or services that are valued by customers. For example, product engineering is a core competency for an industrial company that makes specialized products sold to business customers. Makers of consumer packaged goods compete based on their ability to understand and meet consumers' needs, so marketing is a core competency. The core competency argument is coupled with a differentiation argument, which holds that IT capabilities are equally available to all comers, so it cannot be a source of competitive differentiation.

Table 8.2 Business Considerations for Designing a BI Data Infrastructure

Business View of Comparison of Data Architectures for BI and Analytics

Points of Comparison	One-Tier	Two-Tier	Three-Tier	Comments
Business Users' Degree of Choice of Data	High	Moderate	Low	Choice is a two-edged sword: data can be gotten quickly, but lack of data standardization promotes conflicting views of business reality.
Business Users' Data Management Reponsibility	High	Low	Low	Many business analysts and power users complain about having to manage data because it takes a lot of time that could be focused on business analysis and problem solving.
Commonality of Views of Business Reality	Low	Moderate	High	One-tier promotes well-documented "data chaos" whereas two-tier and three-tier promote delivery of common views of basic facts of the business and performance metrics.
Comparative Ease of Data Sourcing	Low	Moderate	High	Many transaction systems and their database are not well documented, and the same or similar data can be found in multiple systems, both of which make one-tier systems more challenging for BI purposes.
Data Quality	Managed by individual analysts	Quality is managed as imported to data marts	Quality is managed as imported to data warehouse	When there are multiple data marts, data quality is managed by policies for data mart development. In a data warehouse environment, quality is managed as a data intake process, that is, as data is fed to the warehouse.
BI Application Sustainability Risk	Highly dependent on individual analysts	Low - BI applications developed using best practices	Low - BI applications developed using best practices	A one-tier architecture typically promotes a craftperson approach to BI, whereas the other architectures promote a systems engineering approach.
Comparative Deployment Time	Fastest for simple situations and nonenterprise uses	These architectures take more time intially, but promote fast deployment after initial builds and are typically more suitable for enterprise BI uses		The biggest challenge to BI deployment if often found in sourcing the data from transactional systems and other enterprise systems, understanding what the data means, and integrating it for business purposes.

Proponents then suggest that since IT is essentially a commodity that does not enable differentiation of companies' products and/or services, it cannot or should not be considered a core competency, and thus it should be outsourced. This would take IT assets off the balance sheet, reduce IT infrastructure costs due to economies of scale the outsourcing contractor may be able to achieve, and ensure that IT is "professionally managed."

Whether or not IT in general is a core competency for nonIT companies is a debatable proposition. Here are some ideas to considering when evaluating the argument as it pertains to IT in general and/or BI in particular.

- Just as all manufacturing companies are not equally good at manufacturing, or all distributors are not equally good at distribution, not all companies are equally good at leveraging IT within their businesses. Further, there are observable differences in how well companies leverage BI.
- A substantial number of business systems used to run a company depend on IT—some that pertain to noncore tasks like updating and distributing organization charts, and others that pertain to core competencies. For example, most manufacturers use a manufacturing execution system to run their manufacturing processes, which means that their core competency depends on IT.
- The fact that IT assets and skills are available to all does not necessarily negate the possibility of using IT for competitive differentiation. In this regard, IT assets and skills are no different than any other functional assets and skills. For example, product merchandising skills and techniques are available to all, and that does not mean that merchandising is not a core competency or a source of differentiation. The same can be said with regard to BI assets and skills.
- There may be a useful distinction between leveraging the cloud for transactional IT systems versus using it for BI. Transactional systems automate recurring business tasks according to defined operating processes. BI systems have to do with how business people assess and think about their areas of responsibility. The former may be an undifferentiated capability, whereas BI may offer opportunities for differentiated products and services.
- Contrary to utilities, which are regulated, cloud operators have a profit motive and in some cases substantial pricing power. Building

capabilities in core competency areas that depend on partners a company cannot control is riskier than controlling one's own destiny. The degree of risk depends on switching costs, the availability of alternate sources for cloud services, and the business terms and conditions of the cloud services contract, whether for IT in general or BI in particular. A cloud service provider could end up with a more-or-less permanent claim to a share of a company's cash flows.

- BI-as-a-Service is a cloud-based option where a company can lease basic reports and/or set up a cloud-based BI capability. The reports are standard, and more sophisticated uses of BI are not part of the basic package. This option does not solve the source data integration challenges discussed earlier, and it does not offer differentiation to any meaningful degree.

The weight any company accords the above ideas will vary, and sometimes investors will drive companies to outsource for purely financial reasons, such as deploying available capital for nonIT uses or moving assets off of the balance sheet to improved return on assets and return on invested capital. We may also want to acknowledge that many business leaders and managers think of IT as a hassle and are glad to outsource as much of it as possible.

8.5 SUMMARY

Much of what needs to happen on the technical side of BI can be left for the CIO and his or her people to handle. From a general management perspective, the focus needs to be on working with senior IT and business people to ensure that the BI program has the technical infrastructure and data infrastructure needed to deliver BI quickly and effectively. Providing the right infrastructure—cloud-based or otherwise—impacts investment levels, total cost of ownership of BI infrastructure, ability to execute, switching costs, pace of adoption, ability to differentiate, and the return on BI investment.

BIBLIOGRAPHY

In concert with my general management and BI strategy consulting experience, the sources listed below are some that have informed my thinking about how to leverage BI to improve profitability and how to "look under the hood" of the marketing techniques used by vendors in the BI, analytics, and big data arena.

[1] Wren D, Bedeian A. The evolution of management thought. New York: John Wiley & Sons; 2009.

[2] Shapiro J. Modeling the supply chain. Pacific Grove, CA: Duxbury; 2001.

[3] Watson G. Business system engineering. New York: John Wiley & Sons; 1994.

[4] Kaplan R, Norton D. The strategy focused organization. Boston, MA: Harvard Business School Press; 2001.

[5] Kaplan R, Norton D. The balanced scorecard. Boston, MA: Harvard Business School Press; 1996.

[6] Ross J, Weill P, Robertson D. Enterprise architecture as strategy. Boston, MA: Harvard Business School Press; 2006.

[7] Weill P, Broadbent M. Leveraging the new infrastructure. Boston, MA: Harvard Business School Press; 1998.

[8] Hammer M, Champy J. Reengineering the corporation. New York: Harper Business; 1993.

[9] Marakas G. Decision support systems. Englewood Cliffs, NJ: Prentiss Hall; 1999.

[10] Porter M. Competitive advantage. New York: The Free Press; 1985.

[11] Slywotsky A. Value migration. Boston, MA: Harvard Business School Press; 1996.

[12] Hayes R, Wheelwright S, Clark K. Dynamic manufacturing. New York: The Free Press; 1988.

[13] Michigan State University. 21st century logistics. Chicago, IL: Council of Logistics Management; 1999.

[14] Simchi-Levi D, Kaminsky P, Simchi-Levy E. Designing and managing the supply chain. New York: Irwin McGraw-Hill; 2000.

[15] McClellen M. Applying manufacturing execution systems. Boca Raton, FL: The St. Lucie Press/APICS Series on Resource Management; 1997.

[16] Ptak C, Schragenheim E. ERP tools, techniques, and applications for integrating the supply chain. Boca Raton, FL: The St. Lucie Press/APICS Series on Resource Management; 1999.

[17] Davidow W. Marketing high technology. New York: The Free Press; 1986.

[18] Hall R. The streetcorner strategy for winning local markets. Austin, TX: Bard Press; 1994.

[19] Simons R. Levers of organization design. Boston, MA: Harvard Business School Press; 2005.

Note: Page numbers followed by "*b*," "*f*," and "*t*" refer to boxes, figures, and tables, respectively.

Printed in the United States
By Bookmasters